Lucius Bellinger

**Stray leaves from the port-folio of a Methodist local preacher**

Lucius Bellinger
**Stray leaves from the port-folio of a Methodist local preacher**
ISBN/EAN: 9783337283070
Printed in Europe, USA, Canada, Australia, Japan
Cover: Foto ©Lupo / pixelio.de

More available books at **www.hansebooks.com**

FROM THE

# PORT-FOLIO

OF A

# METHODIST LOCAL PREACHER.

BY

REV. LUCIUS BELLINGER,

OF SOUTH CAROLINA.

PRINTED FOR THE AUTHOR,
By J. W. BURKE & CO., MACON, GA.
1870.

To my Wife,

JANE BRUCE BELLINGER,

MY BEST EARTHLY FRIEND, WISEST COUNSELLOR,

AND

CONSTANT HELPER IN MY PILGRIMAGE TO A BETTER LAND;

AND TO

MY MANY FRIENDS,

IN

SOUTH CAROLINA, NORTH CAROLINA, AND GEORGIA,

WITH WHOM I HAVE OFTEN HELD SWEET COMMUNION, AND

WHOSE CHRISTIAN SYMPATHIES HAVE CHEERED ME IN THE

WAY TO HEAVEN,

THIS HUMBLE RECORD OF MY WANDERINGS,

IN THE SERVICE OF THE MASTER,

IS RESPECTFULLY DEDICATED,

BY THE AUTHOR.

# EDITOR'S PREFACE.

The Author insists that the Editor say a word to the Public, to introduce the "Stray Leaves." But there is little need. The narratives here brought together, are not altogether new to the Author's many friends; and it is at their solicitation that they were first committed to paper, and, now, to type. The name and fame of the "Strange Preacher," the love entertained for the "Wandering Arab," the interest already awakened in the "Stray Leaves," by what is known of them by the numberless friends of the Author, will guarantee this book a circulation, without a word from the Editor to stimulate it.

It is proper to say, that the Editor has been embarrassed, from the large amount of matter put into his hands with the responsible privilege of following his own judgment, in selecting from it the best material for the contemplated volume. As *part* of the purpose of the Author was, very properly, to get some pecuniary profit from his book, thus to repair the heavy losses of the war, its cost was to be considered; and had all the material put into the Editor's hands been used, the book would have been too bulky to be remunerative. In making the selection, the Editor has been compelled to follow his own judgment; and he may, therefore, have left out some "Leaves" which both the Author and his friends would have preferred inserted. If so, the full discretion given him by the Author must be his warrant; and the peculiarities of his own taste and judgment must bear the responsibility.

In other respects, the Editor's labor has been confined principally to compressing into smaller compass what was written *currente calamo*, by one not much accustomed to writing, and whose excitable temperament naturally led him into diffuse narrative. In this condensation, however, whatever is characteristic of the Author — as a man, a Christian, a friend, and a preacher — has been faithfully preserved; and the Editor flatters himself, that whoever knows LUCIUS BELLINGER, will find him faithfully reproduced in these pages.

Wishing for the Author many readers, and for his readers much of that spirit of love for the Master that glows through these pages, this unpretending volume is commended to a generous public.

E. H. MYERS.

MACON, GA., *Feb. 1st*, 1870.

# CONTENTS.

PAGE.

LEAF I.—Birth and Early Years—First Serious Convictions—How they were Lost............ 9

LEAF II.—My Second Conviction — Stronger than the First — but Lost in the same way............ 15

LEAF III.—My Third Conviction even more Powerful than the last— Hell is Defeated—Heaven Triumphs—I am Converted............ 22

LEAF IV.—The Dream that was Repeated; and how Dr. S—— was Convicted and Converted............ 34

LEAF V.—How Dr. S—— Joined the Church, and the Merchant did not Sell the Heavy Bill that day as was expected............ 39

LEAF VI.—Dr. S—— in his First Love-feast............ 42

LEAF VII.—Dr. S——, after Advising and Entreating his Friend to refrain from Shouting at an Expected Meeting, is the First heard from............ 46

LEAF VIII.—Old Shiloh; or, the Sanctified Preacher............ 50

LEAF IX.—A Memento of my Departed Friend, the Rev. James C. Postell; or, a Night at Cattle Creek Camp-ground in the Olden Time............ 56

LEAF X.—My First Visit to old Cane Creek Camp-ground, Union District, why I went there; or, the Beginning of my Roving Life 59

LEAF XI.—My First Visit to Rock Springs Camp-ground, North Carolina; and a Wayside Meeting............ 67

LEAF XII.—The Black Swamp Camp-meeting, where the Colonel of the Beaufort Rangers surrendered his Sword, and the Captain of the Gillisonville Guards left his Post............ 73

LEAF XIII.—A Camp-meeting in the Up-country, from which I found out Something I did not know before............ 83

LEAF XIV.—Centre Camp-ground, North Carolina, and the Low-country Dinner; and how the Class-leader's Wife was Convicted and Converted............ 88

LEAF XV.—How I got the Names of "War Preacher" and "Wandering Arab."............ 95

| | PAGE. |
|---|---|
| LEAF XVI.—My First Visit to Gully Camp-ground, Darlington District | 99 |
| LEAF XVII.—My First Visit to Pleasant Grove Camp-ground, North Carolina, where two long Letters on Controversy were Answered | 104 |
| LEAF XVIII.—Camp-meetings in Georgia | 107 |
| LEAF XIX.—Meetings at old Springtown; or, the Preacher who, while Working for others, Enjoyed himself very much | 116 |
| LEAF XX.—"In Union there is Strength;" or, the Two Flags Waving together; or, Judah and Simeon together, with Locked Shields, pressing the Battle to the Gate | 125 |
| LEAF XXI.—Meetings in Alabama | 131 |
| LEAF XXII.—A Memento to my Departed Friend, Rev. H. H. Durant; or, a Visit to Sandy Spring Camp-ground, South Carolina | 138 |
| LEAF XXIII.—A Memento to my Dear Departed Brother in Christ, Rev. W. C. Kirkland—the Man whom the Church and the World loved | 146 |
| LEAF XXIV.—Remarkable Dreams | 154 |
| LEAF XXV.—Remarkable Presentiments which came to pass | 160 |
| LEAF XXVI.—The Strange Preacher Trying his Bob | 163 |
| LEAF XXVII.—The Heroes of the old Walterboro Circuit | 168 |
| LEAF XXVIII.—A Memento of my most Beloved Friend, Brother Thomas Raysor, the Model Steward; or, the Man whose Mantle no one has yet been found Worthy to wear | 184 |
| LEAF XXIX.—Camden; Meetings at Salem Camp-ground, and Lancaster Court-house | 189 |
| LEAF XXX.—The Strange Preacher Counting Chickens before they were Hatched; or, Expecting Great Things, was quite Disappointed | 195 |
| LEAF XXXI.—A Memento to my Departed Friends, the Three great Heroes of the old Barnwell Circuit, and Binnakers Camp-ground —Brothers Henry Holman, David Felder, and George Riley | 205 |
| LEAF XXXII.—Meetings at old Zion; and the Last Freshet in the Edisto | 211 |
| LEAF XXXIII.—My Second Visit to Rock Springs Camp-ground, North Carolina, and the Star of H. H. Durant again in the Ascendant | 222 |
| LEAF XXXIV.—My First Visit to Spartanburg, where I had to preach more than the Two Promised Sermons | 232 |

|  | PAGE |
|---|---|
| LEAF XXXV.—How the Protracted Meeting at G—— was broken up, when the Ghost shook his Gory Locks.................................. | 237 |
| LEAF XXXVI.—Two Visits to Georgetown by the Strange Preacher | 245 |
| LEAF XXXVII.—English Chapel; or, the Wandering Arab, taking the Water with Fear and Trembling, comes out better than he Expected, with the exception of pulling his Boots off.............. | 251 |
| LEAF XXXVIII.—The Protracted Meeting at D—— Closed and Renewed again; or, the Best of the Wine at the Last of the Feast. | 258 |
| LEAF XXXIX.—Meetings on the Cooper River Circuit, with my much-loved Friend and Brother, the Rev. J. W. Kelly............ | 264 |
| LEAF XL.—Providence Camp-ground, Fish Dam, and Belmont, Union District, South Carolina................................................ | 274 |
| LEAF XLI.—Mesopotamia, Union District...................................... | 283 |
| LEAF XLII.—Meetings at Cannon's Camp-ground, and in the Town of Spartanburg............................................................ | 289 |
| LEAF XLIII.—Jacksonville, Florida; or, the Strange Preacher requested to stay till after Supper.................................... | 297 |
| LEAF XLIV.—A Visit to Black Swamp Circuit—Elegies of the Old House and of the Oak-tree................................................ | 300 |
| LEAF XLV.—The Conclusion and Farewell..................................... | 310 |

# STRAY LEAVES

FROM

# THE PORT-FOLIO

OF A

LOCAL PREACHER.

---

## LEAF THE FIRST.

BIRTH AND EARLY YEARS—FIRST SERIOUS CONVICTIONS—
HOW THEY WERE LOST.

I was born in the town of Walterboro', S. C., October 5th, 1806. I was the second son of Dr. John S. Bellinger, who, when I was quite young, moved to Barnwell District, and settled a place, which he called "Pine Forest," where I lived until my mother's death. As I was growing up, my father often told me that as a child I was very hard to rule, very quick tempered, and that I caused my dear mother much trouble. He said, that she often talked to him of me, and told him just before she died, she was much more distressed about me, than any of the other children. She tried, however, to bring me up aright, making me say my prayers regularly.

Soon after my mother's death, my father sent off my elder brother and myself to an Academy called Mount Prospect, in Union District. I was then only eight years old. I remained there for two years. While still quite young, I was sent to another school, ten or twelve miles from Columbia, at Platt Springs. I remained there several years.

There was a large number of boys at that Academy, from different parts of the State. We had some very rough scenes to pass through. It was no holiday business in those days, to go to school so far from home. The boys were very careless concerning religious things—many of them being desperately wicked—awfully profane. Sunday was very little respected, and we enjoyed ourselves in various ways—all sinful in the sight of God. It is doubtful if there was a pious boy among us. The man with whom we boarded was a wicked, drinking bully—a terror to all around.

Once every year, I paid a visit to my home. I well remember those annual returns to the home of my childhood. It seems to me now when I think of those stated returns, that it was to me then somewhat like an exiled son of Abraham returning to the land of his fathers. My youngest brother, Edmund, was then with us at the Academy. My father was noted for his punctuality, so that he had a fixed day both for our going from, and returning to, our home—the first day of January and the last day of November. During the many years I was at Platt Springs, I do not remember having missed the appointed time, but once; and then affliction in the family prevented our returning at the usual time. Oh, those happy days of my boyhood! how pleasantly were they spent in the company of my brothers! How can I ever forget them! Even now, I remember with what transports of joy we would leave Platt Springs and the Congaree creek. During our homeward ride, we noted every hill we passed as bringing us so much nearer the Mecca of our hearts. And when we had crossed the North Edisto at Orangeburg, and the South Edisto at Cannon's bridge, we felt more than we could express, for then we were only ten miles from home. But on, and still on, the boys go—their old horses, "Fear-not" and "Capt. Hull," seem to feel as glad as their young masters—they move so fast on the good road. And now, first Lemon swamp, and then Baring's Hill, are left behind. That house you see on the right leaves only two miles more. Let us now turn down the old avenue. As fast as they are travelling, the boys are becoming impatient, and wish they could go even faster. Hear how they clap their hands and laugh out—"There is old Pine Forest." Edmund spies the homestead first, and then his less fortunate brother, Lucius. And now we are at home. Our dear father is coming down the steps to welcome his three boys. So anxious is he that he has forgotten his hat. Then come Maum Cilla and Kate, and Uncle Cudjo and Paris, to shake hands with us; and now we realize that we are at home at last. It is with a mighty effort that we can prepare for bed that night. And then the next day we follow our inclinations, and roam all about the woods, proving quite a terror to squirrels, rabbits, and birds. Imagine our disappointment though, to find it raining on the second morning after our arrival, and father counsels us to remain in-doors, else we may take cold. We hail with genuine joy the re-appearance of the sun, and go to work to entrap partridges, larks, and other birds. We thought our brother John quite a hero, because he killed two ducks while flying—thinking in our boyish ignorance, that it was one of the most wonderful shots that had ever been made in Barnwell District. And then again, on another day he shot an old fox squirrel, which ran into his nest, putting us to the trouble of cutting down the tree. We found that he was in excellent order, having laid aside all ceremony in visiting father's rice patch. Our vacation has ended, prematurely we think, and we have to return to school again—feeling sad at heart to say "good-bye" to the home-folks. We have travelled many miles before I can muster courage enough to keep back the tears—and in anticipating the future it seems quite an age ere I can return to my old home. And thus many years pass by.

It was well for me at this time that I had been blessed with a mother who was a pious member of the Protestant Episcopal Church, and who required me to repeat my prayers regularly. I have never forgotten her instructions. Our teacher little cared how the boys passed the Sabbath. All that he required was strict obedience to his rules during the week. If they missed their lessons, they might look out for trouble—which came usually with a severe flogging.

They would often resort to any means to mitigate the severity of the thrashing, by putting bark under their shirts.

We usually spent our Saturdays fishing, hunting, etc., which was real sport to school-boys who were, for the time being, free from all restraint. But after a while, quite a change came over Platt Springs. A new teacher took charge of the school. He was a member of the Presbyterian Church—a man of upright conduct and strict morals. He strictly observed the Sabbath, and his walk was upright. This was quite a wonderful day for the entire school—each pupil having his own opinion regarding our future prospects. Here was a large field before this man of God, much of it being stony ground. A very poor crop of righteousness might be expected; but the good teacher went to work. His first effort was to establish a Sunday-school among the boys. At first, he met with but little encouragement; but finally, others joined the number, and I think there was a little improvement among us, morally, which happy change went on gradually.

An old Lutheran preacher, Mr. Franklow, whose life was nearly worn out in his Master's service, at this time preached to us once a month. I was now a Sunday-school scholar. The good seed sown in my young heart years ago began to germinate. Will it spring up? Will it bring forth fruit to the glory of God? Time will tell. Let us hope for the best.

I remember one evening well. It must have been—now, in 1866—more than forty-five years ago. Let me try to draw the picture. The sun was nearly down. A youth—say about fifteen—was walking by himself—an old man now, writing these lines. This was no chance work; I think the Lord must have drawn him to this spot. The last rays of the sun were shining on the bold, rapid Congaree creek. An old man on the other side was walking slowly, tremblingly along, leading his horse. He intended to walk over the foot-log, while he led his horse through the water. This was the aged Lutheran preacher, coming to preach for us on the morrow. I crossed over the foot-log, and hastened up to the preacher, who extended his hand, saying:—

"I am so glad to see you; I suspect the Lord sent you here; I have been fasting to-day, and feel weak and weary; I was afraid to attempt to ride over, and am glad you have come to help me across."

He prayed the blessing of the Lord upon me. I first assisted him over, and then led his horse through the creek. I think that the blessed spirit of my mother looked down from heaven upon her prodigal son, from whose heart all good impressions were not entirely gone. The old man seemed very grateful; he thanked me with tears streaming down his venerable face.

He preached to us the next day. I heard him frequently during those years long gone by; but that which is most distinct in my memory is the hymn with which he usually dismissed us  Even now, at this remote period, in imagination I hear him repeat these lines—

"Give every fettered soul release,
And let us all depart in peace."

About this time there was an examination of the Sunday-school scholars. One of the first prizes was awarded to me. I valued the book given to me on that occasion very highly. The preaching and the counsels of that good man, and the prayers of my blessed mother, which had been so often offered for her wayward son, were answered now, in my first serious convictions. They were strong and powerful. I was bowed in spirit, with no one to advise or comfort me. The preacher would not be back for weeks, and the teacher, though a good man, did not attempt to win the love and confidence of his pupils, but rather kept aloof from them. Consequently, I was all alone with my great grief, not knowing how to approach my God. I have always thought, that if I could have been blessed at that time with the prayers and advice of some Christian man, I might have started that much sooner by many years for glory. I tried to pray; but there was no one to point me the way. How well do I remember those days of trouble—away from home, with no one to counsel me. I think my brothers were ignorant of my feelings.

I remember the last Sabbath I passed in that state of mind. I absented myself from my companions, during the entire day, and tried hard to compose my thoughts, and to engage in prayer. I read the entire book of Psalms on that day.

My distress was very great; but the devil knowing my weak point, kept his eye upon me. I feel truly sorry, even now, when I recall, with shame, how he overthrew me, and deprived me of the great blessing that my Saviour was even then waiting to give me. I was of very quick temper, very easily angered, and my great enemy knew this, and here he got advantage over me. Shortly after that Sunday, I arose from my knees one morning sad and troubled, and joined the boys, which was sometimes unavoidable. I passed through the crowd with my head bowed down, feeling much depressed in spirits. One of my companions struck me a heavy blow on the back with some missile. In a moment all my deep convictions were gone—the tempter had gained the victory. I turned round, filled with awful anger; and when I discovered who the offender was, I rushed upon him; but we were separated, and it was in vain that I tried to reach him. Alas for me! my convictions had been swept away like straw before the mighty wind. The sun rose on me that morning an humble, mourning soul, not far from salvation. The same heavenly orb went down on me, with my good intentions all gone—my angry passions ruling me with a mighty power. I turned from my Bible and prayers, and from my search after the Saviour's love. Hell had triumphed, and I was on my way to ruin.

## LEAF THE SECOND.

#### MY SECOND CONVICTION—STRONGER THAN THE FIRST—BUT LOST IN THE SAME WAY.

My years at Platt Springs were over now. I left there more than forty years ago, and I have never visited the place since, notwithstanding my desire to re-visit the old Springs, the Congaree creek, the old school-house, and their never-to-be-forgotten surroundings. I sometimes think, that the hand of Providence has so directed it, that I should never walk over those grounds again. So be it! The Lord's will be done, not mine. But old Platt Springs, thou art not forgotten! I have thought of thee times without number. And thou, Congaree creek, rapid and bold, hastening on to the river, in imagination I have often, again and again, sported in thy strong current! It was there that I took my first lessons in swimming, and in time became one of the most expert of the hundreds who spent very much of their time in the water.

I well remember the last night of my stay at Platt Springs. The examination was over; father had sent for us. After paying all our debts, and bidding Mr. Stafford farewell, and taking leave of Mrs. Bell, Mr. Boughman, and Mr. Geger's family, and shaking hand for the last time with most of the boys, Edmund and myself were left alone, and we awaited very impatiently the dawn, that we might make an early start for Pine Forest. While we were thus waiting, three or four of the boys entered our rooms. They had come to bid us " good-bye." Let me say here, that even then I was trying to do what I have endeavoured to do ever since—that is, to have as little to do with ardent spirits as possible. But there were boys among us who were too fond of them, and these boys were among that number After remaining for some time, they proposed a parting drink, which they insisted on our taking. We at first declined, but finally yielded to their persuasions. The bottle was brought out. We drank standing, without water, and then parted—some never to meet again. That was the first and last drink of that kind I have ever taken.*

I reached home safely, in due time. After the lapse of some years, I found myself even more wicked than when at school—being headlong, passionate, travelling with rapid steps the road to eternal night. I entered upon the duties of life—farming on a small scale. I hunted, fished, and enjoyed myself in various ways. Occasionally, I went on the Sabbath in company with some wicked young men to a place called Clear Pond, and, by my great skill in swimming, astonished the lookers-on so much, that the report of my feats was heard far and near. I very seldom attended church—having no use for preaching—but I went to camp meetings. I was often, however, at Spring Town—the nearest place of worship—for the sake of the crowd that went there. I went to "muster" regularly, and finally became Captain of the Fish-pond Company, and began to feel a little big. I was very wicked, perhaps more so than my friends imagined. Time rolled on. There was then a very popular preacher on the old Orangeburg circuit—the present Bishop Wightman. I heard so much of him that I concluded to go to Pine Grove Church to hear him. I there met several friends and relatives. I remember it as well as if it were only yesterday. The old log house was crowded. I heard a very fine sermon. A local preacher, famous for his loud praying, concluded, with a voice like a war trumpet. Some of the fashionable ladies present complained afterwards of severe headache. A pair of fine horses became frightened at that trumpet-voice: the carriage pole was broken; and the owner—a lady of great respectability—became so provoked with Methodist preachers, that she never, during her life, attended another Methodist meeting.

---

* Very many years afterwards, when on my way to Camden, to be ordained deacon, one evening about dark, some persons passed me. By their actions, I knew they were drunk, and I was at once suddenly impressed that among them were some of those who took that parting drink with me at Platt Springs, and it required an effort to restrain my tears. I found out afterwards, that I was right—that they had thrown themselves away entirely.

The young Captain of the Fish-pond Company never once thought, during his occasional visits to old Pine Grove in those days, that, in a few years, he would become one of the class-leaders of the little band who worshipped there, hoping to get to heaven, when the warfare of life is over.

During the same year, there was a quarterly meeting at the same place. I attended, and found quite a crowd for the place. Dr. Capers, whose fame had spread all over his native State, and to many others, was expected to be there. Old Pine Grove had never seen such a turn-out for many years—perhaps, a greater gathering had never been there. The people came from Buck-head, from Green-pond, from Wesley Chapel, and from the other side of the Edisto— came in crowds. The Lord blessed his children with a most lovely day for that season of the year. Brothers Howell, Eason Smith, Steadly, Barton, R. Stephens, and Curry were there, singing as the old-time Methodists used to sing. The preaching was out of doors, and to almost every tree there was a horse fastened. In imagination, listen to that singing. Hearts are engaged in the work, expecting and praying for a glorious time; and that day's history will tell, both in time and eternity, that they were not disappointed. The crowd continues to increase, and song after song climbs the hills of heaven, and the holy angels are hovering over, more in number than for years before, perhaps; while hell is trembling to its centre, but musters all its strength for a desperate battle. The negroes are out in great crowds, and sing with voices that make the woods ring. The hour of public worship arrives. Brother Wightman preaches the first sermon—his text, "Woe to the world, because of offences,"—a sermon long to be remembered. He paints the awful fate which awaits all sinners, who not only ruin themselves, but draw others down with them to the realms of endless night.

The young preacher not only sustained, but added much to his rising fame by that day's well-arranged and finished sermon, which was preached at old Pine Grove Church.

When the preacher sat down, Dr. Capers rose before that tremendous throng. His face alone was a sermon, whether in the pulpit or not. Who that looked at that man would not feel that a Christian stood, before him, in all the grace and loveliness of religion. Such a face and such a smile are not often seen in this vale of tears. I think, that was the first time I ever saw him. The crowd was silent and respectful throughout its wide limits. How those expressive words of Virgil suited this heavenly-minded man, whenever he stood up before the church and the world in behalf of his blessed Saviour and Lord—

"Ille regit dictis animos et pectora mulcet."

His text was—"And the Saviour saw the multitudes were as sheep having no shepherd, and he taught them many things." Oh, that sermon! who can describe it? The holy blessed Son of the Father stood before our eyes in all his condescension, his meekness, and his great pity for a lost world, who are like sheep without a shepherd. As the holy man went on, we could see the scene before us. We traversed the realms of earth—we crossed the mighty deep, and the old Canaan of the Scriptures was before us. There rolled the Jordan—the sacred river. We saw the sacred mountains, Carmel, Tabor, Hor, and Gilboa. Hebron, Nazareth, and Jerusalem stood before us. We saw the sea of Galilee, with its palaces mirrored beneath its blue waves, and the fishermen with their vessels following their trade; and the many thousands from all parts of the holy land seated upon the green grass before the eternal Son of God. The halt, the blind, the lame, the lepers and those possessed with evil spirits; the rich and the noble of the country; the scribes and the doctors of the law, were there. The immense throng was before us, and the Blessed Teacher taught them the way of salvation. The preacher tells us of man's danger and his only way of escape; tells us of the joys of the redeemed; of the green fields of Eden on the other side of the flood; of the harps of heaven; of the crowns of glory reserved for the faithful at the right hand of the throne for ever.

Though it has been some forty years ago, I frequently hear persons allude to that meeting. I doubt much if there has ever been such another in these lands. A vast crowd stood spell-bound before the preacher. My much-loved father was present. Having heard much of Dr. Capers, he was anxious to hear every word, and he, therefore, sat quite near, and appeared deeply interested. Whenever he was interested, he usually nodded by way of agreement; but, on the other hand, if he did not agree with the speaker, he would shake his head. On this occasion, he appeared much pleased, and began to nod—a sign that all was right. He finally, however, ceased nodding assent, and dropped his head and wept, being much affected. More than once afterwards he was heard to tell how deeply interested he was; but he said, that he never would sit so near the pulpit in a Methodist meeting again, as he considered it quite a dangerous place; for he was compelled to weep in spite of every effort of his to refrain from doing so. He also acknowledged having been nearly caught by them on that occasion. I wish from my soul they had succeeded in doing so.

But how about the Captain of the Fish-pond Company? How was he coming on all this time? Why, he was more strongly, more powerfully convicted than he was before, at old Platt Springs. He was made to dread the wrath to come, more than ever before; and he felt the longings for salvation more than ever—having been completely carried away with the scene which had been presented to him, and the heavenly face that was before him, now covered with smiles, and then again with tears of love and joy. He was transported with strong emotions, and listened, entranced by the soul-stirring eloquence of the holy man of God, and thought, that if that man would only pray for him, personally, he would at once get religion. He was taken a willing captive by the love of the Saviour, as it was described to him that day. He even yet remembers that he had made up his mind, should mourners be called up, to present himself at the throne of grace. And to this day he believes, that he would not only have gone up as a mourner, but that he would have joined the church, had the opportunity been offered. Towards the close of the sermon, his feelings were powerfully wrought upon, and he was anxious for the sermon to be concluded—having fully resolved when mourners were called up to go too. I think mistakes are frequently made, by having other preachers to close. On this occasion, Dr. Capers did not conclude the service; and I remember how much disappointed I was. I am fully convinced that I would have joined the church many years sooner than I did, had he done so. I had heard enough; I only wanted to be prayed for, and then I would have gone home happy in my Saviour's love. The preacher who succeeded him spoke of the terrors of the law, of sinning away our day of grace, and of our being beyond the reach of mercy in this life. Oh, my soul! what a change came over me! I was at once impressed that my chance was gone. How badly I felt! I at once concluded, that it was too late for me. When mourners were called up, I stayed away, feeling as badly, perhaps, as any who knelt for prayer.

The memorable meeting was over. I felt a strong desire to go to Dr. Capers, as he was about leaving, and ask him to pray for me; but he did not know me, as I had never spoken to him, and, therefore, I concluded it would be wrong. Doubtless it was the tempter at work. At last, however, I did resolve to approach him; but too late, for he was gone, and with him my hope of salvation for that evening I was so much distressed, that many noticed it and have since spoken to me of it. I was so much troubled, that it was with difficulty I rode home. I rode with head bowed down, fully convinced that had Dr. Capers called up mourners, I would have gone and been converted. My state of mind can never be forgotten while life lasts. It was very similar to my depressed feelings, during my first conviction while at Platt Springs.

At that time my father was not a member of the church, and there was no one at home with us, except the negroes, some of whom doubtless loved the Lord, and could have given me some comfort; but I confided in no one. I tried again and again to pray to the Lord; but there was no one to advise, no one to direct me how to approach the throne of heavenly grace. What days and nights of awful gloom and anguish of my soul! I began to read the New Testament as soon as I got home, and finished it by the next Saturday morning, trying very hard, in my imperfect way, to obtain the forgiveness of my sins. I fully believe, that had I been at some meeting, where the Spirit was poured out, I would have found my blessed Saviour. But alas! my great enemy was preparing for me another overthrow, fatal to my hopes of religion.

The Saturday succeeding the one of the meeting, was the regular muster-day for the Fish-pond Company. Had I known what my experience was to be, I never would have gone, but would have rather paid a double fine. I do not remember whether I commanded on that day or not; but I remember full well how earnestly I tried to pray, before I left home—without, however, experiencing any change. I was much depressed in spirit—scarcely speaking to any one—only replying when spoken to. I resolved to return home as soon as my duty had been discharged. But I had a friend and relative on the ground—a man fond of his glass, and very quick tempered. There was also another man on the ground, of the same habits—a large man, while my friend was rather small. While I was standing some distance from the crowd, engaged with my own sad thoughts, I heard a noise and, on turning round, found that the strong man had struck my friend, and the blow had been returned by him. The scene of Platt Springs was enacted again. Great rage took possession of me. I rushed between them, and took the place of my friend. My antagonist and myself were finally separated. I went home—all my convictions and distress of soul gone. Hell had triumphed the second time.

# LEAF THE THIRD.

MY THIRD CONVICTION EVEN MORE POWERFUL THAN THE LAST—HELL IS DEFEATED—HEAVEN TRIUMPHS—I AM CONVERTED.

After my second overthrow, I wandered much farther in the broad road to destruction than ever before. I thought and cared very little for religion. I hardened my heart more and still more. I ceased praying to the Most High, and stopped reading my Bible. Yet, there were some of my friends who had not given me up, but still expected me to come out on the Lord's side, and start for the better world.

Let me here say, that it appeared to me the Lord had, on more than one occasion, told me what was to be my fate—that is, so far as my becoming a preacher was concerned. My father had two very old and faithful servants, who loved the Lord, and were on their way to heaven I placed implicit confidence in their professions. During my wildest days, they often told me that I would join the church and become a preacher, that they expected to hear me preach, and nothing I could say would make them think otherwise. Their predictions were fulfilled, for they both lived to hear me preach.

Again, there was a gentleman of high standing—a worthy minister of the Baptist church, who had known me from boyhood, and he often told me that he knew there was work for me; that I would be called to preach. He also told me that he had been noticing me for some time, and that the idea was a permanent one. I remember that one day, while he was thus speaking to me, I told him how little prospect there was of that ever happening. He replied, with a serious face that I can even now recall, "Captain, you *will have to preach;* I have a lease of my life till that takes place." That good man lived to see the pleasure of the Lord fulfilled. I have had the happiness to be with him at some very interesting meetings.

But I continued on in the downward road that leads to

eternal night and endless despair. I remember one holy Sabbath how I sinned against the Lord. What a great mercy it was that in those days, he so often bore with me, during my rebellion against heaven. I had broken my gun, and had to send it to a gunsmith, who was a member of our church. I knew when it would be finished, and I went for it on the Sabbath. He did not wish to give it to me then, and told me that he was a member of the church, and considered it wrong; but I insisted, for I was determined to have it. On my way home I rode carelessly by the church, where they were holding class-meeting. The good leader, Brother Holman, told me afterwards that he saw me pass, but little thought that he would live to hear me preach in that same church. That blessed man of God has years ago gone to the green fields of Eden on the other side of the flood. The old church, too, has passed away; but I am still here, trying to call sinners to repentance.

I went on still in the way of the transgressor, and was still exceedingly wicked. I remember to have wounded the feelings of my dear father, who attempted to counsel me; but I little regarded his advice, and rushed on madly to destruction. I frequently attended large gatherings at Methodist churches, particularly at camp-meetings, where I made sport at holy things. I laughed at, and ridiculed, the excitement witnessed at such places. I did not believe one word of what I heard, for I did not understand it; and I was apparently farther than ever from the church.

About that time our State became much excited on the subject of Nullification, and I became a warm partizan on the Union side. We had meetings, gave dinners, and made speeches. The whole country was aroused from the mountains to the sea-board.

Meanwhile, my heart was closed against all religious impressions; but the time was fast approaching for my conviction the third time—more powerfully than before. And ever since the day of which I am now going to write, I have thought that that occasion was to be the last offer of salvation to me—that mercy would have been extended to me no more, had I then refused to be saved; that my day of grace would have departed never more to return. Such is my serious conviction, while now I am reviewing those past scenes of my roving life, and I expect to go to my grave with this same solemn belief.

In September, 1831, the annual gathering of the Methodists was to take place at Binnakers, a famous camp ground some twelve miles from my home. The two political parties were to meet at Buford's bridge on the Saturday after the meeting, where they expected to have their dinner and speeches. My father had requested me to make a few remarks on the occasion, which I had tried to prepare to my satisfaction, hoping thereby to give some aid to our side. He also gave me some pamphlets for distribution at the camp-meeting; but requested me to do nothing during service, but should opportunity offer during the intervals, to take advantage of them. I went alone to the camp-meeting. Taking a private way, before reaching the public road I stopped, and repeated to myself the speech which I had prepared for that day week, and then passed on to the camp-ground, situated near the banks of the Edisto. 'Twas a beautiful place, regularly laid out, which had been used as such for several years. Persons attended it from some distance; sometimes from across the Savannah. The Methodists were there in great numbers, and many ministers, men of talent and experience, were present. The Rev. Henry Bass was presiding elder—a man much beloved by the church.

On my arrival, after mingling with the crowd for some time, I concluded that there was but little chance for me to work politically. Nevertheless, I made an effort and distributed my pamphlets, speaking in the intervals on the subject which brought me there.

On Saturday evening, I heard a portion of a sermon, after which I made much sport of the man of God. Having concluded that I could do but little for my party, I proposed to go home; but I was persuaded by a much-loved friend to remain. He was very wicked, and I think if he could have foreseen events, that he would have been as urgent for me to leave as he appeared anxious for me to remain; but the devil is much disappointed sometimes. I guess if he had suspected what was to happen on the morrow, he would have left no stone unturned to get the young Captain away from that place.

I had, too, another friend on the ground, whom I respected much, notwithstanding he belonged to the opposite party. I thought that, in visiting the place, he was prompted by the same political motive I was, and I concluded that it would be to my advantage could I persuade him to leave. Some one informed me, that his wife and children were sick; so I believed that he was in my power. I therefore approached him in the presence of others, and remarked that I was much surprised to meet him, telling him at the same time why I came, and acknowledging that I was ashamed of myself for having been actuated by such a motive in visiting the place. But I told him that I had no family, and that I left my father quite well; while, on the other hand, I had been told that he had left his family sick, and yet came there to discuss politics I asked him if he was not ashamed, and advised him to return home immediately. He made no reply till I was through; so I concluded that I had gained the day. But I soon discovered my mistake; for he replied in a manner I never expect to forget. I was overwhelmed with astonishment as Dr. Ayre replied very calmly—

"You have made a great mistake. I left my wife and children much better, and requested Dr. ——" who lived near, "to visit them regularly during my absence."

He also told me, that he did not come there to take part in politics, but for something far different. that he had recently found out he was fast going to hell, and would be lost unless the Lord saved him; that he came, hoping to get religion; that, on describing the state of his mind to his wife, she advised him to attend the meeting; that he had committed his family to the Lord's care; and further, he advised me to follow his example. He silenced me at once, and I left and kept aloof from him until after I, too, had become convicted.

Not having an opportunity to work politically, I became

reckless, and behaved much worse than I had ever done before at places of worship. I gathered some friends around me—among them the wicked young man to whom I have alluded. We made up our minds to have fine sport. Oh, my soul! sporting over the pit, while the fiery billows were raging below. My friend and I were very much attached to each other; we called ourselves "The Two Gentlemen of Verona." I was Valentine, he was Proteus—by which names we usually addressed each other. I behaved so badly, that a gentleman present, who had married my sister, after requesting me in vain to desist, finally told me, that he would not remain in my company any longer, not even in the same tent; that he knew my sister would be much worried, when she heard of my conduct. He left me, and I went on in my wicked course—not to be stopped but by the power of the Most High. Among other things that we did for pastime, I being the leader of the party, was the following—the wrong of which I can now see. A gentleman and lady of respectability were present—she was the daughter of a Methodist preacher, who served the Lord faithfully during his life. They were engaged to be married; I proposed to my party that we could have fine sport by being very attentive to her, thereby depriving him of her company; and furthermore, to mention it where he could hear it, that we were much pleased with her. In this way, we annoyed them very much—walking with her alternately, and intruding ourselves whenever we could. We even went so far as to step in between them, while they were walking together, thereby making him quite indignant.*

On Sunday morning, a gentleman to whom I had just been introduced—a man of the world, requested me to

---

* Many years afterwards, when I had become a zealous preacher, I met that same lady at a meeting, where we had an opportunity of conversing alone. During the conversation, she told me of my conduct at Binnakers; and told me also, that whenever she left the "stand," she went to the tent to cry, and to ask the Lord to convict and turn me from my wicked course. You can imagine how I felt—how much I regretted my conduct.

step aside with him, and, apologizing for the liberty he was taking in speaking to me regarding my conduct, he told me that he was well acquainted with the gentleman I was annoying, and that he was much shocked at my behaviour. He informed me further, that unless I stopped, the gentleman intended to have satisfaction. He also requested me to give him my address, telling me also, that he knew that his friend would not submit to an insult; and that *he* would advise me to desist, or perhaps our party might be invited across the Savannah river to settle the difficulty. My reply was, that I was more determined than ever to go on, and he left me, with a sad face. I then sought my friends, and told them of the interview, and we were fully resolved to persist in spite of all consequences.*

The 8 o'clock sermon had been preached. We were all drilled and prepared for the execution of our plan, and at the conclusion of the next service, it was to be my turn to annoy the couple—we having made up our minds to be more insulting than ever. So far, I had not heard the whole of a sermon since I had been there. While our party was in a tent at lunch, and the 11 o'clock service had been going on for some time, all at once I felt impressed that I ought to go to the stand. I made known my intention to my friends, who tried to persuade me to remain; but I told them that on my return home my father would question me about the meeting, and that it would never do for me to tell him I had not heard one sermon. I was resolved to go, and I left them thinking that they had no idea of attending; although, soon after I took my seat, they came and sat just behind me, as I was afterwards told.

I went to the stand, as I then thought, only through respect for my father. Since then, however, I have thought that it was the influence of the Holy Spirit which drew me to the place where, as I now believe, I was to have my last offer of mercy—if accepted, religion—if refused, no further

---

* I have often thought, what melancholy results were arrested by my being struck down by the power of the Lord; for that stopped our plan at once. I never met the gentleman afterwards without feeling ashamed of myself.

offer; that it was the Saviour of my dear Episcopalian mother, long gone to heaven, about to give her prodigal son his last hope of meeting her in the green fields of Eden when the warfare of life is o'er. And I have often thought what a momentous crisis of my life that was—how my eternal destiny hung tremblingly in the balance. And moreover, I have ever felt thankful, that I did not know who was to preach at that hour; for had I known, perhaps I never would have gone, since it was the same preacher of whom I had made sport the preceding day. I was much disappointed when I ascertained that he—the Rev. William Crook—was to preach.*

The text on the occasion was—"For the great day of his wrath is come; and who shall be able to stand?" And many have since pronounced it to be the best sermon that Brother Crook had ever preached.† The sermon was almost half over before I became interested. The preacher finally spoke of those who will not stand. He dwelt with much force on this portion of his text, and I felt the drawings from above. The preacher draws near the conclusion of his sermon, and describes the day as *now* come—the whole world *now* stands before the face of the dread Eternal—the countless multitudes are judged as they have lived—the final sentence is passed—the crowd is divided on right and left—the last parting takes place—the father bids his son, the mother her daughter, an eternal farewell. My

---

* I have since heard more than one preacher, who was present, say that the presiding elder, previous to the blowing of the horn to call the people to the stand, called the preachers together in the tent, and told them that the meeting had not been as good as he expected, and that he was aware, that there were many very wicked persons on the ground; and he requested them to engage in serious prayer before service—which they did, not without experiencing much good, for the Lord blessed them, and it was from His presence they went to the stand. Those preachers were not disappointed, for one of the best meetings ever held at Binnakers was the result of their prayers.

† That meeting has been long remembered by many. Even now persons often speak to me of that time. Recently, one of our Bishops told me, that he was there at the time—a little boy, only seven years old—but that he remembers my distressed face as I went to the altar.

feelings at this time can never be imagined. Horror, awful, indescribable horror, took full possession of my soul. I saw myself weighed in the balance and found wanting. I felt that my doom had been declared to me—that I was on the left hand of the Judge, and without the saving mercy of God I would remain there at the judgment day. My sins stared me in the face; I felt that should I die at this moment, I would be doomed eternally. I trembled under the conviction that was upon me. I had never felt so much before in all my life. I thought that the last offer of mercy was now extended to me.

The sermon over, the great moment of action arrived. Mourners were called up. I had never before exposed myself thus to even a few persons. Shall I now go up before these thousands who are gazing at me? Shall I, who had been conducting myself so shamefully, now approach God's throne? Shall I go up to be laughed at by my gay friends, who will say, "those shouting Methodists at Binnakers had you down at last"? But then, to be lost for ever! to be separated from my sainted mother eternally! I started for the altar, still ashamed of what I was doing.* I remember even now, how ashamed I felt at that moment. You may form some idea of this when you are told that at first I would not kneel; but I stood up, holding on to a post, trembling most violently. My convictions were overwhelming: while the others were kneeling I stood up, yet expecting every moment to fall prostrate.† It occurred to me that I had better kneel than fall; and I was soon on my knees, praying for mercy—my proud notions all gone. My agony of soul cannot be described. I dreaded sinking into

---

* Several persons have since told me, that my friend Proteus caught at me as I left, and that he barely missed my coat. I feel grateful that he failed; for had I at that moment met with the least resistance, I would have yielded, perhaps to my eternal ruin. I think, that if he had said, "Oh, Valentine! 'tis your much-loved Proteus who calls you; come back," I would have stopped.

† Persons have since told me that they did not expect me to keep my feet many minutes.

that eternal fire, and I resolved to pray to the last—that, if lost, I would die praying for mercy.

The prayer was over—all had left; but I remained praying for mercy, pleading the name of Jesus, my only hope, my only plea. The Captain of the Fish-pond Company remained for many hours at the altar, in bitter agony.\* There I remained until near sun-down, nor left till the friend whom I had tried to induce to leave the ground—Dr A.— came to me, and asked me to go into the woods with him, where the two friends, now more closely united than ever, conversed together and advised with each other I felt somewhat relieved, but was still much depressed in spirit.†

The last night of the meeting had arrived. So far, I had not thought much about joining the church. I was still unconverted. The door of the church was opened, and I joined it, and never have I regretted it. I had come out as fully from the world as I could. I had burnt the bridge behind me. I was in the way of salvation. I felt something within me that convinced me that I had done right. My distress, though not all gone, was much lessened. I retired to rest late at night. Oh, what a change! The sun rose upon me that day so very wicked, so very near the gates of hell. That same sun went down on me an humble mourner, so near the redemption of his soul! At a very late hour I was still awake, and the impression was strong upon me, "if you will now, even at this late hour, give your heart to God in earnest prayer, you shall now be

---

\* Some gentleman expected me to dine at his tent, and I was told afterwards that he waited for me for a long time, sending a servant to inquire for me, who reported to him that I was still at the altar.

† It was noised abroad that I had gone to the altar. My brother-in-law afterwards told me, that "Proteus" was much distressed; that he was seen walking about much troubled; that he asked him what was the matter; and he replied with a sigh—"Valentine has left me ; he has started for heaven, and Proteus is not ready to go with him." I suspect as soon as I went to the altar, my mother saw me, and blessed her Lord that her prodigal son was coming home to the church; and that her spirit hovered over me in all my agony, and was near to rejoice when my sins were forgiven.

converted, your sins forgiven." It seemed to me that the spirit of my mother was whispering to her son to pray, that the Lord would bless him. I was on my knees again directly, and I then and there received the blessing, though not in all its fullness. A sweet peace came over me, which no unrenewed heart has ever felt. A blessed calm filled my soul. My troubles, my sorrows were gone. My mother seemed to whisper to me. "Son, did I not tell you so!" Oh, that never to be forgotten hour! I was blessed. I was converted. The prodigal had returned to his heavenly Father—that Father had thrown his arms around his neck, and had welcomed him with a kiss of love.

My friend, Dr. Ayer, seemed quite surprised at my joining the church, as I did not tell him that I was going to do so. He had informed me that he had made up his mind to do so, but did not know when; that perhaps several months would pass before he would be able to do it. But he now said, that if he had been present when I joined, he would have gone with me, and appeared much pleased that I had done so. The next morning he concluded that he could not wait any longer, and he joined also.

On Monday morning, Brother Bass called up all who thought they had been blessed at the meeting. We both went forward among the happy number. Oh! how happy I was when I left the camp ground, having been blessed again at the last prayer. I set out for home, exulting in the forgiveness of my sins; the love of the Lord was shed abroad in my blood-washed soul. Hell had been defeated; Heaven had won the glorious day. There is joy in heaven over the conversion of one sinner.

Now let us follow those young converts, the Doctor and the Captain, rejoicing on their homeward journey. How they commune, and converse, and exult together, happy in the blessed hope of heaven. After riding thus for some distance, the young Captain was struck very forcibly with the thought that perhaps his father would not approve of his joining the church without first consulting him; for though not a member, he had a strong preference for the Episcopal church. This thought troubles him, and he concludes to say nothing about his having joined, but to let his changed course speak for him. His friend asks, if he is going to tell his father at once, or to wait. He replies, that he will not broach the subject for some time. What a picture is now presented! It is now time for the two young converts to part, as their roads separate here—having just crossed the Cedar Spring ford. The Captain will now turn to the left; the Doctor will continue in the same road. Dr. A. takes his friend by the hand, and says to him, "I will not leave you, until you promise to tell your father as soon as you reach home—even before you have your horse put up;" and he held his hand until he gave the desired promise, telling him at the same time to continue to ride at the same gait at which they had been travelling, so that he could form an idea when he would reach home. He tells him, "When I think you are telling your father, I will be engaged in prayer in your behalf. I am convinced that all will be right." We part; and I ride on slowly, feeling happy, and trying to sing. Unfortunately, I belong to that class who cannot raise a tune; still I try to sing—

"Jesus, my all, to heaven is gone,
He whom I fix my hopes upon."

I reach the place where I delivered my political speech to the trees on Saturday last. There I stop, dismount, and fall on my knees, thanking the Lord for what he has done, and begging for more grace. I set out again as agreed upon, sometimes thinking that my father will be angry with me, and then again hoping for the best. Although I have not been a member of the church quite a day, still I put much confidence in prayer, and expect my friend will soon be remembering me before the throne of grace. I at last reach home, and hitch my horse without taking off the saddle, and then proceed to the house, and tell my father what has taken place, at the same time begging him to forgive me for all I had ever done to wound his feelings. He is much moved, and forgives me all—telling me he had heard of it before I got home. He told me, that he would have preferred my joining the church of his choice, but that next to that, he liked the Methodist church; and that he hoped I would do well, and that the Lord would bless me. He told me also, that he had seen some of his friends that day, who thought he was sorry I had joined the Methodist church, and that they told him they had clubbed together, and would have me back in the world in six months at most. But my father said, he hoped that, with the help of the Lord, I would disappoint them. I knew that I alone could not resist them. More than thirty five years (October, 1866) have passed by, and I am still in the church, and I hope on my way to heaven.

Before my six months' probation had passed, I was appointed junior class-leader by Brother Adams, at Pine Grove church, to which allusion has already been made. Brother Dunwody received me into full connection; I remember the occasion well. He told me, that they were satisfied with me; but that if I desired to withdraw my name I was at liberty to do so. With tears in my eyes I told him, that my wish was to live and die with them.

I remained class-leader for some time, and after the lapse of some years I began to exhort; but I was in the church for several years before I was licensed to preach, which was I think thirty-one years last July. As my papers were burned some five years ago, I may have forgotten some of the dates. I think Bishop Andrew ordained me deacon, in Camden, in the year 1840, and four years after I was ordained elder by Bishop Soule, in Columbia. I owe all that I am to my Heavenly Father, to whose name be all the glory. I have again and again said and done things for which I have felt very sorry afterwards; but I hope that my blessed Saviour has forgiven me all.

## LEAF THE FOURTH.

### THE DREAM THAT WAS REPEATED; AND HOW DR S—— WAS CONVICTED AND CONVERTED.

More than thirty-one years ago (1866), there was a gentleman, a physician of much intelligence, well known to me, and I respected him very much. I will call him Dr. S. Though he was an upright man, and highly respected in his neighborhood, he was not a member of the church, and very seldom attended our church. At that time I was an exhorter, and I often wished that the Doctor had religion; for we met frequently, and usually spent our time very pleasantly together, and I thought that if he were a Christian it would be a great help to me. I had often desired to speak to him on the subject, but at that time I was young in the cause, and I dreaded the opposition with which I might meet; for I was easily repulsed if I met with a smile of ridicule or contempt, and was afraid of making him more distant towards me, should I fail in persuading him to come out on the Lord's side.

What I am now relating happened so long ago that I cannot recall to mind all the incidents connected therewith, but those of most importance can never be forgotten.

Time passed on thus for years, with Dr. S. and myself, when one night I dreamed that I saw the Saviour, as I had once seen him in a dream years before. He was standing quite near me, as described in the book of Revelation, and said to me, speaking of my friend Dr. S., "Unless he gets religion, and joins the church in twelve months, when he dies, he will be lost."

The vision vanished. I was very much impressed, and slept but little during the rest of the night. It seemed to me that I must tell the Doctor about it—that it was the Lord's will that I should do so. I knew not what to do. I dreaded being laughed at. Oh! how well I remember that day, and how I tried to pray for him. The next night, strange to say, I dreamed the same thing again. My feelings cannot now be told. It seemed to me more than ever that I ought to tell him about it.

I have often thought the Lord brought Dr. S. to see me the next morning, that I might tell him the dream; for soon after breakfast he rode up, and asked me to ride with him. We were alone for several hours—my thoughts dwelling on the solemn dream. Duty prompted me to tell him. I made many efforts to do so, but failed each time, being afraid of being laughed at or repulsed in some way. The Doctor saw, and said, that something was on my mind. I told him he was right; but even then I dreaded to tell him. We travelled on. I have seldom had such an unpleasant ride. At last he said, that he knew I was much troubled, and felt hurt that I would not tell him the cause, as he thought he was entitled to my confidence. Even then I could not speak of it. Thus we parted. I was much cast down, and felt that I had done wrong, and was sorry for it. I have always being willing to bear with persons, who, when they first join the church, are timid and dread to take up the cross; for I remember so well my neglecting to do my duty, being afraid of being laughed at. I was in the church for years, before I would hold family prayers in the presence of persons who were not members. I would wait until after they had retired, and then do that which ought to have been done before them. When I recall the past, I see so many things which I regret—so much want of Christian fortitude and firmness—so many duties neglected—and so many things done, for which I felt sorry afterwards.

Dr. S. and I parted; and for a long time I prayed for him twice daily; but after a while I ceased praying so often, and the time came when I did not pray for him individually in my private devotions. The twelve months were passing away. I sometimes thought of my dream, and felt very sadly; but the Lord was then drawing the Doctor to himself. He had a servant who ran away, and was taken up and put in jail, some distance from home. He heard of it through the papers. He left for the place, which I will call R——, where, not many years before, there had been quite an outpouring of the Holy Spirit. Very many persons had been converted, and had joined the church. The good impression made then was not all gone, and the citizens often met in different houses for singing and prayer. Now, it so happened that Dr. S. arrived in town on one of those evenings devoted to prayer. He told me, that he was seriously affected by the singing, and wished that he had religion. He found when he arrived at the friend's house where he expected to spend the night, that the prayer-meeting was to be there, and not feeling worthy to remain with them, he went to the hotel—thinking that if he only lived in R——, he would get religion.

One day some time afterward, he dined with me. He observed to me suddenly, that he had a great mind to go to R—— to live. I asked if he was going there for the health of his family? He said, no. I then inquired if he was going there to practice medicine? He replied, that in that respect he would do better to remain where he was. Up to this moment I had no thought of his being under serious impressions; and was much surprised when he said very seriously, that if he could live there for three months he would be converted; and that he would give the world, if he had it, for religion. I was overwhelmed with astonishment. I remained silent for some time, but replied after a while, "You can get religion at home just as well as there." He could not believe it; but said, he thought R—— was the best place in the world. All this was so unexpected, that I failed to improve the opportunity of speaking to him on the subject he had introduced. We separated without my saying anything more; but in my secret soul I felt thankful, and afterwards I began to pray for him frequently.

Some time after this, he attended one of our camp-meetings, and became seriously impressed, and went to the altar for prayer. He went home without experiencing a change, but deeply convicted, and began holding family prayer. He afterwards told me how much surprised he was, that I did not speak to him on the subject of religion while at my house—that he fully expected me to do so, and was much disappointed that I failed to do so, expecting to be invited there to prayer meetings; and he said he thought me a poor exhorter. Thus was I reproved, and I embraced the offered opportunity, and spoke for my blessed Master. I told him that I would be glad to see him at my house on such a day, which was near at hand—that I expected a brother-exhorter to be present on **that** day, and that we would have a prayer-meeting for him. He said he would be glad to come. He said he thought that a great difficulty with him would be, that he did not believe in the Saviour as he ought to do—that for years he had been praying to the Father, but not to the Son, and when that difficulty was removed he thought he could get religion. Thus we knew how to advise him and pray for him.

On the appointed night, Dr. S. was there, much distressed. The wife of one of our preachers was with us. She was a sweet singer. We had a good meeting. My brother-exhorter was a good man, full of faith, and spoke much to the point while addressing the Doctor — who complained of a great oppression in his chest. After a while, he begged us to walk out with him. When on the road, he requested us to pray for him right there, and knelt down, his heart almost broken. We remained with him for more than hour, and then told him, as it was quite late, perhaps he had best go home, as his family might become uneasy. I told him that such a preacher would be at our house on a certain night, and that he must come, and we would have prayer for him again.

The appointed time had come, and the preacher was present. It was a lovely night; the virgin moon shone most beautifully. As the sweet Swan of Avon would say—

"She tipped with silver all the fruit-tree tops."

Dr. S. arrived, more distressed if possible, than before. The same scenes were passed through again: we sang and prayed for some time, Dr. S. being most powerfully impressed. He begged us to go out with him again, and proposed another direction. He was so troubled that he could not walk alone, and we supported him on each side.

"Doctor," said the preacher, "what would you give for religion?"

"Sir," said he, "I will give my wife and two children; and the Lord only knows how I love them."

He would have fallen, had we not been holding him. "Doctor," said the preacher, "you are very near conversion; there is but one step between you and salvation." Dr. S. said he had been laboring for some time under a great oppression in his breast; that he had been thinking a strong dose of calomel would relieve him. I suspect only myself and the virgin moon saw the slight smile which passed over the preacher's face as he said, "Doctor, 'tis religion you want; the weight will be removed when the Lord blesses your soul, which I believe he will soon do."

We went only a few yards farther, when he fell on his knees, and the preacher prayed for him, and he felt that his sins were forgiven. We arose from our knees, and he threw his arms around the preacher's neck, and said, "Oh, sir, you do not know how much I love you." Then Dr. S. exulted aloud; he was very happy, and we rejoiced with him. On our way from the house we had to support him, he could not walk for the sorrow of his heart; on our return, we still supported him, he could not walk then for the joy of his soul. I regard that night as one of the happiest of my life. As we passed on to the house the preacher said, "Now, Doctor, how about that oppression at the heart?" Dr. S. replied, with a heavenly smile, which I see even now upon his face, "Oh! sir, it is all gone."

We had arrived at the steps; he was perfectly carried away with his happy emotions. Just as we were on the top step, the Doctor shouted aloud. We entered the house, and Dr. S., in passing across the room, came near falling; but he approached my wife, and shook her hand heartily, saying, "Oh! I feel so happy." He said, it was much easier to get religion than he thought it was; it was only to give your heart to the Lord.

Some days after this, my wife said to me, "How about that dream?"—some ten months having transpired since I had the dream. But Dr. S. had been converted, and was rejoicing in his God.

## LEAF THE FIFTH.

HOW DR. S —— JOINED THE CHURCH—AND THE MERCHANT DID NOT SELL THE HEAVY BILL THAT DAY AS WAS EXPECTED.

Dr S. had been happily converted, and the oppression at his heart was all gone, and he rejoiced in the great hope of his salvation. He told me, that on that famous night while going home, it appeared to him that he was stepping higher than the trees along the road. He asked me if I remembered having spoken to him on the subject of religion, in his own house, and in my eagerness placing my hand on his shoulder, and that he turned suddenly round, with his back to me. I told him that I remembered it well; and that my reason for leaving so soon afterwards, was because I thought his feelings were wounded. He said his reason for turning from me was to conceal his emotion, for he was weeping while he had his face turned away; that had he followed his inclination he would then have asked me to pray for him.

The great object of Dr. S. now was the salvation of his much-loved wife. He often told me of his anxiety on her account. She appeared rather indifferent; but we often prayed in her behalf. I sometimes went over and had prayer at his house; and thus things remained for some time. This was prior to his joining the church; his family believed in another communion, and I said nothing to him on the subject, thinking that they might conclude I was trying to persuade him to unite with our church. During my whole life, I have ever been careful on that point—always counselling friends to join the church of their choice; notwithstanding I have always been glad to have persons unite with our church—doubly so, when I thought they would become a help to us, with the blessing of God. Some months after this, Dr. S. told me he had made up his mind to join our church—knowing full well that some of his near relatives would object to his doing so; one particularly would be much hurt, and it would be a great cross for him to take up; but he would put his trust in the Lord, and go where his heart was. He, however, said nothing to his wife about it, wishing it to be kept a profound secret, and wanting to take her by surprise. He said he wanted her to go with him; that he would be much hurt if she joined any other church, and he requested me to say nothing about it to any one except my wife. He did not know when he could unite with us, as he wanted his wife to be present when he did so. He thought a sudden surprise would make a good impression on her, and perhaps she herself might unite with the church at the same time, or soon afterwards.

He told me finally, one day, that his wife had at last promised to go to church with him, not knowing what were his intentions. He also wanted my wife to go with us. Some time after, the Doctor's wife told mine that she had no idea why her husband was so anxious to have her go with him on that occasion; that he begged her very hard to go, telling her he would give her anything she wanted; and that she finally promised to accompany him, provided he would let her go to a store near by, and buy anything she wanted. He promised to let her do so, if she would first go with him to church. She said she had made up her mind to get a great many things, whether she needed them or not, and that she rather thought he would have a heavy bill to pay that day. The day arrived, and we went to the church—situated near the Edisto river. The preacher had not yet arrived, and we were much disappointed. There were not many persons present, but among them was the exhorter at our first prayer-meeting held in behalf of Dr. S. We were told that the preacher would not come, and Bro. C. and myself had to conduct the meeting. Several persons had come out for the purpose of joining the church, and did not wish to wait any longer, and they requested us to open the door, which we concluded to do. We agreed to conduct the meeting thus:—Brother C. was to open with prayer, giving each one an opportunity to relate his experience, after which we would have an exhortation and prayer, and then open the doors, which would conclude the service. The blessed Spirit was present, and we had a glorious time. First one and then another, would tell us what the Lord had done for them. I spoke to the Doctor's wife about religion; she appeared provoked, and I left her. She afterwards said, she never was so angry in her life as then, to think that I should presume to speak to her in the church concerning her soul! The meeting went on under the blessed influences of the Holy Spirit; we were sitting in heavenly places. I no longer thought of speaking to Dr. S.'s wife; she was sitting on the opposite side, looking very defiantly. She afterwards said, she was determined to show the Methodists that day that she would not be moved—that she would not shed a tear; no, she would not; and that she was determined the Doctor should have a heavy bill to pay for bringing her there that day.

The time for those who wanted to join had come. While the hymn was being sung. Dr. S. came forward; then followed a venerable man, and then others. I then turned to look at the Doctor's wife. She had fallen from her seat, overpowered with strong emotions. She told her friends afterwards, that she was never so surprised in her life. Her first thought was—"If he had only told me of his intentions, I would have gone with him;" but the second thought which occurred was—"You are unworthy to do so; for did you not get very vexed just now, when spoken to about religion?"

After this, we remained in church for some time, singing and praying. I will not try to describe the feelings of the Doctor; for who can tell the thoughts of his heart? The meeting was then closed; but the store was not visited; the merchant did not sell the heavy bill; for the Doctor's wife appeared as much troubled as he had been while under conviction—he having to support her as she left the church. She went home in great agony of soul; but at last found the pearl of great price, and united herself with the church.

3

## LEAF THE SIXTH.

### DR. S—— IN HIS FIRST LOVE-FEAST.

Dr. S. and his wife were now united together in the Lord, and we were united with a few others, who loved the Lord, in having meetings sometimes, where we enjoyed ourselves in singing and praying. In some respects, the Doctor differed from myself and others around him. He said we ought to enjoy ourselves in a calm, silent way—that it was better thus to pass along through an unfriendly world to glory and to heaven. When alone, he often spoke to me on this subject; but I thought there was no harm for a man, whose sins the Lord had forgiven, when he felt so inclined, to shout aloud and praise his God—knowing that the old saints thus praised their Maker, there being proof of this in holy writ. We often spoke of our difference of opinion, but always in a friendly manner. He told me, he knew he had praised the Lord aloud when he was converted, but that was an extraordinary occasion, and he could not help himself. He did not think, though, that he would ever be so moved again; for he had made up his mind to pass through this life very gently—manifesting no violent emotions at any time—that no one should ever know he had religion, unless they saw it in his changed life.

Thus things passed on—the Doctor happy in his Saviour's love. Some time after this, there was to be a two days' meeting near by, and I prayed for, and expected, a gracious outpouring of the Spirit. Some time before, the Doctor said to me, "I expect you will speak in the love-feast." I replied that I expected to, as I had never been in one without saying something for the Lord. He thought it but right that preachers, class-leaders, and exhorters should speak if they felt like it; but other members ought not to say anything; that he expected to enjoy himself as much as any one who would be there, but had made up his mind never to speak in love-feast; that as he sailed along the river of life there would be no noise, no ripple in the water; that persons would never find out that he had religion, if they depended on his speaking in public. I told him I thought his friends would be glad to hear him speak in love-feast; but to do as he thought best.

The time for the meeting at the chapel arrived. Let us imagine that holy Sabbath morning, more than thirty years ago. The hour for love-feast had come—there being a good turn-out for the neighborhood. That blessed man of God— that primitive Methodist minister—Brother Bass, conducted the meeting, other ministers being present. The house was closed, and singing and prayer were over; the exhortation had been gone through with, and the bread and water were being passed round; and our never-to-be-forgotten love-feast had a happy beginning. Brother Bass told us something of the dealings of the Lord with him—of his long course of trials and sorrows. The tears stole down the veteran's face as he begged us to pray for him, and told us of the strong hope he had of reaching the happy land, where all is peace and joy for evermore. In conclusion, he told us he would be glad to hear from any of us how we were coming on, on our way to glory. There was much feeling among us.

I remembered what Dr. S. had said, and glanced at him. He seemed to be under some emotion, but looked as if he had made up his mind to master it. Another preacher arose, and carried us back to his early life, when he was a wicked, graceless youth, bound for perdition, without Christ and hope. He spoke of his praying mother, who often told him of the love of the Saviour; and that he was at last made to see his condition, and know there was no hope for him but through the redemption of God; but that one day, which he could never forget, the Lord pardoned him.

Some one then—Brother Holman, I think—sung a few lines of a beautiful hymn; and there was then a shout in the camp. I again glanced at Dr. S., who appeared so much excited that he could not keep still.

I then arose, and had much to say of what the Holy One of Israel had done for my poor soul. I spoke of my mother, who I knew was in heaven. I alluded to my past life—spoke of my wickedness during my first years: that before that memorable meeting at Binnakers I had been extremely wicked; but that I was then powerfully convicted, and joined the church before I got religion, but was soon after converted. I told them I expected to get to heaven, and knew I would there meet my sainted mother. After which, I asked an interest in their prayers, and sat down.

Dr. S. was under powerful impressions, but was trying hard to retain his seat—holding on to the bench in front with both hands. There seemed to be a giant effort on his part to adhere to his determination not to say anything in his first love-feast. We had a blessed time; the Lord was in his holy temple, and his servants were exulting in the God of their salvation. Another beautiful hymn was sung by Brother H., and we had another shout in the camp. Another member then got up, but was so excited that he could not say much; he told us though of his boundless love for the Saviour, and hoped he would never return to the world, preferring, if it was the Lord's will, to die rather than backslide and quit the church.

I again glanced at the Doctor, who was still holding on to the bench, looking as if he would soon fall prostrate. There was another shout and clapping of hands, in which the preachers joined heartily. Dr. S. could stand it no longer; hell was disappointed, heaven had triumphed, and the holy angels were rejoicing. Oh, my soul! what a glorious time we had! He rose, and told us he could hardly speak for his strong emotions; that he had made up his mind never to speak in love-feast, for he thought it wrong to do so, and that he had told a friend he never would do so; and he had never tried, in all his life, as he had done that morning, to keep his seat, but could not do it. He told us, how happy he was that he was bound for heaven, and his dear wife was going with him. He requested us to pray for him, hoping we would all meet in heaven to part no more for ever.

I think there is more than one ransomed soul in glory who remembers that blessed love-feast, which was as good as I have ever been in. Brother Bass seemed as if he was looking over the flood into the green fields of Eden, and that he was listening to the harps of glory by the banks of the river, which makes glad the city of the Lord. The glorious tide of deep feeling swept on through the joyous throng present in the church, while some of those who were outside, waiting for the preaching of the word, were impressed by the great Spirit. Among them, a brother told me, he saw my father looking through a window, with the tears streaming from his eyes. On went the love-feast, with the tide of devotion bearing everything before it. Several others spoke near the close of the meeting. Dr. S. again rose, with a smile of joy on his face. I have no doubt many holy spirits were hovering near. He said, if we would excuse him, he would speak again. Brother Bass said we would be glad to hear from him. Among other things, he said, he could not tell us how happy he felt, that although he did not expect to speak at all, he now wanted to speak the second time. If I had never clapped my hands and shouted "farewell world" before, I think I would have learned how, at that love-feast.

" Jesus, all the day long
    Was my joy and my song:
O that all his salvation might see!
    He hath loved me, I cried,
    He hath suffered and died,
To redeem a poor rebel like me.

" O the rapturous height
    Of that holy delight
Which I felt in the life-giving blood!
    Of my Saviour possessed,
    I was perfectly blessed,
As if filled with the fulness of God."

## LEAF THE SEVENTH.

DR. S——, AFTER ADVISING AND ENTREATING HIS FRIEND TO REFRAIN FROM SHOUTING AT AN EXPECTED MEETING, IS THE FIRST HEARD FROM.

Did you ever, brother preacher of the gospel, have a friend, that you thought much of, who did not think it right for persons to give way to their feelings, and thought that sometimes harm was done by it, and made great efforts to control himself, but who could not always succeed, as now and then he would be heard from like the sound of many waters, but afterwards be much mortified and ashamed of it, and go to work to recover his self-command? Such a friend was Dr. S. to me. I used to think in those days, that I preferred to hear a shout from Dr. S. more than any man I knew. He used to make a brave and gallant effort to restrain himself, and often succeeded; but once in a while the tide of emotion would be too strong for him, and he would then be heard from like the mighty whirlwind, sweeping everything before it; and after the excitement would pass off, he would be in the very depth of the valley, low down, very low down. No text would suit him so well as, "Why art thou cast down, oh, my soul; and why art thou disquieted within me?" He would now have very little to say; his head bowed down like a bulrush; thinking everybody was looking at him—some in sympathy for, and others finding fault with, him; it would be some time before he would recover the even tenor of his way. It would now take a tremendous power to arouse him to the strong fever heat again.

For several weeks after our love-feast, Dr. S. seemed to be uneasy while with me, appearing to be much troubled about something. I suspected what it was, but said nothing, thinking, though, that I knew a thing or two. He did not appear as much at home in my company as formerly. Thus several months passed off. I suspected he was gathering fresh strength for another effort for self-control, and that he would not again approach the debatable subject until he thought he was master of his emotion. I understood it all, though I said nothing.

The Doctor was called on by some of his friends to pray in public. He never refused, but did not like it, and told us as much. He prayed fervently, as if the words came from his heart, and they never failed to reach the hearts of others. The time came when he thought he could approach the subject in a proper manner. Once, when we were alone, he said to me, he suspected I was much surprised at his speaking twice in our love-feast, after making up his mind to say nothing. I told him I was; but thought it added much to the interest of the meeting. He replied, that he was ashamed of himself afterwards; but he knew it would never happen again, for he could control himself much better the next time, as he was prepared, and had made up his mind more fully on that subject. I made no reply. He went on to say that he supposed, that some thought he had made quite a display of himself on that occasion, and he was determined it should not happen again, for he had prayed for strength, and felt that he could control himself. He wanted to know if I had heard the preachers or any one object to his speaking the second time that day. I told him, all who spoke to me of it seemed much pleased, and thought with me, that it added much to the pleasure of the meeting. He was still quite sore on the subject, and appeared to be making a mighty effort to be able to command his feelings. I told him he was too sensitive; for I did not think it was wrong in any one to thank the Lord aloud if he felt like it, but rather thought it wrong for any one to attempt to restrain his feelings on such occasions; as we were taught in the Bible that in olden times God's people praised him aloud; and that it was wrong to wish or attempt to please the enemies of the church, as there were some who would make sport of religion and all things connected therewith.

Time rolled on, and the Doctor recovered, as he thought, still better command of himself. I was present at several meetings where he sailed along very quietly, there being no noise, no ripple in the water. About this time, there was a minister on our circuit whom we all loved very much—even sinners revered him. He accomplished much good, both in and out of the church. He was a whole-souled Christian; and both the Doctor and myself respected and loved him. We expected to attend a quarterly meeting some distance off, and to stay with a friend who lived near.

Once, when Dr. S. and myself were alone, he told me there was something about which he wanted to speak very plainly, that he had been long wanting to do so, and he hoped I would not feel hurt with him. He said, he had often thought that I would do more good to the church, and enjoy myself better, if I had my feelings under better control; that at times he thought my giving way to my feelings did harm, as he had heard some members of the church object to it. He said, that his motives in speaking to me were pure, and begged me, as a friend and brother, to make a great effort to control my feelings while at the approaching meeting. He told me further, that he was afraid the sight of the minister of whom I thought so much would excite me. I told him, at one time I was of the same opinion, but I was changed; and, when I felt like shouting, I did so, whether people liked it or not. I warned him not to be too confident of his position, as I had not forgotten our love-feast at the chapel. I thought he winced a little, and said, if I would forgive him, it should never happen again, as he was much stronger.

We went to the quarterly meeting. Dr. S. was in fine spirits, and said he expected to enjoy himself in a quiet manner—no one knowing it but the Lord and himself. On Saturday we had a good sermon, but apparently but little feeling in the congregation. In company with several of the preachers, we went to the house of our brother, to whom allusion has been made, who was a good and true man in every respect. We were kindly received by him and his gentle wife. Dr. S. embraced the first opportunity to tell me how much he had enjoyed the meeting, saying, he supposed I had noticed how well he controlled himself, and added, he wished I could do the same. Night hastened on. Several preachers were present, and we retired to a room for private prayer. We closed the door, and bowed our knees in humble prayer. For some time, we remained silent, with only a few brief prayers from some of the preachers. But what noise was that, like the roaring of the mighty whirlwind? Dr. S. could hold in no more; the avalanche had fallen, and borne everything before it! Such a shout had been seldom heard in the chamber of private prayer. I have heard nothing to surpass it for more than thirty-five years. Dr. S. rose from his knees, and shook hands, first with one and then another. He was completely cut loose from all his moorings. All his boasted self-control had been swept away like straws before the mighty winds of heaven. His loud shouts rang through the evening air. A tide of happy feeling passed through the room—the preachers all rejoiced with the Doctor.

We had been there some time, when I went to the back door, and opened it to let in some fresh air. Many negroes had gathered outside, to know what was going on within. Dr. S. came out, completely overpowered by his emotions, which, like noble horses, long held in check by bit and bridle, now having broken loose, rushed with headlong speed wherever they pleased. He went among the servants, and shook hands with them, and praised the Lord.

Finally, though a reaction took place with Dr. S., family prayer was over, and we retired to the same room, but he scarcely closed his eyes, being very low down in the valley of despondency, and having hung his harp on the willows. All his self-control was gone; how could he ever raise his head again? He who had so earnestly, so affectionately, entreated me to restrain my emotions—to follow the example he would set me—he who would sail along so gently, so quietly, with no ripple on the waters—was the first heard from—he praised God aloud. He passed a sleepless night. Whenever I awoke, I found him tossing from side to side, sighing mournfully. He was afterwards taken with a violent headache, and remained on the stool of repentance for a long time, regretting much what had happened, and resolved to go to work to recover his self-control; but he said nothing to me for many years about restraining my feelings, and following the example he would set me.

# LEAF THE EIGHTH.

### OLD SHILOH; OR, THE SANCTIFIED PREACHER.

Brother preacher, have you forgotten the little wayside church in which you preached in olden time? It stood not far from the high-road, just after you crossed the branch or creek; or, perhaps, in the edge of an old field, with a few short leafed pines near it; or, perhaps near a little pond, full of water in winter, and very dry in summer; or it may have stood on the top of a little hill, with large tall trees near it. Such was the situation of old Shiloh, when I first began to preach. And, brother preacher, do you not love to return, in imagination, to those times when to go to a two days' meeting at one of those little wayside houses was the height of your ambition? And if the weather was good, and the friends had laid by their crops, and their corn and cotton were not in the way, and there was no other meeting near to draw off a part of the expected congregation, and if you had something over a hundred rank and file of all classes and colors, you would think you had a tremendous crowd, and would have to preach out of doors on Sunday.

Such was the Shiloh of my hopes and fears in the days of "auld lang syne." But the much-loved church is gone, and I see it no more.

And then, you sometimes got to the church, after your long ride, ahead of your congregation, and hitched your horse to a swinging limb, and sat down on one of the rough benches in the little log-house, thinking about your sermon; and after a while the people would begin to come up; perhaps first a woman, with a child in her arms, and two or three little ones walking close behind; and then an old horse with both shoulders rubbed raw, in a small cart full of folks; and then two young women, with a young man walking between them, all with flowers in their hands; and then, again, a man on an old field pony, with a woman behind him, and a crop-eared, stump-tailed dog trotting close behind them; and presently an old gig, and a heavy, old-fashioned carriage, belonging respectively to the Squire and the Major on the other side of the swamp; and now, you are ready to say to yourself, "I do believe there is one dog to every four persons present." And after you got into the pulpit, and had said your prayers, the class-leader would come and beg you, in a whisper, to preach from such a text, as the Squire and the Major are out. Such was old Shiloh to me in the olden times.

And after preaching, when you said to the brother who was with you, "I feel so tired; I think we had best not have preaching to-night," and Brother V. would say, "I am afraid there will be a great disappointment; for old Sister N. told me, that her girls would be quite put out if there was no preaching to-night; for they had to stay at home to-day, to fix up, and have some dumplings and tarts for the big dinner to-morrow." So you had to publish night meeting; and then Brother V. fired off his big gun; and the Squire's daughter—Miss Sallie, and the Major's sister—Miss Mary Louisa, first came up and knelt at the little table—for there was no altar. And now, Mrs. P. came up, with a child in her arms, and a little boy holding to her skirts; and then Charlie R., and Billy H., and several other young men knelt at their seats; and the Major clapped his hands, and the old Squire said "glory!" and we had a great meeting that night.

Such was Shiloh of the olden time.

And then, such a fine turn-out we had on Sunday. Some of the quality, from near the Court House, came in, when the sermon was half over. And when the second sermon was almost ended, and Sister N. had shouted out aloud, and the Squire had twice said "glory!" and we were counting on a tremendous time, and we expected to have to protract the meeting—Mrs. G.'s little boy began to cry very loud, because he could not get another biscuit, and two horses which had been tied to the same tree began to fight, and the Squire's old dog Hector jumped on Mr. E.'s crop-eared, stump-tailed dog Pompey, and they had a big fight, and some of the boys ran out to stop the fuss—and the meeting was spoiled. And when you told Brother V. "good bye," he said "O, Brother B., what a pity those dogs began to fight; if it had not been for that, there is no telling what a glorious time we would have had!"

Such a place was old Shiloh to me in the days gone by.

But, my good brother preacher, after a while you began to spread out from home more than you used to do, and sometimes you got to a camp meeting on the other side of the river; and the preacher on another circuit sometimes told you he wanted you to help him at a big meeting at the Court House; and the presiding elder told you, that night he stayed with you, that you must "branch out more," for you would do more good by it. So you cannot go to old Shiloh now as often as formerly. And the last time you were there, you had been away for a long while; but somebody told you, that some one said, that the Major said, that the Squire said, that day at the log-rolling at his house, that "he was afraid the parson would soon be too large for his pants;" so you said to yourself, "this will never do; I must go there once more, even if the old house looks more like falling than when I was there last; and I will get some of the preachers to help me, and we will have a big meeting; and I will stay one night at the Major's, and one night at the Squire's, and take dinner at Sister N.'s; and will let the friends see, that the parson is not yet too large for his pants!"

So the long and short of it, my friends, is, I am on my last visit to old Shiloh—for not long after it was replaced by a new house.

The report of the expected meeting had gone far and near, on both sides of the big swamp; for it had been given out months beforehand, that Brothers D., V., B., and others were expected, and the meeting was expected to last over two Sundays; and the candidates for the next sheriff and tax-collector were expected to be there, so the meeting would not be broken up, even if old Hector did jump on and fight Mr. E.'s crop-eared, stump-tailed dog, Pompey.

And now, the preparations were all over, and the young ladies had been to the Court House, and got lots of fine things. But times have changed a little since our first visit. Some fine crops have been made down there since that time;

and the big swamp has been opened for rafting; and some of the quality people have moved into the neighbourhood. But the old church has not changed—there it stands, looking older, and more ready to fall, than when we were there last. The floor has sunk down near the pulpit. But the old house has been scrubbed over, and the yard has been swept and cleaned. Come, friends, be a little careful as you walk in. The old house looks as if it cannot stand much longer. The company appeared to be better fixed up, than when I first went there; and there is not as much going in and out during preaching as usual; neither were there as many dogs there as in days gone by. I did not see old Hector or Pompey; I suspect they had both crossed the flood.

As well as I can now remember, we had a good meeting on Saturday; but Sunday was to be the great day of the meeting. Every body will be out—big fish, little fish, and all. Arrangements were made accordingly—two sermons were expected—prayer-meeting before preaching—friends requested to come early. The blessed Sabbath—the holy day, was now come. Alas, for the expectation of poor mortals! it looked much like rain. We nevertheless start for the church, and have a fine turn-out.

Prayer-meeting was over, and we were in a crowded house, which looked as if it could not stand much longer. Old Shiloh had not had such a fine turn-out of the quality folks for many a day. A good local minister, from another circuit, was to preach the first sermon. He had been on the walls of Zion for some time, and believed in the doctrines of our church fully. He was a man with a sharp, strong, piercing voice. We now have old-time singing—clear, loud, and ringing. Prayer was over. The parson gave out his text, and told us how he would treat it, with the Lord's blessing. He divided it into three parts—first, second, and thirdly. The congregation looked as if they expected him to spread himself on *thirdly*. A gentle rain was falling. I was seated in the pulpit—having to hold forth next. As the preacher went on, he warmed up from time to time; but was reserving his main strength for *thirdly*. On went the parson with his sermon; the rain falls—a little faster, a little louder. The preacher, in his second division, raises his voice louder, and it is more piercing—the people appeared serious and attentive. On account of the depression in the floor, the pulpit leaned over a little. At times, the preacher had to hold on to the book-board to keep himself erect, and I had to lean back the other way to keep myself upright. The parson was now entering with his full strength on the last division; and the people looked as if they expected him to spread himself on *thirdly*. His glance seemed to say, "you need not be afraid; there will be no mistake, if the Lord will help me." The rain was falling now faster and louder; the old house seemed to lean more towards the middle than when we first came in. The preacher was spreading himself on *thirdly*. The people looked as if they thought so too. His voice was louder, and more piercing than ever. It rang through the church and the woods around. He was swinging clear now under very high pressure; his broad banner was unfurled and waving.

But now, that full justice might be done to *thirdly*, the preacher must press home on the waiting congregation, the doctrine of perfect love. He pauses, only for a moment, to gather all his powers for the final effort. While he pauses, if you listen, you can still hear the rain falling from the old house. The preacher was now making his final effort; and full justice will be done to *thirdly*. He proves his position—he tells us we must reach that point of perfect love by experience; he tells us of many of the old-time saints who lived in the enjoyment of this blessing; now he comes down to modern times, and makes honorable mention of many of the primitive Methodists who possessed it, and went home to glory. The old house seemed to lean a little more. Before taking his seat, the preacher begs his friends to excuse his speaking of himself; he does not wish to press so strongly this great truth upon them, without saying he was in the enjoyment of this great blessing himself. He was glad to think, he possessed himself what he preached to others, and had been happy in its enjoyment for some time, and was living in full stretch for the better world; the roots of bitterness were all removed, and he was free to say he was living each revolving day as if it was his last; he had no will of his own—had not had for some time—it was all swallowed up in his heavenly Father's. He was only waiting his Master's time; he was ready at any moment, by night or by day—in July's heat, in December's cold, if called he was ready—at home or abroad—on horseback or on foot—on the land or at sea—if called then and there, he would as lief go from that old pulpit, and through that old roof, to glory, as from anywhere else.

The preacher sat down, having done full justice to *thirdly*, calm as a summer's evening when no wind bloweth. I got up, having hardly time to plant myself firmly before the bookboard, when an awful crash was heard—apparently, the old house will be down in thirty seconds at most. A desperate rush was made for the open door, and the preacher was the second man that jumped out. Some said he was first, but the general impression was, that the parson came out second best—proving to all, both saint and sinner, that he *still had a very strong will of his own.* And while the parson rushed out, perhaps a holy angel almost sighed, and a fallen spirit shouted. But the old house did not completely fall down, and the preacher, who had no will of his own, and the congregation, who were more scared than hurt, came back, and I preached my last sermon in Shiloh. For the much loved old church is gone now, my friends, and I see it no more.

# LEAF THE NINTH.

A MEMENTO OF MY DEPARTED FRIEND, THE REV. JAMES C. POSTELL; OR A NIGHT AT CATTLE-CREEK CAMP GROUND IN THE OLDEN TIMES.

Departed brother, safe home in glory, I often think and speak of you, having a strong desire to see you once more, and hear you preach and sing again,

> "Trouble's over, trouble's over;
> A few more rounds of circuits here,
> Then all our troubles will be over."

Who ever heard that gifted brother once, without wishing to hear him a second time? I had heard so much of him, that my curiosity was much excited, and I was anxious to see and hear him. I saw him, I think, for the first time, at old Providence, near Midway, in Barnwell District, and was much pleased with, and interested in, him, being at once convinced that as a preacher for protracted and camp meetings, he had few equals. He invited me to come to Cattle creek camp meeting, soon to take place, and I promised to do so.

The day came, and I went. The meeting had been going on for some time, and much interest was manifested. Reader, were you ever at Cattle-creek years ago, when travelling was not so easy as now—when you had to ride some distance, and cross more than one deep creek; and were you not glad when you reached the place? After you had been there only a little while, and had received more invitations than you could meet, did you not feel like saying, "although the friends here have little tents, they have very large hearts." Come, tell the truth now; you were not long on the ground, were you, before the Bartons, the Fredericks, the Bowmans, the Snells, the Izlars, the Berrys, and others, were, sometimes more than one of them at once, requesting you to go with them? There is such a thing as a man getting too many invitations at camp meetings; at least, it has been so with me, as I am rather forgetful. It happened that the Strange Parson once, at Broxton's bridge camp meeting, received so many invitations (as was afterwards proved), that he promised four different persons to dine with them, and when the time arrived, a fifth man came, and the parson went with him, having forgotten the others. So I felt, while at Cattle creek, more than once like saying, "although the tents are small, these people have very large hearts."

Soon after I reached the ground, I was met by Brother Postell, who gave me a warm shake of the hand—which I can even now remember, though near thirty years ago—saying, "Well, Brother B., I am glad to see you; I think we are going to have a fine meeting to-night, for I have been praying for it, and I have faith to believe it." My hopes concerning the meeting, I confess, were not strong. The night was gloomy, and we had to go through the rain to the stand, and I suppose the unpleasant weather had affected my spirits. The old church was the only place in which the crowd could be accommodated, and even there I was afraid they would not be comfortable, and that we would not have a fine meeting; but he said, "Oh, yes, you will see it; for I have been praying for it, and expect it; as, you know, 'according to thy faith so be it.'"

"Brother B.," said he, "I have something to tell you; but you must not say anything about it for a while. If I have a chance, and I think I will, as I expect to exhort to-night, I wish to make use of something which happened on my way here." He then told me what it was, and said he thought he could make good use of it. Nothing more was said, and we parted.

The hour for preaching had come, and the horn had been blown. There was to be service in several tents, but I went with the crowd to the old church. There was a perfect jam, every place being filled with persons either standing or sitting. Such glorious old-time singing we had—even now in imagination I hear it. Every now and then I found myself thinking of what Brother P. said about our having a good meeting. In all my life, I never looked over a congregation as often as I did that night, trying to discover the wonderful things to be done; but I saw nothing during the sermon. Brother Forster preached well. When he concluded, I looked over the crowd, but saw no signs of what I had been led to expect. During the sermon, I had more than once discovered Brother P. regarding me with a look, which seemed to say, "never mind, we are going to have a fine meeting; for I have been praying for it, and have faith to believe it."

Brother P. now got up. He was a popular preacher, and drew crowds after him; and I suspect that the house was so full because it had got out that he was to exhort that night. The large and unpleasantly-situated congregation became very still when he rose. He observed, that he hoped to have the prayers and attention of all present, and exhorted the brethren to exercise faith, and to expect a large outpouring of the Spirit—that he looked for and expected it. He said, he was afraid there were several present who did not expect much, but that he hoped to see many mourners and several conversions. I turned, and looked again, but saw no manifest signs of the great out-pouring which was expected. He hoped the mourners would not wait for singing to commence, as he wanted to see them coming up promptly. During his exhortation (which ought never to be forgotten) he several times requested us to pray, and not to fear, and said that we would have a glorious meeting. I looked round frequently, but saw no marked signs. He more than once gazed at me with his piercing black eyes, which seemed to say, "do not fear, Brother B., we will have a great revival."

He compared himself to an archer, with his quiver full of arrows, and said he was going to shoot them at the sinner, the backslider, and all cold-hearted Christians, and he hoped every one would feel a smart—that he had more than a score of them, and as he shot them off, he hoped the church would pray as they heard them whizzing through the crowd. In his very impressive manner he proceeded fixing the arrows. His soul-stirring words followed one another like a mighty torrent rushing down the mountain side. I soon forgot to turn again, for the last time I looked I saw the marked signs, not to be mistaken. If the rain continued to fall, that torrent would sweep everything before it—trees, houses, rocks, and all. He would every now and then, after some strong expression, tell us another arrow was shot off, and beg us to pray as we heard it flying from the string.

On, and still on, the archer of the cross went—getting at length to his last shaft. He then paused, as if to recover full strength for his last effort. Oh, my soul! what a pause was that! It seemed as if immortal souls were trembling in the balance, while angels and devils held their breath as they looked and listened. Before shooting the last arrow, he said he would put a new string on his bow, and he begged us, if ever in our lives we had prayed with faith, to do so now—and I doubt if a more general or fervent prayer was ever offered up in old Cattle creek church. He then told us, that an interesting young lady, whose parents loved the Lord, and were on their way to heaven, who came there with him, was very gay and fond of fashion, and he was afraid she would never meet her parents in glory. He said, he had begged her to try to get religion, and he would pray for her as long as he lived.

The last arrow went sounding from the string. As I turned round to look, I almost sprang to my feet; for I saw a young lady fall from her seat as if she had been shot through the heart; and now, from the outside of the crowd, came a young man, forcing his way, stepping from bench to bench, crying for mercy. And then a crowd of mourners rushed up as if for their lives; and then Brother Postell came down from the pulpit, singing—

"Trouble's over, trouble's over;
A few more rounds of circuits here,
Then all our troubles will be over."

We had, indeed, a glorious old-time meeting. I remained until eleven o'clock, and then, not being able to reach the door, got out through a window. I hope to remember that night, in heaven, where all our troubles will be over for ever.

## LEAF THE TENTH.

MY FIRST VISIT TO OLD CANE CREEK CAMP-GROUND, UNION DISTRICT—WHY I WENT THERE; OR, THE BEGINNING OF MY ROVING LIFE.

After joining the church, and being class-leader and exhorter for some time, I began to preach; but for years did not go much beyond my own circuit. Brother James C. Postell, being sent to the Union circuit, invited me to come and spend some time with him, which I was glad to do—both to be with him, and to re-visit the old place in that district where I went to school when only eight years old. When circumstances allowed, I went; and this, then, was the beginning of my roving life, though I confess that preaching the gospel was only a secondary consideration.

After travelling a long distance, tired and worn out, I arrived one day about noon, at the house of that much-respected and whole-souled preacher, Brother John Jennings. I was told that Brothers Postell and Picket, and a few others, were going to hold a camp-meeting at Cane creek, and wanted me to attend. I told them what brought me up there; but, that after I had re-visited old scenes, I would be glad to attend. I had found out that the most of Brother Jennings's sons were not members of the church. After dinner, I went up stairs to rest; but the Lord was beginning to lay the burden of immortal souls more heavily upon me than ever before, and I could not rest; for the desire to see the preacher's sons converted took full possession of my heart, and for a time almost everything else was forgotten. Again and again, during the evening, I was on my knees, engaged in ardent prayer for those young men, begging the Lord to convict and convert them. I humbly besought him that they might be among the first at the altar, and among the first to embrace religion at the camp-meeting.

The next day I went on to Unionville, and was warmly welcomed by Brother Postell, and became acquainted with Dr. Dogan and others, good men and true. And now, reader, you find me at the place which I so long wanted to see—the old grounds of Mount Prospect stood before me. I roamed all about, thinking of Mr. Campbell the old teacher, and Mr. Wright with whom I boarded; and I went to the spring at the foot of a steep hill, and drank from it. I then knelt, and thanked the Lord for his protection to that hour; and then my thoughts went back to the death of my dear mother. I saw the whole scene before me—my gentle, heavenly-minded mother lying in her coffin; and I again listened to the reading of the funeral service, and remembered how filled with grief was the little boy's heart, yet no tears fell from his eyes; and how an old gentleman came up and put his hand on my head, and said, he suspected the little boy who could not weep felt as sorry as any present. And then I recalled the time soon after, when my brother John and myself were sent from old Pine Forest to Mount Prospect to school. I then went to the old house, and went in and around it, and then my melancholy feelings soon departed; for I then thought of the wild sports and frolics of the boys, and it seemed as if it were only a few days since we were there. I must leave old Mount Prospect now, and start for Cane creek.

I hastened on my way to spend the night at Brother Glenn's. It was near sunset, and I was approaching one of the happiest evenings of my life, for I was soon going to see one of the noblemen of heaven—the much-loved and highly-respected Dr. G. We met then for the first time, and have ever since been dear friends, and I hope we shall meet in heaven. I asked the stranger to direct me to the Rev. Mr. Glenn's. He told me, it was too far to be reached that night, and asked me to turn back a short distance, and spend the night with him. I declined at first, but he still insisted, and I yielded, for it was near night. We heard a noise in the distance, and rode on nearer to it; it proved to be water running over the rocks. I asked the name of the river, and was told it was the Enoree, which I had greatly wanted to see; and I enjoyed the sight, for I had now seen all that I wished of the places of my boyhood. We passed over the Enoree, and Brother G. took me to the house of a Brother Clark and his wife, where I met an interesting young man—a Mr. Sims. Thus in one evening, I had found four friends, who, since that time, have possessed a life-time hold on my affections; and I have always regarded that night, and the scenes therewith connected, as one of the green places in my roving life.

The morning came, and I was soon to leave for the meeting. Brother C. had a man attending to business, a Mr. B., who seemed inclined to have some sport with the preacher before he left. He took me over the place, and every now and then told me he thought it was unhealthy on the Walterboro circuit, and was surprised to see me looking so well, as I came from that country of grave-yards. He continued in that strain for some time, but it was not very entertaining to me. After a while, he insisted on weighing me, to ascertain how heavy I was. My horse had been ready for some time, so I told the family farewell, and turned to Mr. B., and spoke to him on the subject of religion.

"O!" said he, "I care nothing about it now; I have time enough to think of such things. If I thought I was going to die soon, I would like right well to have religion; but as I expect to live a long time, I will put it off."

I begged him to attend our meeting. He said, he had no time. I entreated him to come; telling him he might be benefitted. He said, he did not care about it then; but would put it off until just before his death, which would be ample time. At last, my faith in reference to Mr. B. became stronger, and I told him, if he would come to the meeting, I believed he would join the church. But he told me, he did not wish to attend, or to join the church. My faith became still stronger, and I told him I believed he was afraid to come, and dared him to do so—that I was going to pray for him, and I thought he would join the church; and thus we parted, and very soon I arrived at old Cane creek.

Let me say here, that it has been one of the greatest pleasures of my life to attend camp-meetings. Among them all, Binnakers and Cane creek camp-meetings are the dearest to me. At the former, I embraced religion, and joined the church in which I hope to live and die; and at the latter, I became more fully convinced than ever that I was called to preach, and that so far my labors had been blessed. I have always regarded my first meeting at Cane creek as the best I ever attended in my life. When I arrived there, the tents had been pitched, and the stand prepared, and everything was ready. There was an old church there in which the Quakers worshipped many years ago, but which was now used by others. I found several preachers on the ground, both travelling and local, but high above us all stood Brothers Postell and Picket. The meeting began with the marked presence of the Lord, deepening and widening from hour to hour. I forget who preached the first night in the Quaker church; but there was much feeling manifested. I had been praying every day for Brother Jennings's sons, and they were among the very first mourners to come to the altar. They were also among the first who were converted and joined the church. The powerful work continued for many days—at the stand, in the tents, in the woods, and everywhere. Perhaps such a time had never been known in those parts before. Day after day more interest seemed to be manifested. By common consent, Brother Postell was made the presiding elder of the meeting, he having had much experience in such meetings.

A gentleman of wealth, a Mr. Kelly, not a member of the church, came on the ground. One day, Brother P. changed his programme, and by this new disposition of his forces, he hoped, by God's help, to gain a complete victory over the enemy, who seemed to be yet strongly entrenched on some portions of the field. He appointed a love-feast in the church, and preaching at the stand, at the same time, and said, that he wished both services to close at the same moment. O, that love-feast! such a time of power and glory. All present seemed to enjoy it. It finally closed, and, the preaching having ended about the same time and singing just begun, we went there from love-feast, and the two bands of happy, rejoicing worshippers met together. Everything yielded to them, and a tremendous victory was gained—many were converted, many joined the church.

On another day, we had preaching at the stand, and prayer-meeting in the woods, at the same time. Both were well attended, and both closed at the same moment. The party from the woods—among them many happy converts—now came up to the stand, singing and praising the Lord; and a second time the exulting bands met together, and made a general charge—forcing the enemy to abandon every position, and leave the field. I have never witnessed such scenes in all my roving life. The gentleman mentioned above, was the father of the Rev. J. W. Kelly, both of whom I have always ranked among my best friends. Every day I prayed for Mr. K., and the Mr. B. of whom I have spoken. He had not yet arrived, but I still expected him. The meeting continued to go on with tremendous power—the young converts seeming to be deeply interested on the Lord's behalf, hunting up their worldly friends, and entreating them to come to Jesus. The preachers were fully engaged, with all their might, helping the Lord against the mighty. Brother Jennings and the two Brothers Glenn, did much good. They were seen everywhere, pressing the battle to the gate, driving all opposition before them—while hell raged in vain, and heaven rejoiced. Quite a large number had been converted, and up to this time about one hundred and fifty had joined the church. Some of the most promising young men of the country had come out on the Lord's side, and were soon to commence preaching the gospel. Men, whose names will never die, had thrown down the arms of their rebellion, and had started for the better world.

The morning came for me to leave, or break an engagement to go to another meeting, and as the time drew near, I became much cast down, and I was sorry that I had to go. I was entreated to remain; and Brother P. said, if I would go, that I must preach the 11 o'clock sermon, open the doors, call up mourners, and take my farewell. As I was walking over the ground, I was met by Mr. B., who had just come. He said, with a smile, that having heard so much about the meeting, curiosity had brought him over. I told him, I had been expecting him—that he must not forget what I told him. I then left him, and went to the woods to pray before preaching my last sermon. The congregation assembled, and I preached from, "He that goeth forth and weepeth, bearing precious seed, shall doubtless come again with rejoicing, bringing his sheaves with him." After the sermon was over, I opened the door of the church, and twenty-seven persons joined, among them Mr. B., who had made so much sport of me, and who did not want religion until near his death. My feelings at seeing him weeping can never be described. He soon afterwards was converted; and many years after, when he was a pious class-leader, we met at the same place.

Many mourners came up, and my work for the time was nearly done. Mr. K. and his son still kept away, and I thought I must make another effort; so going up to him as near as I could, I said to him, "I may never see you again until we meet at the judgment seat; I would be glad to pray for you." He knelt down, and I prayed for him. When we arose, I felt more resigned. He thanked me, but said, he thought we would meet again in this life; but if not, he would try to meet me in heaven. He then said, he wished to join the church. Years after, Brother J. W. Kelly told me, that he and some other young men used to be afraid of me when they saw me coming out in the congregation, and that on that day he first thought he would leave, but finally went where several young men were standing; that he afterwards saw me praying for his father; he then could remember no more, but was told that he fell between the benches, and when he came to himself he found himself at the altar, with his head in his mother's lap, and asked for me, but was told I had been gone for hours.

It required a mighty effort on my part to leave, but I thought I ought to keep my word. I have always regretted having left at that time, and it seemed as if I could almost feel some invisible hand holding me back. I left the stand; on my way a gentleman, whom I did not know, came up to me and asked if my name was not Lucius Bellinger, and if I, when a little boy, went to school, with my brother John, at Mount Prospect? I told him that I was the same. He said he was there at the time; that he was a member of the Baptist church, and that he had never enjoyed himself so much before. With tears in his eyes, and with his arms about my neck, he begged me, for the sake of the days of our boyhood, to remain. He told me, my labors had been blessed there, but that there was still more work for me to do. But I thought it would never do not to keep my promise. My heart was greatly moved when I parted from my old class-mate.

It appeared now as if the unseen hand was pulling me back; but I still moved on, and met a young gentleman, with a lady on each arm—all strangers to me. He told me who he was, and that he and his two sisters were among the mourners that came to the altar, and that they had never been there before. He said, they had not been converted; but thought if I would preach one more sermon, they would find the pearl of great price. They all wept, and begged me to remain. I told them I was sorry I had to go; that, so to speak, I was leaving my heart behind. They then asked me to pray for them right there, and we knelt in the sand, on the way to the tents. The Lord was present—the brother and one sister were converted, and rejoiced in their Saviour. The other sister, still more distressed than ever, entreated me to stay. I again felt the touch of the invisible hand, but tore myself away and left the ground, with such feelings as I hope never again to experience. I went on a little way. O, how I longed to stay! I turned round and looked back, and could still see the camp ground. I again started on my way, and went some distance. The unseen hand was too much for me—I turned round once more, and rode back, so near that I could see the congregation still at the stand, and could hear the sweet songs of Zion; but I thought it would never do to break my word, so I turned round, and left old Cane creek behind me. It was the best meeting I ever attended in my life. It lasted several days longer. More than three hundred persons joined the church, and nearly all were converted. Farewell to old Cane creek camp-ground, with its immortal memories.

## LEAF THE ELEVENTH.

#### MY FIRST VISIT TO ROCK SPRINGS CAMP-GROUND, NORTH CAROLINA; AND A WAYSIDE MEETING.

My friends, have you never been to the far-famed Rock Springs camp-ground? I will tell you then, of my first visit there, many years ago. I had my curiosity much excited by a Brother Carr, who was then on our circuit. He told me, if I wished to see the largest place of the kind in our church, to go there. I started on my long journey all alone. Brother Carr had told me, the meeting would commence on Thursday preceeding the first Sunday in August. I got to Yorkville in due time, and was much surprised when told I was a week too soon. I was an entire stranger, and knew not what to do at first; but I concluded that Brother C. must be right, and those who said otherwise mistaken. Some one told me, there was a class-leader living some fifteen miles a-head, who always kept the time, and he directed me to him. So I started, more than once wishing myself at home. I was then young in the cause; I had not yet learned to trust in the Lord as much as in my after life. I at last got in sight of the house, which stood on a high hill. As I was driving slowly up, I saw a buggy coming down the hill, in which there were a lady and gentleman. I was suddenly impressed that they could tell me something about the meeting, so I stopped until they came up. I asked, and was told it was a week off. I still thought Brother C. must be right, and these persons wrong. I told them I was on my way there, and would go on to the house, and find out all about it. The man said, he was on his way home from one camp-meeting, and expected to attend that one, and he knew he was right. As I was moving off, I saw the lady whisper to the gentleman. who asked me to stop, and then observed, "My wife says she knows you are a Methodist minister; and that I would regret it, if I did not stop you." He told me, he was the preacher on that circuit, and had been ordered to

Rock Springs next week; and he inquired my name. I told him who I was.

"Oh!" said he, "Brother B., I have heard of you, and you are the very man I wished to see. My name is McKibben;" and he told me he had a three days' meeting some thirty miles below, and that he wished I would turn back, and go there with him, and afterwards we could go to Rock Springs. I did not like the idea of turning back so far, but at last concluded to do so. And that was the place and manner in which I first met with Brother McK.—a whole-souled man and true, if there are any such in this unfriendly world.

"But," says some one, "what of the wayside meeting?" That was the one to which he turned me back. We retraced our steps to an old school-house, in which it was held. We stopped at the house of a sister Postell, the wife of a brother of the Rev. James C. Postell. She was a widow, and I found her to be a kind and good lady. That was my only visit to her house—it was a time of much pleasure, of which I often think, and hope never to forget. There were not many out the first day; but the number continued to increase during the continuance of the meeting. It was then I first heard Brother McK. He was plain, practical, strong, always to the point. He always followed his text; and, in my opinion, was neither too short nor too long. On Sunday, as there were a great many out, we had to preach out of doors. The presence of the Lord was evidently felt; and Brother McK. gave us a strong sermon. The feeling was such that he thought the meeting should be continued, though he had to leave for another appointment. He requested me, with some others, to remain until it was time to leave for Rock Springs. The interest appeared to increase; the Holy Spirit was powerfully present. Sinners were deeply convicted, and some mourners happily converted, and I think several joined the church. Preaching was again given out for the next day, and I stayed at sister Postell's—a night long to be remembered.

I might as well say here, that some of my friends have long known, that I often have had very remarkable dreams, which came to pass—that I sometimes preach, and exhort, and become very happy while asleep—sometimes disturbing the family, where I happen to be, very much. Sometimes I can recall every incident of my dream; and at other times, I know nothing of what has happened. I was told, the next morning, that I had disturbed the whole house, by making quite a noise, clapping my hands, shouting, etc., and I was asked what was the matter.

I pledge my honor for what I am going to relate. I told them, that I thought we would enjoy our best season that day; for I dreamed I was at the meeting, and we had a most glorious time; and that a young man, who had black eyes and hair—the latter being worn rather long, and who was of a dark complexion, came up to be prayed for, and remained there until happily converted, when he praised God aloud; and then turning to me, said, "Sir, I wish to join the church;" adding, "I would rather give my hand to you than any man I have ever seen; you need not be afraid of me; for, by the help of God, I will fight the whole warfare through." At that time I praised God aloud—which was the noise they heard. I told them my faith led me to expect it would all come to pass. Had some of my friends, who have long known me, been there, perhaps they would not have been as much surprised as that family seemed to be; though they only said, there was such a young man there, who was much respected.

The time for the meeting drew nigh—my hope in the Lord remaining firm and steadfast, never for a moment doubting the result; for I believed that our Lord was just as willing to answer prayer in these days as when those words were spoken, "ask, and ye shall receive; seek, and ye shall find."

Service began, and the text was taken from II Kings vii. 3, 4. The strength of Israel was gloriously present on that momentous occasion. Near the door stood the young man whom I had seen the night before in my sleep—a fine looking youth, black eyes, and hair that hung very low, and of a dark complexion. If I had given way to my feelings every time I looked at him, I would have said, "I saw you last night; and I am counting on you to-day;" and it was with an effort I restrained myself. At the close of the sermon, I called up mourners. At once several came up, among them the young man, who seemed much affected; and before he reached the place of prayer there seemed to be a great impression in the assembly. He fell on his knees, and remained there for a long time. We sang and prayed with him, and the feeling seemed to increase among the congregation. I have seen but few scenes in my life of more than thirty years as a preacher, that can be compared to that of which I am now writing. I think heaven was as near me then, and hell as far off, as at any time during my life. At last, the dark-eyed youth sprang quickly to his feet, with a tear and a smile on his countenance, and, "O," said he, "I am so happy!" He then turned to me, and said, "I wish to join the church; I would rather give my hand to you than to any man I ever saw. You need not be afraid of me; for, by God's help, I will fight the whole warfare through." I will not attempt to describe the effect of these words of the young convert upon myself and the congregation. I heard some of the old members say, "we will have a class-leader now." Some years after, while passing through that neighborhood, I spent a night with that young man. He was then a class-leader, and had a wife and one child, and seemed to be bound for heaven. I have never seen sister Postell since; but I suspect, if any of her family are living, they still remember the Strange Preacher, and the dark-eyed young man who joined the church that day.

It is time now to proceed to Rock Springs camp-ground, where I did not expect to know any one but Brother McK. I arrived there safely in due time, and found that scarcely the half had been told me. I had never seen such a vast crowd before. The famous London of camp-grounds was before me. My mind was so impressed by the sight of the multiplied thousands there, that I did not notice as much of the preaching, and the effect produced on the people, as I generally do. Binnakers, Black Swamp, Cane-creek, Providence, Cattle-creek, Mount Carmel, and Broxton's Bridge—are all small places, when compared with Rock Springs. There stood the tents, three rows deep, with more than a hundred in each row; while some distance farther off were

## MODES OF AMUSEMENT. 71

seen vast numbers of cloth tents, like hills of snow, on which the rising and setting sun shone so bright. While writing of Rock Springs, and the vast multitudes which I saw there, some of them more than a hundred miles from home, I feel like saying to myself, "if all those men, women, and children, who were present, were whole-souled, thorough-going Christians, what a vast amount of good might be accomplished, and how gloriously might our Saviour's kingdom be advanced!"

I was introduced to many members of the church, and was treated with much respect, and had more invitations than I could meet; but still, there were so many thousands there of whom I knew nothing, that I felt like a stranger during my first visit. I confess, that I looked more at the multitude before me, than at the single man who was preaching. At each successive service, though there were many thousands who listened with apparent respect to the word, there was always a very large crowd who stayed away. One day, I went out among them, and found them amusing themselves in different ways—some laughing, some talking, some reading, some writing, some eating, some getting drunk, others buying or selling horses, some cursing, others whooping as if they were on a fox-chase; some were asleep, partly opening their heavy eyes as I passed, others so buried in slumber that you might think nothing would rouse them up but a tremendous blast from Gabriel's trumpet; some looking very serious, as if they were sorry they had not gone to the stand; while others were separated from the rest, as if they wanted nothing to do with any but those belonging to their own party. But the Holy One of Israel was present to bless the word preached in faith, and also those who prayed for the salvation of Israel.

During the intervals of service, prayer and singing could be heard before the tents, and sometimes a preacher or exhorter would stand up and preach, the Lord blessing their labor. Brother McK. and others preached with spirit and power, and seemed to be used to such vast crowds, and knew full well what was best to be done. At times, the great crowd seemed to be moved by tremendous impressions, and there was singing that seemed almost loud enough to be heard for miles. And then, when a general shout went up from the hundreds of rejoicing souls who were not ashamed for sinners and devils to hear them, you might almost imagine that the dwellers on the other side of the river of death heard the praises of God's people.

Saturday night arrived, and many thousands had assembled; and you felt like asking, if they would at last settle down, and be as quiet as the occasion would permit? Yes; for the mighty ocean sometimes ceases its raging, and reminds you of a quiet inland lake. The trees of a mighty forest do not always bend beneath the strong winds of heaven, for those winds do not always blow. So the tremendous, moving, restless crowd at last quieted down, and was as a sleeping infant on it mother's breast. But now, the singing again begun, and those loud voices appeared to rise towards the heavens, and then that throng bowed in humble prayer before the Lord of hosts. The Spirit was powerfully present, and the arrows of truth flew through that dense crowd. The impression was strong, and all seemed to participate in the feeling of the presence of God. A crowd of mourners came forward, and their friends gathered around them, urging and encouraging them to go to Jesus. And the shouts of the new-born souls were heard at all hours of the night, from all parts of that immense camp-ground.

The time for the 11 o'clock sermon on Sunday came, and the crowd was much larger than before—that immense place was filled to overflowing. Carriages and buggies were ranged round, and benches and chairs were brought from the tents, and filled, and yet hundreds remained standing. A powerful impression seemed to be upon the dense throng, and tears of repentance were falling from hundreds of weeping eyes—while heaven-born smiles were seen on hundreds of happy faces.

My first visit to Rock springs, the London of camp-grounds, is past; and many are now in heaven, who then and there praised the God of their salvation; but, O, my soul! how many are now in hell, who then and there refused the offer of mercy.

## LEAF THE TWELFTH.

THE BLACK SWAMP CAMP-MEETING, WHERE THE COLONEL OF THE BEAUFORT RANGERS SURRENDERED HIS SWORD, AND THE CAPTAIN OF THE GILLISONVILLE GUARDS LEFT HIS POST.

Old Black Swamp camp-ground—holy place! time-honored spot of earth! never can I forget thee. O! ye friends of mine, who have gone to heaven from that once happy neighborhood, and who are now safe in glory, if you ever in your holy home above remember brethren on earth, I hope you sometimes think of me. Blessed spirit of Brother Joseph Manor Lawton!—much-loved class-leader of old Union church—hast thou, throned and crowned in heaven, no thought of those friends still left on earth—preachers and others, who were always made to feel at home under thy friendly roof? Loved friend! gone to a happier Eden than man first lost, dost thou not often think of those left behind—some of whom even now at times imagine that they still hear thy kind greeting? Blessed spirit! dost thou ever spread thy golden wings to revisit thy fatherland here below? If thou dost, I know thou art often hovering over Black Swamp campground, and thy much-loved Union church. O! ye friends of Christ and the church, who, in these troublous times, have your tents still pitched within the bounds of Black Swamp circuit, I hope you sometimes think of the preachers who used to sit with you in heavenly places in Christ Jesus. I often think of you, and hope your faith is still firmly fixed on the Rock of Ages, and that you will land safely on the other side of Jordan when life's pilgrimage is over.

Come, let us now, in our imagination, visit the old place, and record some scenes connected with that well-remembered meeting.

The time for the meeting had come, and the presiding elder—whole-souled Dr. Boyd—with his staff had arrived. The meeting began well, and continued to increase in interest. The second evening had come, and it was almost time for the sun to set, and the camp-fires would soon be brightly burning—and perhaps the heavenly guard, which had been around the camp all day, was to be enlarged. The preachers, who were still expected, came in due time, and their many friends gathered around them—Major G. among them; and who, that has ever felt the grasp of his hand, can ever forget it? There, too, was Major R., with his smile of friendly welcome; and Brother E. M., with his kindly greeting. But who is that, approaching with quick step, to shake hands with Dr. W., and him who now writes these lines?. It was the much-loved class-leader of Union church—Brother J. M. L., the perfect Christian, and the noble gentleman—who came more fully up to old Horace's description of the "*factus homo ad unguem*," than the best Roman who ever crossed the Tiber in those immortal days.

The meeting continued on with blessed results; and, O, what a happy time we had from the Lord! The Holy Spirit came down, and the friends of Jesus sung the sweet songs I loved so much—"There is a happy land, far, far away;" "Our bondage here will end by and bye;" "I would not live alway;" and many others. The preachers appeared to be full of the blessed Spirit; Christians rejoiced; sinners were deeply convicted; and mourners were happily converted while the shouts of the exulting servants of the Lord rang through the grand old woods that border on the Savannah river. I can never forget how much I enjoyed myself when Brother Bond English was preaching about the heavenly gardener, and of Mary weeping over the yet undiscovered Jesus, and saying, "if you have carried him away, O! tell me where you have laid him." Brother E. went on, and the heavens seemed to be coming nearer the earth; and many who listened and wept as they hung on his eloquence, will often remember those moving words, "O! tell me where you have laid him;" and many, who had with much pleasure heard the preacher before, thought that he was then preaching his best sermon. In the intervals of service, the time was well spent in some of the tents—exhortation followed prayer, and song followed song. The holy feeling seemed to widen more and still more. I went into the woods with others, to pray for the trembling mourners who were still unconverted, unblessed. They cried for mercy, and entreated their friends not to leave them. When we got there, Brother J. M. L., with a heart full of love and eyes full of tears, spoke to those weeping souls, begging them to go to Jesus just as they were, with no hope, no trust, in any other name; and then the woods rang with the sweet songs of Zion; then Brother Blunt prayed, and the Lord heard; and Colonel J. A. and his brother seemed full of happy, holy thoughts.

But who is that now coming up so gallantly to the help of the Lord against the mighty? Who that knew him well can ever forget that war-worn veteran of a thousand battle-fields—that sanctified knight of the cross—a preacher "without reproach"—Brother McPhail. How he moved about, speaking suitable words to all; and then he prayed; and first one and then another was happily converted. And then the good man clapped his trembling hands together, and passed through the throng, singing, with a voice that trembled too,

"O! brethren, will you meet me, In Canaan's happy land?"

And then, Brothers Lawton, Martin, Davis, Solomons, Blunt, Allen, Roberts, and others, all sung together,

"Yes, by the grace of God, we'll meet you, In Canaan's happy land."

We then went to the stand where Dr. B. was to preach, and the meeting still continued to increase in interest, for a prince of Israel was now on the walls of Zion. The large crowd appeared to be still more interested as the preacher went on gathering holy strength, and the mourners came up more willingly than ever, even before the singing commenced. Those who were never there before came then, as if they thought death and hell were close behind them; prayer followed prayer, and song succeeded song; and holy angels who were hovering near, carried the blessed tidings that the dead had arisen and the lost were found.

Now, my friends, let me introduce you to the young Colonel of the Beaufort Rangers, and the gallant Captain of the Gillisonville Guards. See the Strange Preacher seated by a gentleman, who appears very glad to see him. They are conversing in a low voice; now they draw closer together— the preacher taking his friend by the hand, and speaking with a serious face. See how the gentleman hangs his head, apparently listening, but for a while saying nothing. That man is the Colonel; and his friend is now telling him of the time when he was a young man, not yet of age—of the time when he joined the church and professed religion; and how his sister, the sweet singer of the Barnwell circuit, and many others, thought he would be a preacher in after life. That young man, who was then on his way to heaven, is now the the Colonel of the Beaufort Rangers, and is on his way to perdition. He remembers full well those better days. After a while, he recovers partly from his emotion, and raises his head, and says to his friend, "Those, sir, were by far my happiest days; for I felt that I was called to preach when I first joined the church, but would not do so, and then I lost my religion." He then added, with a serious face, "Prince Immanuel has many officers in his service; and if I ever feel like enlisting again, I would much prefer surrendering my sword to you." The preacher replied, that whenever the Colonel is ready to do so, he will with much pleasure receive his sword, in the name of Prince Immanuel.

And now, my friends, come with me to another tent. Let us wait and listen. There is a strong mind present, who leads in the general conversation—to whom all are listening with much interest. Would you not know him again among a thousand? He is the Captain of the Gillisonville Guards.

But we are again summoned to the stand. The Strange Preacher says to himself, "I must pray in private for those two friends; for the Colonel has given me a hint. If I am called to the pulpit, I will try to paint a picture for them which I hope they will not soon forget. The Colonel was once with us; O, how I wish he would come back again! And, O, that the Captain's heart might be reached! If he were to come out on the Lord's side, a great victory would be won, and the kingdom of darkness would tremble almost to its foundation."

## THE GREAT BATTLE. 77

The congregation at the stand was large. The seats were all filled—carriages and buggies were rolled up and occupied—benches and chairs were brought from the tents—and yet several remained standing. This was the most important hour of the meeting. Dr. Wightman was in the pulpit, and expectation was very high. He had many friends present, who had often heard him with much pleasure, and their hopes were now fully realized; for, by the help of the Lord, the great sermon of the meeting was then preached. The interest which was at first manifested grew deeper; but the great battle had not yet been fought. Dr. W. rose and soared in one eagle flight after another. By the help of the Lord, he bent the far-famed bow of Ulysses, and shot all the arrows through all the rings. But I must hasten on.

At the 3 o'clock service, the Strange Preacher occupied the pulpit, and the friends, by his request, were singing a song he loved very much—hundreds were singing—

" I've listed, and I mean to fight
Till the warfare is over."

The preacher told the congregation, near the close of the sermon, that the meeting would soon end, and that much depended on the results of the passing hour. He told them, that perhaps the report of the great battle then going on, had not yet reached the court of the King of perdition; and he attempted to paint the scene which was soon to take place, when the news of what was now going on should be known in hell's dark empire; and he begged them, for a little while, to imagine themselves present when the great Enemy of man first hears the report of the Black Swamp meeting.

The gloomy King was represented as seated on his fiery throne, with his chief princes around him. The black plumes of the vulture of despair waved over the Monarch's brow, and his relentless guards were about him. All the court was in full dress, and the ambassadors from different parts of the empire were present. It was a grand public day in hell. All the great master spirits, who drew their swords with him when he first unfurled his flag of rebellion in heaven, stood close around the archangel fallen. The standing army of perdition was seen in the distance, passing in awful review on one of the ever-burning plains of damnation, before some great spirit, who for the time represents the absent Monarch. Suddenly, a loud knocking is heard at the closed outer doors of the palace, and there is a slight stir within. Some one steps up and whispers to the Monarch. He speaks out aloud, "No secrets here, when I am on my throne, and my court in full dress before me. Let the expected messengers from distant lands enter one at a time, and report what news they bring."

The outer doors are opened now, "and their hinges grate harsh thunder." First one comes, and then another, each in due form saluting the King. The news generally, if not pleasant, does not alarm him. He nods, or smiles, or looks slightly serious, or speaks to some of the lords close by. One after another they come—from Africa, from Europe, from America, from the Isles of the Sea—from all the world. One comes at last, with signs of distant travel about him. He is just now from Burmah. He says—

"My lord king, every thing is going on generally well there; except that the Baptists are gradually winning their way; and Dr. Judson is much respected, and may in time render your Majesty much damage."

The Monarch replies, that he is aware of that, and will strengthen those places. The messengers still come, some with news so pleasant, that he claps his hands, and says—"that will do; I am very glad to hear it. You may expect promotion soon."

And now, one comes who has not been seen there for a long time. He pays his respects to the throne, and seems to know right well how he will be welcomed. He says—

"My lord king, good news from China. Every thing is going on there as well as you could wish. There is no sign of danger." He is about to bow low now, and depart, but adds—"My lord, one thing I had almost forgotten. On my return, as I was flying over the deep, I saw, far down below me, a distant ship. Some strong impulse drew me near the vessel. There was a crowd on board. I found out, by some talking I heard, that there were two preachers among them, from the Methodist Church, South, on their way to China, to convert the people. They were not in the best of spirits. One of them said to the other, 'You know, brother, the great difficulty will be to learn the language.' 'Yes,' said the other, 'it will take almost a life-time to master it.' I think, my lord, you need not fear those men for a while.".

"No," says the king, "not for a while; but those preachers must be looked after. You may expect promotion soon. Have they not all come," inquired the King.

"No, my lord; there is still one absent."

"I wish he would hasten; for I am expected to be present at the close of the review."

"He is come now," is heard from the outer courts; "He is come," is spoken still nearer the throne. A spirit enters in haste. He has no wish to change his dusty robes for his full court dress. He enters, with sad news full, with a face far more woe-begone than that man who at dead of night drew aside old Priam's curtain, and told him, more than half his Troy was burnt. He bows not the knee; he pays no respects to the throne; he does not kiss the Monarch's ample robe. "Arrest the traitor," cries the King; "hurl him into the lowest prison." The guards rush up. The messenger stands unmoved, with sad news full. "Stop, my lord king," says he, "you have no truer servant here than I am." The King signs to the guards to pause.

The spirit says, "Excuse my abrupt entrance, my unbent knee; no time for courtly respects now. I am just from Black Swamp camp-ground. I never flew so fast on my dark wings before. Sad news, my lord, from Black Swamp; and I, the unhappy messenger."

"What!" said the Monarch. "from Black Swamp, did you say?"

"Yes, my lord."

"Why, I feared no repulse there. Come, tell me all, at once! But stop, first close all the inner and the outer doors; let no one leave the presence. Come, now; the news!"

"Well, my lord; as I was returning, on rapid wing, from where I had first been sent, I passed near the place, and heard the sound of song and prayer, offered up to our Dread Enemy. I paused, I turned aside, I joined the crowd, and found much more than usual interest manifested. Every sermon preached seemed to make an impression on those who listened; while every now and then, some of those whom I thought true to you, were confessing their sins, and begging for mercy from Prince Immanuel. Dr. Boyd preached one of his best sermons; the congregation was much excited; the mourners rushed up in crowds. But the great effort was made by Dr. Wightman; and you know, my lord, he can preach, for you have heard him."

"Yes," says the King, "the Doctor knows how to preach; but go on."

"When the Doctor finished," said the spirit, "I said to myself, 'without help all is lost.' I heard your great friend, General R., from the other side of the Savannah river, say to some one at his side, 'let us go to the altar,' and on they went."

"That is strange news," said the Monarch, as he shook his black plumes; "strange, indeed. But I have not time for all. How is it with the Colonel of the Beaufort Rangers, and the Captain of the Gillisonville Guards? I know they are still true to me."

"Ah, my lord! the worst is yet to be told. I have not seen the Colonel so much affected for years. I am afraid he is lost to you."

"What of the Captain? I know it is all right with him."

"My lord, the Captain was still at his post; but he was bleeding from more than a score of wounds. He had lost his battle-axe; he was fighting bare-headed; his keen Damascus sword was broken at the hilt; he had shot his last arrow; and he had nothing but his long lance left—he leaned against it, only for a moment, to breathe, and said to me, 'help, at once, or all is lost. Tell your king, without instant help, all is ruined.'"

The Monarch springs from his throne, shaking desperately his black plumes. He draws his sword, he throws away his scabbard. And now a cry is raised throughout all the court, "Volunteers! volunteers for Black Swamp."

"But one word more," says the spirit. "Stop, my lord king. As I was spreading my wings for flight, I heard that old preacher, McPhail, whisper to Dr. B., and say, 'If you will order a general charge of bayonets soon, you will sweep the field; you know they cannot stand that.' And Dr. B. said, 'Yes, brother; and you shall lead the charge, when the time comes.'"

The cry is now heard all over perdition's gloomy empire—"Volunteers! volunteers for Black Swamp!"

The preacher then told the congregation, that the fallen spirits were then present on the ground, determined on their ruin; but that the hosts of the Lord were coming to their help; that the glorious news had reached heaven; that the cry too was heard all through the shining throng around the throne above; that the glorious cry was heard on both sides of the river that makes glad the city of the Lord—"Volunteers! volunteers for Black Swamp!" He told them that the blessed angels were there, with crowds of their departed friends—all there for the help of the Lord against the mighty. He told them, that the contending hosts of heaven and hell were now meeting in awful combat above and around them. And now he cried out, "once more to the charge, dear friends, once more."

Then Dr. B. gave Brother McPhail the sign, and the war-worn veteran passed through that crowd, with the dust of a thousand fields fought and won upon him, singing at the top of his trembling voice, as he clapped his hands together—

"I feel the work reviving, I feel the work reviving,
  Reviving in my soul.
O! brethren, will you meet me, In Canaan's happy land?"

And hundreds of happy souls replied—

"By the grace of God, we'll meet you, In Canaan's happy land."

And now, the Captain could keep his post no longer though he has been strongly re-inforced by the legions of hell, and though the stern, relentless guards of the pit fough as they always did while under the eye of their dread monarch. The Captain left his post, upheld by his long lance, apparently soon to fall from more wounds spiritually, than those that took the life of Rome's great Cæsar. Among the mourners at the altar was seen the famous Colonel of the Beaufort Rangers. The Strange Preacher, more than usually excited, rushed up, and waving his handkerchief, cried out aloud—"Colonel, I receive your sword, with much pleasure, in the name of my Master, Prince Immanuel."

Now, farewell to Black Swamp camp-ground and the Union church! If I see them no more on earth, I hope to remember them in the happy land, far, far away.

---

"I would not live alway: I ask not to stay,
Where storm after storm rises dark o'er the way;
The few lurid mornings that dawn on us here,
Are enough for life's woes, full enough for its cheer.

"I would not live alway; no—welcome the tomb,
Since Jesus hath lain there, I dread not its gloom;
There sweet be my rest, till he bids me arise,
To hail him in triumph descending the skies.

"Who, who would live alway? away from his God,
Away from yon heaven—that blissful abode,
Where the rivers of pleasure flow o'er the bright plains'
And the noontide of glory eternally reigns:

"Where the saints of all ages in harmony meet,
Their Saviour and brethren transported to greet;
While the anthems of rapture unceasingly roll,
And the smile of the Lord is the feast of the soul."

## LEAF THE THIRTEENTH.

A CAMP-MEETING IN THE UP-COUNTRY, FROM WHICH I FOUND OUT SOMETHING I DID NOT KNOW BEFORE.

The Strange Preacher started for a camp-meeting in the up-country, in an old sulky of happy remembrance. Did you, my friends, ever have one of those old-fashioned sulkies, with high wheels, and a high seat, from which you would be thrown every now and then, either by your careless driving, or by the axle-tree breaking in the same place where it had been mended before? But your old horse was gentle, perhaps—and, above all, Providence was kind to you—and thereby you missed being thrown into mud or water, and were never dashed against a tree. Well, friends, I once owned such a sulky, in which I travelled for many years; and I cannot tell you how much I thought of it. If I did not get turned over, or thrown out, once in every three months, I would become cast down and depressed, thinking something dreadful would happen to me or my friends. But as death at last separated David and Jonathan, so time and rough roads parted the parson from his much-loved old sulky. I suspect some of my friends at times wonder why Brother B. does not come up to their houses, singing, as he used to do—"I have listed in the holy war;" "I want to live a Christian here; I want to die a-shouting." One reason is, I miss my old sulky too much. If some of my kind friends were to ask me what they must do for me, to make me feel like old times, I would say, "Please give me an old sulky, with an axle-tree that has been broken and mended in the same place more than once, with high wheels, and a high seat, and a horse that will stop quickly and stand very still when I have been dropped or turned over."

Well, I left my home, my much-loved "Mamre," as I called it, in the famous old sulky. I was in fine spirits, for I was expecting a good meeting, though I was on my way to a place where I expected to see but few persons with whom I was acquainted. It mattered not, for I had become accustomed to such things. I expected to see Brother Talley there, who first licensed me to preach, and who was so kind to me as to wait on me until I got over my fright at that quarterly meeting at Green pond; and Brother Crook, who preached his best sermon at Binnakers, when the young Captain of the Fish-pond Company struck his flag and came out on the side of Prince Immanuel. I went on in fine spirits. I was passing along a good road; the woods were quiet; and more than one old large forest tree, not far from the road, with wide-spreading limbs and green leaves, seemed to say to me, "You had better stop, and bow your knee, and pray to the Holy One of Israel, for a blessed time at camp-meeting, and to take care of the loved ones at Mamre; for you will soon be travelling where you will see nothing but straight lanes, and large open fields on right and left." So I stopped, and prayed to the Blessed Hope of Israel, and started off again, and travelled for miles, seeing nothing but large open fields on both sides, till I began to sigh for the large trees with their friendly shade, and the murmuring brooks with their little waves kissing the smooth pebbles, and for the singing birds. And on I went, until I came once more to the grand old woods, and I passed along the shady road; and I said again to myself, "I hope the owner of this land, who has spared these time-honored trees so long—beneath whose friendly shade some brave soldier of Sumter and of Marion may have rested for a while, during a sultry summer's day, in the olden days of Seventy-six, and dreamed as he slept of the gentle maid of the Enoree or of Lynch's Creek, who wept as she thought of her absent lover—I hope he will go to heaven when he dies, and rest in that happy land, far, far away."

On I went, still travelling through the grand old woods; and after a while, I said again to myself, "what a suitable place to preach one of my Old Testament sermons." I then looked up and down the road, and seeing no one in sight, I gave out the text, "And Moses said to Hobab, come thou and go with us, for we will do thee good," and preached a sermon, with the old forest trees for my congregation. My old horse moved along slowly, taking his own time; sometimes he would trot along, and then he would walk slowly, and then again he would stand still. I had got nearly through the sermon, having more than once asked the church to pray for me, and my horse was standing still, with his head turned back, and I said to myself, "I hope he is listening well pleased with the effort." Then he moved slowly off. My sermon was over, and I turned to the sinners—I entreated, I implored them, to give their hearts to the Lord, and come up to the altar for prayer. I gave out the hymn, "Come, ye sinners, poor and needy," etc., and said, I hoped the mourners would come up, weeping as they came. But what noise is that? Nothing but my old sulky, which had broken down again—the axle-tree having given way in the same old place where it had often broken before. I was dropped softly in the road, and my horse stopped very quick, and stood very still. I got up, and returned thanks to the Lord for my deliverance; and after a delay of some hours the old sulky was mended again. Myself and horse had been well cared for; and the kind Presbyterian brother, near whose house I then was, and who fixed me up, would take no pay.

The next day I arrived safely at the camp-ground. Brother T. was not there; but Brother C., who had charge of the meeting, was the first to meet me—for which very thing I had been praying on my way. He greeted me with a smile, and a shake of the hand which went to my heart. I was then presented to others, and was soon made to feel quite at home by those up-country friends of our Saviour and his church. Did you ever hear Brother C. sing, when his voice had not yet failed? Well, so he preached, and prayed, and sung; and the Strength of Israel was with him. We had a well-behaved and respectable congregation. I found some of the old-time Methodists there, who did not care what the world and the devil thought—when they felt like shouting they did so. Brother C. put me up to preach more than he ought to have done; but I thought perhaps it was because I was a stranger, and might never be there again; and because also I was a son of his in the gospel. I preached three times; but I do not remember my two first subjects.

I thought I was getting on as usual, and the church was praying for me. The third sermon was at 3 o'clock on Sunday. I went into the woods, as I often do, to pray before I tried to preach; and when I had gone where I thought no one but the Lord would see me, or the holy angels, or the little birds which were singing around me, I bowed down, and prayed for help, that God would bless his poor servant, and that some souls might be converted—that I might have some sign that I was in my Master's work. My text was, "I would not live alway." The Lord was with me. The Holy Spirit was abroad in the congregation. A large crowd of mourners came up, and the services went on for some time after preaching was over. Many were converted. Some of the brethren professed perfect love. A preacher, who did not believe in shouting, was completely carried away by his feelings.

The meeting was over. I started to go to another one still further up. I had not ridden far, before I was overtaken by a young man, with a message from Brother C. and some of the chief members, requesting me to come back, and hold a protracted meeting in a neighborhood where they thought much good might be done. I turned back; the meeting was renewed, and the Lord was with us to the end.

"But," says some one, "you have not yet told us what it was you learned that you did not know before." What I am going to tell you now I did not know for several years after. Some friends, who were at the meeting, afterwards told me, that there had been no good impression made by my first two sermons, but quite the other way—that my style of preaching was so different from what the people had been used to, that neither saint nor sinner wished to hear me again. After my first sermon, several of the members went to Brother C., and requested him not to put me up any more. Again, after my second sermon, the same request was made; and during the intervals of service, one could hear both Methodists and Baptists saying, "I hope that Strange Preacher will not be put up again." Now, my friends who have known me long, know full well that if I had heard all that, I could never have faced that congregation any more—that I would have struck my flag at once, and started back for the Walterboro circuit. I was told, that on Sunday evening, after I had left the tent for the woods, the principal members came to Brother C. once more, and asked if it was possible I was to be put up again; that no one wanted to hear me; that I had already been imposed upon them enough; and that there was no preacher, or exhorter, or class-leader that they would not rather see in the pulpit than me; and they begged him to change the appointment. But he told them he did not have the heart to do it, that I was then in the woods at prayer, and that the Lord blessed me sometimes, and he was hoping for the best.

Under these great difficulties, I went to the stand, and preached my third sermon, and with God's blessing I was able to turn the tide of feeling for the first time, with great power bearing every thing before it. After this, those same persons went back to Brother C., and told him they were very sorry for what they had said, and that their minds had undergone a complete change: that I must be brought back and the meeting renewed. From that time, I have learned that I get along better after the people become accustomed to my ways; and that I ought not to expect much when I stand before a congregation for the first time; and that I never can pray too often to the Lord, before preaching.

## LEAF THE FOURTEENTH.

**CENTRE CAMP GROUND, NORTH CAROLINA, AND THE LOW-COUNTRY DINNER; AND HOW THE CLASS-LEADER'S WIFE WAS CONVICTED AND CONVERTED.**

The time had come when I was to take another ride in my old sulky. Brother James Stacy was the presiding elder—a man for whom I always had the highest respect. He had always treated me with much kindness. When I think of Brother Stacy, how many places of my wandering life rise before me! Georgetown, Marion, Centre, Gilbo, Bennettsville, Fayetteville, Binnakers, and others. Where I have heard him once, I wish it had been many times. I do not remember the names of many of the other preachers, but I know Brother Simmons was there.

While recalling my visit to Centre camp-ground, a certain famous low-country dinner on Saturday is the first thing I think of. Let me make a confession, and throw myself on the kindness of my friends in the upper part of my own State and North Carolina. Though I have so long been roaming to and fro, I have never lost my relish for a good low-country dinner. When I first began to rove, though every thing was always so bountiful on the tables of the up-country, yet the low-country style of cookery was very often missed by me. Now you know, when a long-absent and much-loved friend turns up unexpectedly, the pleasure of meeting is all the greater, if not looked for. So it was with the Strange Preacher on that memorable occasion. Now, friends, fancy you see the parson sitting down unexpectedly to a fine low-country dinner. I will not tell you of all the very nice things which passed in due order before us. Suffice it to say, I enjoyed myself very much from the first to the last, or as old Horace would say, "from the egg to the apple." Brother Stacy had told me, before we went to the tent, that he wanted me to preach the 3 o'clock sermon. It was to be my first effort there, and he told me he was much interested in it. He said, he was anxious for his friend, the War

Preacher, to swing clear. I was fully convinced, that as a general rule, a preacher must not eat too much, if he has to preach soon after. When thus situated, I usually refrained somewhat; and if it was left to me, I would always avoid preaching after dinner. It was said of the greatest of all the Cæsars, that he "came, saw, and conquered." But, alas, for the Strange Preacher! he came, saw, and *was* conquered. I did not know till years after, how the presiding elder trembled when he saw what an impression even the sight of that dinner had made on me. If I could have seen the anxious looks he cast at me from time to time, I might, as I thought so much of him, have made a desperate effort to hold in. A friend present told me long after, that Brother S. was very restless, as he saw how much I enjoyed that famous dinner—that, as the good things on the parson's plate, as often as it was replenished, disappeared like "foam on the river," he every now and then would touch my friend's hand, or press his foot; and that when he saw the Strange Preacher swallow down his second large tumbler of buttermilk, he whispered to him that there was no preaching in Brother B., and dismissed the table as soon as possible. We then retired to the preachers' tent. Brother S. remarked to his friend that there was no preaching in Brother B., after eating such a dinner, saying, "my last hope left me when I saw him drink his second tumbler of buttermilk; it is all over with Brother B.; I wished so much to have him make a good impression this evening; but there is no hope for it now, and it is too late to change the appointment." I did not know what was passing in his mind; but I knew that I had eaten too much—there was no mistake about that. I felt dull and sleepy, and went to rest a little, as I thought it would be some time before preaching. I did not know for a long time after, how anxiously my friends watched my every movement. My much-respected Brother S. drew a long sigh, as one that thought his last lingering hope was gone. He whispered to his friend, "it is all over now, there is no preaching in him; my last trust was, that he would not lie down, but keep moving about slowly, and thus at last become roused up a little. What a pity!" The Strange

Preacher laid down, and the buttermilk — the crowning offence—began its work. Old Somnus was going to lead me off a willing captive. I do not think hard of what my friends did on the occasion, though, at the time, it was very unpleasant to me. When they remembered how the War Preacher's flag had often waved so freely on many stricken fields, I suppose they dreaded very much the expected passage of arms for that evening, when they thought that perhaps the slightest touch of hostile lance would throw him from his gallant steed upon a dishonored field. Their next effort was to keep me from falling asleep. When they saw I was going to drop off, first one and then another would come up, and say, or do, something to arouse me. I would about half open my dull heavy eyes, and look at them with a vacant glance, and then close them again. I wished they would leave me alone for a few minutes; but, no, they kept it up. It was at last thought that the influence upon me would in the end prove too strong for their united efforts, and that I would pass off into a deep, profound slumber, from which even the loud sounding horn would scarcely arouse me. Look at the picture—there lay the Roving Preacher, having indulged himself too much at that famous low-country dinner, the crowning sin of which was the two large tumblers of buttermilk. Between us, my friends, remember that what I am now going to tell you, is in confidence. As a last resort, the friends resolved to have the horn blown about a half-hour earlier than usual—that some cold water should be brought from the spring, and that the parson should be aroused up at once, and persuaded to bathe his face and head well, and his arms up to the elbow, and to open his eyes in the cold water. I tried hard to go to sleep, but they would not let me; I was nearly gone, and if I had been left undisturbed for five minutes, I would perhaps have been dreaming of the loved ones at Mamre. But Brother S. came up and shook me, and told me it was time to get up— that the horn was blowing. He then advised me to try the cold water. I felt a little relieved; but still there was a heavy influence upon me. There was a little time to spare, so I stepped into the woods, and offered a brief prayer to the

Strength of Israel for help. Something seemed to whisper to me—perhaps it was the spirit of some loved preacher gone to glory, it might have been Brother Higgins or Brother McCall—"Try, 'Solomon, my son;' and make the ghost shake his gory locks, and remember the casting off for ever."
We went to the stand; and I gave out for my text, David's charge to Solomon on his death-bed. I imagine, if ever there was a time that strong, urgent prayer was offered up for me, both by preachers and people, that was the time. I doubt very much if Brother Stacy ever thus remembered a preacher before. I was as "clay in the hands of the potter." The set time had come to favor Zion. The Spirit was present, and the Lord's word did not return unto him void. I heard afterwards, that Brother S. said, "Brother B. got through much better than I expected, although he had enjoyed the famous dinner so much, and finished off with the two tumblers of buttermilk."
I have never forgotten that time; but since then I have tried to be more careful when similarly situated. The meeting went on, Brothers Stacy and Simmons preaching with the Holy Ghost and with power. Did you ever hear Brother Stacy, when the Spirit was present, and everything was right with him? That was the way it was with him at the Centre camp-meeting. I remember well what a glorious meeting we had on Saturday night—time of immortal remembrance. I think Brother Simmons preached. He was clear, impressive, and powerful; and many mourners were at the altar. The church was seen, "coming out of the wilderness, leaning on the breast of her beloved; fair as the moon, bright as the sun, and terrible as an army with banners." Many persons went through the crowd, and implored their loved friends to come to the altar. The father went to his son, the mother to her daughter, the sister to her brother, and the husband to his wife—and many were thus persuaded to come
There was a class-leader there, who had very recently married his second wife. He seemed to love her very devotedly. She was beautiful, and fond of dress and display. He went to her, and pressed her to come to the altar; and

at last prevailed on her to come. She went rather reluctantly, and did not kneel; but sat down with a frown on her face. Her husband seemed to feel deeply for her, while she remained unmoved. I was very sorry for him, and thought I would talk to her; but I met with such a reception that I soon left. After we went to the tent, I heard the preachers say, they wished the brother had not gone to his wife, as they were afraid it did more harm than good. I felt sorry for him, and I made up my mind to pray much for his wife. Often, when at such places, I become more interested in some persons more than others, and make them the objects of earnest prayer; and I have often had the pleasure of knowing, that they had come out on the Lord's side. I even now recollect many such instances. At the 11 o'clock service on Sunday, the right man was in the right place—Brother Stacy was well prepared, and preached a finished sermon to a large and attentive congregation. He had recovered from his fears of the day before, and told the Strange Preacher that he wanted him to try the 3 o'clock sermon again; and I determined not to indulge too much, and I held in somewhat, and did not drink any buttermilk. I retired to the woods, and entreated the Lord to bless my last effort; I prayed that the class-leader's wife might be convicted and happily converted. I made up my mind to paint a picture, at the close of the sermon, if the Lord would help me, that she would remember for years.

The horn blew long and loud. My faith was strong, my trust in God firm. I had hold of the blessed Rock. Some of my much-loved songs were sung, and my hopes were high. The subject was, the resurrection of Lazarus; and for the introduction I read the greater part of the chapter. I begged the Lord to grant me, "the thoughts that breathe, and the words that burn." The death-bed, with its heavenly surroundings, was described; the scene at the grave was dwelt on; also the rising from the grave. I then told the members of the church, I wished to give them some parting advice, as we might never again meet in this vale of tears. I told them not to count too strongly on their relatives and friends coming out from the world, and starting for heaven, for many of them would be lost for ever; and that they would be sadly disappointed if they expected to meet them in heaven. No matter how much they loved them in this world—in eternity they would have to bid them an eternal farewell; that we would be saved on the right hand of the throne—they thrust down to hell; that parents must not expect to see all their children in glory. I told them, I knew full well it was a sad, a heart-breaking thought, to think of their being separated in all eternity from those we love so much on earth; hence they should not count too strong on meeting them in the green fields of Eden. I begged them to remember what I was going to say—to follow my advice, should they never see me again. I then told them, perhaps it was best not to say any thing now to those of their friends whom they thought had made up their minds never to come out on the Lord's side; but to try to make them pass pleasantly through life, to grant them every wish, and to render them as happy in this world as possible, as they would never enjoy the happiness of heaven. I told the father thus to treat his wayward son, the mother her daughter who would not live for the Lord, the sister her brother, the wife her husband—and thus through all the relations of life. The Strange Preacher now took his sharpest arrow from the quiver, and he placed it to the string, and drew it to the head. It was for the class-leader's wife. He said there were many husbands on their way to heaven, who loved their wives dearly, but there was no hope for them—they would be lost for ever. He advised such a husband to love his wife, if possible, more than ever—to give her a heaven below, as there was none for her in the world to which she was hastening; to try to grant her every request, and to anticipate her every wish, but never to urge her to attend church—that he must gather sweet flowers for her all through life, for there would be no flowers for her there—that he must never use harsh words to her, nothing but words of love—and that he should request preachers never to speak to her of her soul's salvation and of heaven—that he must be careful of her health, to try to save her from the cold of winter, and the heat of summer—that, as she would never give her heart to the Lord, she must have sweet flowers to walk on, on her way to hell.

The arrow was shot, and the sermon ended. Mourners were called up, and among the many who came was the class-leader's wife. She was in such distress, that a lady who sat near her told me afterwards, she expected her to go into convulsions; and she said, loud enough to be heard by those around her, "I know the preacher meant me; but I will not go to hell, even if I have nothing but sweet flowers to walk on." Brother McA. seemed ready at that moment to go to heaven from the Centre camp-ground, when he saw his much-loved wife, who had been bowed down for a long time, realize the forgiveness of her sins. I fancy I see her now, with happy heart, with smiles and tears, praising the Lord, going among the ladies at the altar, and begging them to give their hearts to their Saviour. The rejoicing class-leader threw his arms around me, and said, "I never can forget you, no, never; for, by the help of the Lord, you have saved my wife."

I have often longed to see my friends of the Centre camp-ground; but we have never met since. May we meet in heaven to part no more!

"O! for a glance of heavenly day,
To take this stubborn heart away;
And thaw, with beams of love divine,
This heart, this frozen heart of mine.

"The rocks can rend; the earth can quake;
The seas can roar; the mountains shake;
Of feeling all things show some sign,
But this unfeeling heart of mine.

"To hear the sorrows thou hast felt,
O Lord! an adamant would melt;
But I can read each moving line,
And nothing moves this heart of mine.

"But something yet can do the deed;
And that blest something much I need:
Thy Spirit can from dross refine,
And melt and change this heart of mine."

## LEAF THE FIFTEENTH.

HOW I GOT THE NAMES OF "WAR PREACHER" AND "WANDERING ARAB."

As far back as I can remember, I was very fond of reading of wars—of wars by land and sea. I was anxious to learn all I could of heroes and warriors, both of olden and modern times. I had always been so fond of such reading, that when I became a preacher, I was disposed to treat of warlike scenes, with which the Old Testament abounds. And though I have been preaching for nearly thirty years, this habit still clings to me—it has become, as it were, a second nature.

In years gone by, I had an appointment at a church called Bethlehem, near a Brother Izlar—a much respected friend of mine. Near the church, I passed the tents of several travellers, on their way to Florida from the old North State, and some of the strangers were among my congregation. I preached, and as usual indulged in some warlike pictures, though not as much as I had on other occasions, as I did not think the subject called for so many. It was Jer. xiv. 8. During the sermon, I noticed that one of the strangers was very attentive. When the meeting was over, I was introduced by Brother Izlar to them, one of whom, a Brother Terry, said he was a class-leader—I think, from Anson county, North Carolina. We dined with Brother I. that day, and spent several pleasant hours together. He was a man of intelligence and pleasing manners. He was going to look at Florida; and, if pleased, to move his family out there, which he did, and after some years died there. As he was parting with us, he said, with a marked expression on his face, "you will hear from me again." We did not fully understand his meaning, but told him we would be glad to do so. From Florida he wrote several letters to the *Southern Christian Advocate*, describing his trip, and what he thought of the country. This, we both concluded, was what he meant by saying, "you will hear from me again;" but we were mistaken; for, when he returned for his family, he published in one of the papers of Fayetteville, a description of the preacher and sermon he had heard near Brother Izlar's. I never saw it; but some of my friends told me, that in his article Brother Terry said. he thought, "that man should be termed the 'War Preacher;'" and he was "surprised the name had not been given before; but hoped persons would take the hint, and call him by that name." So several persons began to call me the "War Preacher."

Some months after this, I was at a camp-meeting in North Carolina, and as I was passing over the ground a minister called me to him. There was a stranger with him, who, he said, had read Brother Terry's article, and wanted an introduction to me. He then introduced me in due form, as the "War Preacher from the Walterboro circuit." This was done more than once while on the ground.

I had not paid much attention to it up to that time, but began to think more about it. I thought if the friends were determined to give me a name, I would much prefer another. When I got home, I asked some of my friends to help me; and told them I would rather be called the "Walterboro Preacher," as I was born there. So we started an opposition party, who called me by the latter name. I more than once called myself by it in the pulpit. We tried it for some time, but had to give up at last. One of our preachers once told me publicly, in the congregation, at Broxton's Bridge camp-meeting, that I might as well let them have their own way; that I could not stop them, as the thing had then gone too far. So I gave up, and in time became fond of the name; yet there are some persons who do not seem to like that name as much as another I am often called by—"the Old War-horse;" but I do not fancy that name.

Many years ago, I was at a very interesting meeting up the country, where a lady of intelligence said to me, she did not think I had the right name yet; that as I wandered about so much, she thought I ought to be called the "Wandering Arab;" and thus another name was given to me. Some months after this, I was on a steam-boat, with many preachers of our church. One of them came up to me, and said, there was some excitement on board. I inquired what was the matter. He said, it was noised abroad among the ladies and gentlemen, that the Wandering Arab was among them.

I was once at a meeting of some interest, with one of our preachers. After I left, he wrote several verses, descriptive of the Wandering Arab, and the subjects on which he had preached.

Several years ago, while returning home with some friends, several preachers among them, from a camp-meeting in the up-country, we overtook an old negro woman, who seemed to be in fine spirits, toiling along the highway. Some of the company asked her where she had been. She said, she was on her way from Goshen Hill camp-meeting, and that she had enjoyed herself very much there. And that among other things, she blessed the Lord she had lived to hear Captain Bellinger once more. So it seems I have been called by many names. I was once at a camp-meeting in the up-country, where I found that my singularity, and the different names by which I was called, made me an object of interest to some persons, who followed me about from one part of the ground to another. One morning, quite early, a stranger was seen sitting down, not far from the preachers' tent, watching the door close by. He remained there some time. Several persons asked him what was the matter; if he wished anything. He said, he was waiting for the War Preacher to come out; that he was determined to follow him when he went to breakfast, as he wanted to see all he could of him. Some one told me to remain in as long as I could, to see if he would still remain. I did so, and he kept his post. At last, I came out; he stood still till I passed, and then followed close behind. He went to the same tent, but did not eat any breakfast; he only sat down near by, and watched me all the time.

Being the War Preacher, of course I was expected to have a flag, and to wave it sometimes. I must of course have a gallant steed, harnessed for the battle; the saddle was said to be a Spanish one, high before and behind. I was once at a camp-meeting in the lower part of the State; I did not feel very well, but had to preach that night. Some of the friends wished me to make a successful effort. I remarked, playfully, that I did not feel as if I could even mount my gallant steed, much less make a splendid charge. Several remarks were made; at last a good Baptist brother said he was so much interested in having me mounted, that he would hold the bridle and stirrup for me. Before preaching that night, some one overheard two young ladies talking. One asked the other if she was going to the stand. "O! yes; I would not miss it for the world; for I understand the parson is to mount his war-horse, and I must be there." The other then asked, how would she like to ride behind him. She said she would like very much to do so, if she was only good enough. The horn blew, service began, the singing was fine, and we had a large attentive congregation. I think that was a time when the supplications of the church prevailed; for a most glorious outpouring of the Spirit was granted to us. I told the friends, that by the help of the Lord, and the prayers of the faithful, and the aid of a good brother present, I was at last mounted on my gallant steed; that I felt him pawing the ground; that his neck was clothed with thunder; that he was tossing his head towards the heavens; and that my war flag was waving gloriously. Many mourners came up, several were happily converted; and we had an old-time meeting. Both of the young ladies were deeply convicted, and some time after were converted. One of them has since died, and I hope went to heaven; the other I had the pleasure of meeting last summer.

## LEAF THE SIXTEENTH.

#### MY FIRST VISIT TO GULLY CAMP GROUND, DARLINGTON DISTRICT.

I went to this meeting in company with Brothers Richardson, Felder, and Smith. It was just after we had had some heavy rains, and had some difficulty in reaching the ground. The meeting had been going on for some time when we reached it. We were warmly welcomed by Brother Talley, the presiding elder of the district—a very polished, refined gentleman, much respected by all who know him—one of the war-worn veterans of our church.

This camp-ground was a famous place, where large crowds had gathered from year to year, and where much good had been done. I found the presiding elder well supported by a gallant band of preachers, good men and true, ready and eager to join battle with the enemy, who were strongly entrenched on the ground. The services went on, with some interest manifested; but not so much as you sometimes see at such places. Brother T. and his staff were at their post, enduring hardship like good soldiers; and the battle was hotly contested by the opposing forces of light and darkness—sometimes one side, and then the other, appearing to have the advantage. "Each adverse host was gored with equal wounds." Many persons were there to do and get good, who were deeply interested in the progress of the meeting, and whose prayers were going up night and day for the extension of the Saviour's kingdom; but then, again, there were many careless, indifferent souls—some of them, alas! members of the church—who were there, apparently, only to enjoy themselves after the fashion of the world—to see and be seen, to come to the stand at one service, and then, if they felt like it, to stay in the tents. Others were there, far gone in sin and transgression—open, heaven-daring sinners, who were "madly rushing to ruin as a horse in battle." I have never been at a meeting with Brother Felder where

God's work was not gloriously revived. And this was not to be an exception. He was just the man for such a place—a good preacher, a good exhorter, and one of the best singers of our church; who prayed at times as if heaven and earth were coming together; and who was of a fine, commanding appearance, both in and out of the pulpit. He, with Brothers R., S., and E., and others from time to time, threw himself nobly into the thickest of the fight, causing the enemy, more than once, to retreat from the field, with the loss of many prisoners. During the intervals of preaching, interesting services were held in some of the tents, and those brothers did good service at such times. Whenever I heard Brother F. clapping his hands, and singing, "The warfare is over," or " I want my friends to go with me," or " I will join the army, by and bye," I knew that all was right, and that the work of the Lord was reviving.

Brother Talley, the hero of a thousand stricken fields, with the marks of the war helmet on his brow, and his keen Damascus blade in his hand, preached the 10 o'clock sermon on Sunday. The crowd was large, and generally respectful and attentive. After awhile the work became more serious, as the preacher went on warming with the heavenly fire that filled his heart. The joys of heaven were described to the listening multitude. More than one "amen" was heard; more than one "bless the Lord" was spoken by some happy heart; and there was a strong, deep feeling rising in the congregation. On the preacher went, increasing in strength and and power; now he paused, only for a little while; the church looked, and listened, and prayed; he turned to the sinners and bore down on them with all his might. Some of them had been exposed to these broadsides before, and seemed to dread what was coming. A few left the stand and hastened to the tents; for they had no heart to face the fire. The preacher described the dread judgment day, with all its sublime and awful surroundings. The King Eternal was seen upon his dazzling throne, and the entire world was before it; and the eternal separation took place; the wicked on the left received their final sentence, "depart ye cursed:" they stood on the battlements of glory and looked on the happy throng before them for the last time; they were driven off; they sunk down, hopelessly down, till they reached the dark realms of ruin; they were forever lost; it was one eternal night of endless misery for them; despair, the black vulture of hell, flapped her wings over their heads and bade them hope no more; they sunk down beneath the awful waves; they were lost to sight for hundreds of years. At last they rose again on some distant burning wave of damnation; they lifted their despairing eyes to heaven; they cried out, "Watchman, watchman, what of the night? How long must we remain amidst these eternal fires?" The watchman replied, "Eternity; Eternity." They now sunk down again, lost to view for thousands of years; they now rose again on some gloomy billow; they still heard the hope expelling words, "forever, forever." The sermon was over, and the mourners came up in great numbers; Christians rejoiced, sinners trembled. The kingdom of the Lord was greatly advanced. Brother E. looked as if he saw the green fields on the other side of the flood. Brother F. stood erect and clapped his hands and cried, "Glory! glory!" The Strange Preacher sprang to his feet and shouted out, "Farewell, world, I am bound for the kingdom!"

We had a season of great refreshing, but still there were many who stood off, who would not give their hearts to the Lord. There were many ladies and gentlemen there—in the church and out of it—who seemed resolved to enjoy themselves, pleasantly, as they thought. In the intervals of service they formed in groups and promenaded the ground. Sunday afternoon came, and it was nearly time for the three o'clock sermon. And now a larger number of promenaders than had yet been seen had met, and arm locked in arm were parading all over the camp-ground—before the stand—before the preacher's tent—every where. Many were now hastening from all sides and joining them. The beauty, the talent, the wealth of Sumter and Darlington were circling round, and still round throughout the ground, laughing and talking. The Strange Preacher was very sorry to see that sight; he had to preach the next sermon. He would be glad to see that gay party broken up and dispersed; so he resolved to see if they could be prevailed on to leave off that circling round and round. He gathered a group of friends, and they began to sing some of the much loved songs of the church. They placed themselves where the party would pass very near to them. The revellers were coming nearer and still nearer; and the singing became louder; and the preacher was in hopes that the gay throng would pause—would listen—that some few of them, at least, would come over to his side. But alas! no; on and still on they went, round and still round. The singing still went on—the sweet songs of Zion. The revellers were coming round once more—how the Strange Preacher's heart was beating. A few came over and joined us, but the crowd still continued on. The horn then blew for the three o'clock service, and both parties went to the place of worship. The Strange Preacher said to himself: "If the Lord will help me, I will paint a picture for those revellers which I hope some of them will never forget." Brother F. sang one of my favorite songs. When the sermon was nearly over, the Strange Preacher told the congregation he would paint a picture which he hoped they would remember for a long time; that there was a time, many years ago, when a gay party met near the water's edge for a sail of pleasure; that the sky was clear and the water smooth. The ladies and gentlemen seemed in gay spirits, but their friends who followed them with wistful looks were very uneasy, for not far off was a dangerous whirlpool where many noble ships had been lost. Every effort had been made to induce them to come back, but all in vain. They smiled, and clapped their hands, and laughed, and said there was no danger. For awhile all was bright—the ocean was as calm as a lake where no breath of air was stirring. Their friends on the shore still implored them to return; a mother with tears in her eyes entreated her daughter to come back; the father his son, the brother his sister, but all in vain. The gay party of revellers at last found out their danger, but it was too late; they implored their friends to save them, but it was too late now. Their friends on shore closed their eyes, as the gay party sank down beneath the dark waters, never to rise till that great and awful day. The preacher then told them of that gay party that had so lately been there sporting near that whirlpool of eternal fire, while devils looked on and rejoiced—while the holy angels almost wept as they looked on from the portals of heaven. He told them how some of their friends had tried, by singing some of the sweet songs of Zion, to draw them away from the awful danger so near. But they would not come; though every exhortation they refused brought them still nearer the gulf of perdition that would soon swallow them up. He told them how grieved their pious friends at home would be when they heard how they had been sporting at the Gully camp-ground —that soon, very soon, they would find out their danger, but perhaps when it was too late.

Long will that meeting be remembered by preacher and people; by saints and sinners. Again and again, in my roving life, have I met persons, years afterwards, who told me that they were in that gay party of revellers on that holy Sabbath evening, but that it was their last. Before I left the ground more than one brother in Christ, and others afterwards, told me they thanked me from their hearts for that picture, that the Holy Spirit had blessed the effort, and they believed some souls were saved by the help of the Lord.

---

No room for mirth or trifling here,
For worldly hope or wordly fear,
 If life so soon is gone ;
If now the Judge is at the door,
And all mankind must stand before
 The inexorable throne.

No matter which my thoughts employ,
A moment's misery or joy,
 But oh! when both shall end,
Where shall I find my destined place?
Shall I my everlasting days
 With fiends or angels spend?

## LEAF THE SEVENTEENTH.

MY FIRST TO PLEASANT GROVE CAMP GROUND, NORTH CAROLINA, WHERE TWO LONG LETTERS ON CONTROVERSY WERE ANSWERED.

Many years ago, I received a long letter from a gentleman of standing, and of much intelligence, who belonged to another church, and who left no stone unturned in trying to persuade me to enter into a controversy with him. The writer expressed a strong wish to break a lance with me, even if he should be unhorsed—of which, merely to flatter the parson, he professed there might be some danger. He entered at length into some of the disputed points between us.

Some time after, I received another, if possible, longer than the first, with a request endorsed, that it should be read as soon as received, no matter what I might be doing. I got it at Binnakers camp-ground, when my mind was filled with other thoughts; but still the very lengthy letter was read at once.

Some time after this, I attended the camp-meeting at Pleasant Grove, with Brother M., whom I met at Camden. Of all the camp grounds I have ever been to, Pleasant Grove ranks next to the famous Rock Springs. I saw several thousands of strange faces before me. I was introduced to many persons, and received a great many invitations of a social character. I looked, and gazed, and wondered where all these people came from, and if the most of them were in the church or not. I saw much less of fashion and display there, than I have seen anywhere else in all my roving life. The congregation, though large at first, still continued to increase as the meeting progressed.

If I remember rightly, the meeting was a good one from beginning to end. The prayers at the tents were plain, strong, and fervent. The Strange Preacher missed much his famous low-country dinner; but of course kept his thoughts to himself. When Brother M. preached, he was the right man in the right place. Did you ever hear him? You say, "no." Then there is a great treat in store for you, I hope. Take my advice, and embrace the first chance you have. When you have heard him once, I know you will wish to do so as often as possible. He fired off one of his "biggest guns," and by the help of the Spirit, there was much execution done—there was soon a fine work going on among mourners, backsliders, sinners, Christians, and all. After the Strange Preacher left the stand, where he had enjoyed himself very much, he said to himself, "Now is the best time I will ever have to answer those long letters on controversy." He had a notion in his head, that he could do it after such a fashion as never to be troubled with such tremendous, lengthy epistles from that same person in all his future life. So the parson, when he got to the tent, sat down to reply to those lengthy letters. He wrote with much affection, for he loved his friend dearly. His letter was dated, "Pleasant Grove Camp-ground, North Carolina; Three Hundred and Twenty-one (321) Tents on the ground, all told." He said, he was then enjoying himself very much; that Brother M. had just preached one of his best sermons, which made a tremendous impression on the congregation; that he had thought of and prayed often on the subject, and had at last come to the conclusion, that it would do no good, and might do some harm, for them to controvert the points of difference between them; that he had no thought of ever changing his correspondent's mind; and that he himself expected to live and die where he then was, in the church of his choice. And he hoped, if the Lord spared his life, to come again to Pleasant Grove, where there were "three hundred and twenty-one tents on the ground, all told; and to hear Brother M. preach another good sermon."

I never got any more lengthy epistles from the same person; but understood, some months afterwards, that the Doctor said, he would never write to me again on the subject, as he regarded it a hopeless case; for the last time he heard from the parson, he was at Pleasant Grove camp-meeting, North Carolina, three hundred and twenty-one tents on the ground, all told; and that Brother M. had just preached a tremendous sermon; and he was then enjoying himself very much.

I had already tried to preach; but I suspect it was a poor affair when compared with Brother M.'s sermon. As it was my first visit to that place, it took me some time to get used to what I heard and saw around me. My voice, not strong at best, could not be heard by that vast crowd, unless I spoke much louder than usual. I was again called on to preach, Brother M. cautioning me to speak much louder; for it was thought that at least two thousand of those present before had not heard one word of what I said; and he wished very much that all should hear. So he recommended a plan which he thought would answer—he would stand on the outer edge of the congregation, and if he could not hear, he would shake his head; and if otherwise, he would nod or smile. The hour arrived, and a vast crowd was present—between six and seven thousand. Brother M. was among the extreme outsiders, some of whom, by their glances, seemed to say, "What are you doing here? Your place is in the altar." I began to read the hymn; Brother M. shook his head. I tried to elevate my voice while reading the first few verses; but he continued to shake his head. I then made a still greater effort; he smiled and nodded—all was right. After prayer, I gave out the second hymn; he smiled again. I then began my sermon; he nodded, and then came back to the altar. I went on, straining my voice very much; but was heard by the many thousands. The meeting closed; and as well as I can remember at this distant day, there were a great many convictions and conversions, and several scores joined the church. Brother Talley told me before we left, that at the tent in which he dined, after my second sermon, a brother said to him, "We have got a name for our boy at last; for though he is several years old, we could not heretofore agree about a name; but while we we were coming from the stand, I asked my wife how she would like to call him after the Strange Preacher; and she replied, that she could not be better pleased;" and so the boy was named Lucius Bellinger D——.

## LEAF THE EIGHTEENTH.

#### CAMP-MEETINGS IN GEORGIA.

I have been to several meetings in the Empire State of the South a long time ago. The first one I attended I think was called, Hill's camp ground, in Wilkes county. I had a letter of introduction to the presiding elder, the present Bishop Pierce; and from that day to the present I have felt glad that I formed the acquaintance of that distinguished preacher. I had heard much of him as one of the most eloquent ministers of our church, and my expectations, high as they were, were fully realized. He treated me with much respect, and showed me every attention, which made me feel quite at home while there. It has been so many years since I was with him at those Georgia meetings that many things of interest have been forgotten—my memory being my only reference book. I met while there a Brother Martin, a member of the Conference, and a man of winning manners and address. He made a favorable impression on my mind. I also had the pleasure of forming the acquaintance of a Brother Duncan, who was called the sweet singer of Georgia, a very useful, and a very successful minister. There was also Dr. Pendleton, whose health would not permit of his preaching often; but who, having the respect and confidence of both the church and the world, did much good in pushing on the work of grace, and advancing the Saviour's kingdom. I am very happy to number him among my Georgia friends. He was gentle and kind, full of faith and hope, and love; always ready to weep with those who wept, and to rejoice with those who rejoiced. Brother Pierce was the great object of attraction, but still he would have all to do their full share of work. Because of his kindness and friendliness I have felt more at home with him than with any other of our great preachers, without exception, whom I have seen in my roving life. I also met Brothers Lewis and Branham, both whole-souled, devoted, thorough-going men of God, and much loved by the church. They are brave soldiers of the cross—heroes of many immortal battle fields. All hail to the preachers of the Georgia Conference whom I then met.

The next meeting I attended was the Hancock campground, near Sparta. Previous to my visit there I spent some time with Bishop Pierce, at his home near by that place, and was kindly treated by his amiable wife. How pleasantly the hours rolled by! Having rested, we set off again to endeavor to push forward the victory of the Cross, and to save immortal souls. Dr. P. labored here, both in the pulpit and altar, to win souls for the Lord. I think I have never heard him preach without losing all control of my feelings, and felt like shouting, whether the devil, or the world, or lukewarm Christians were pleased or not. Each time I heard him I thought the last sermon better than the preceding one. The Holy Spirit was wonderfully poured out. The powers of hell mustered strong for the battle, filled with rage and fury; but the the powers of light rallied to the support of the Lord's people, and the camp of Israel moved on in glorious triumph, from one service to another, driving the routed foe from every strong post, till the blessed flag of Calvary waved victoriously over the entire battle field. It did not matter who preached, the good work continued to revive. Many mourners crowded the altar, and many were made to rejoice in their Saviour's love.

There was a respectable gentleman of wealth and position on the ground—one of the chief men of the county, his family all members of the church—in whom the preachers seemed deeply interested; but there appeared little hope of his ever being convicted and converted. He had a son who was then preaching, and who afterwards rose to a high position in the Conference. His eldest son, a worthy member of the church, with tears in his eyes, told me how anxious he was to see his much loved father a member of the church—that as to his morals he was a good man, and did everything he could to add to the happiness of his family. While listening, I became much affected, and, as usual with me in such a case, began to pray for him. I encouraged the young man not to give up, but to pray for and expect his father's conversion.

Brother Pendleton, I think it was, told me that the old gentleman had taken quite a fancy to me, and that he thought I could influence him, if I would go out and speak to him in the congregation. As soon as they would begin to sing he would always leave the stand, and when I was going toward him he would start for the tent. I said to myself, "the next service I will be in time." Dr. Pierce preached the next sermon, and we had a glorious season. Before singing began I started, praying as I went for the old gentleman, and when I reached him, he had his hat in his hand, just ready to leave. I begged him to let us pray for him. He bowed at his seat. How his children, his friends, and the church rejoiced! He was much affected; his heart was fully reached; he was made, by grace, to dread the wrath to come, and the anger of a sin-avenging God. I can even now see the happy smile on the face of his eldest son, when he beheld his much loved father so much interested in his soul's salvation, and trying to close in with the offers of mercy. I was after this, at the tent of Brother S., and he asked me to go into the room where his father was, and talk to him; and I went in and prayed for him. My faith was strong, and I came out and told his son he would soon see the old man in the church.

I was trying to preach to a large congregation, and hoped for a greater revival. When about half through my sermon, I saw a young man sitting at the root of a tree, in the outer circle of the congregation, who was laughing in my face; and whenever I looked at him I became so much disturbed that I would not turn that way some time. When I did look again, he was still laughing. It sometimes seems to me, so to speak, that my faith is almost dead—hardly breathing—so faint, so weak is my trust in my blessed Saviour, at such times, that it might be said that a child of the Lord, whose trust is firmly fixed on the blessed Rock, of only one week old, has at that moment a stronger faith than the Strange Preacher. I feel sorry when I think of this, but so it is. At times I remain thus for several days; but after awhile my trust in the Lord begins to rise by slow degrees, and, at some times, very suddenly, until it becomes so strong that it takes firm hold on the horns of the altar, and will not let go until the request is granted, and the desire of my heart is found. I have often thus claimed a promise, believing it would be granted. "According to thy faith so be it." "All things are possible to him that believeth." Is not this the doctrine taught in the blessed book? I have often prayed to the Lord that some particular persons might embrace the faith, and several times the request has been granted.* The young man still kept on laughing. At last I stopped and pointed him out to the congregation, and thus addressed him: "Young man, you have been disturbing me very much; mark what I say to you. You are laughing now; but, with the help of the Lord, I am going to have you in the altar begging for mercy. Before the services end you will be here on your knees. Stay away if you can; remember—forewarned, forearmed." I called on the church to help by their prayer. I suspect the crowd thought there *was* a a strange preacher before them, surely. Perhaps there were few Methodists present who believed those words would come to pass, but the preacher did. And if he had never found it out before, he would have gone to the judgment seat believing it would be made known, that he had spoken the truth.

I preached on with my faith firmly fixed on the strength of Israel—the Jehovah of Abraham, of Isaac and of Jacob. The power of the Highest descended upon the congregation. The shout of a king was heard in the camp of Israel. The banner of redemption waved gloriously over the host of the Lord. When singing began, mourners came up in great crowds, and the shouts of the Lord's people rang out, and the cries of the weeping penitents were heard all around. My soul exulted in the Lord, my Strength and my Redeemer. Many were happily converted, and the entire congregation seemed under the influence of the Holy Spirit. Prayer after

---

*I was once at a meeting in Sumter District, South Carolina, where a young man was acting very much like the one above. I stopped and pointed him out, and called on the preachers to witness what I said. I told them that same young man would, in a few weeks at most, come and ask an interest in their prayers—that my faith was strong enough to believe it. In the course of the day he came up to the altar.

prayer was offered up; one holy song followed another up the hills of heaven, and entered into the presence of the Eternal. The preachers, exhorters, and leaders were at work everywhere—all were at work at their post, helping on the cause of their Master, comforting, exhorting and encouraging. On and still on the army of Prince Immanuel pressed the routed foe; hell was flying; heaven was pursuing; angels were rejoicing, while devils were howling for the loss of their victims. Preachers were clapping their hands and shouting; pious sisters were rejoicing with young ladies lately converted, who were telling them what the Lord had done for them in the forgiveness of their sins. Hardened sinners had been subdued, and were coming to the altar, or bowing at their seats. Many young converts were passing through the throng, hunting their friends and bringing them to the Lord. On, and still on, went the blessed meeting. The Strange Preacher was seen every where, as many of his friends on the old Walterboro circuit have often seen him. Now he was shaking hands, and then talking to the mourners; now kneeling before sinners, begging them to give their hearts to the Lord, and now passing through the crowd, clapping his hands, and calling out aloud, "Farewell world, I am bound for the kingdom." Now he was at the outskirts of the congregation, praying for some whom he found bowed at their seats, and now coming back to the altar, saying—

> "I want to live a Christian here,
> I want to die a shouting,
> I want to see bright angels stand,
> And waiting to receive me,
> To bear my soul to Canaan's land.

On went the holy work, and among the many who found their Saviour was a young brother of Dr. Pierce, who afterwards became a member of the Georgia Conference. The night was passing away, but still the meeting was kept up; the mourners were so many, that it was difficult to pass among them. The preachers still continued in their holy work; sinners were still being convicted. At last, one of the preachers said to me, that one of the young men at the altar wanted to see me. The crowd was so great, it was some time before we got there. There was a young man, lying on his back, clapping his hands and shouting, happy in his Saviour's love. He was in a constant motion. "Mr. Bellinger," said he, "I want to see you. I am the same young man who was seated at the tree, whom you said you would have at the altar before the services closed. I did not then believe it would be so; but you have got me here now; and I'm glad that I came." He then took me by the hand, pulled me down, and threw his arms around my neck. O, how we rejoiced together! I think it was Brother Pierce who said to me, with a smile I can never forget, "That will be something, Brother B., for you to tell your friends when you go home." O, my blessed Saviour! even now, at this hour, I thank thee, as I have often done before, for the happy moment that proved the truth of what thy humble servant had proclaimed. O, glory to the Lord! that I once, in my roving life, was at the Hancock camp-ground, and enjoyed myself so much, and was treated so kindly by the friends I found there. I have always regarded it as one of the best meetings I have ever attended; and I hope I will never forget those olden days of immortal remembrance.

One day, Dr. Pierce said, he wanted me to preach at such an hour; and that he had something to tell me, which he thought I ought to know. He then told me, there were several young ladies and gentlemen, from a certain town in the State, who had been making sport of me; and who professed to be much amused at my singular manner of preaching. They said I made them laugh every now and then; that I would sometimes repeat a beautiful piece of poetry, which they enjoyed very much; but they said they could not hear all the words, so they were going to come near the altar the next time, that they might hear every word—they expected to be much amused. He told me, the preachers would pray for me; and he hoped these hard hearts might be reached. Brother Pendleton told me the same thing. I went to the woods, to implore divine aid, and to pray earnestly for those particular persons. I have known for a long time, that many persons seem to be much amused at my manner, and say they cannot help laughing at me. I know I have a very singular manner; but it is all natural with me—nothing forced, nothing borrowed. I never say a word with the wish that people should laugh; and I must confess, that I am at times much surprised to see them thus affected. I feel thankful to the Lord, that I have sometimes seen those who had been thus excited to mirth, afterwards weeping as if some loved one had gone.

The hour of trial, of hope, and of fear to the preacher had come. The service began; and the persons alluded to were present, sitting very near the altar. The parson was aware of their presence—a hint had been given to him. He looked at them; every face seemed to say, "We are expecting quite a farce; we will be much amused." He gave out his text, and began to preach; and then looked towards the gay group from the town of W——. The gentlemen were smiling, and looked as if they expected to laugh soon; and the ladies had their fans to their faces, and were evidently much amused. The preacher went on after his own fashion, and asked the prayers of the church—not looking at them again for some time. After a while, he ventured to turn his eyes that way again. The same expression was still on each face, and it reminded him of persons in a theatre, who were enjoying very much what was passing before them. The preacher was quite disturbed, but went on, hoping the Lord would be with him; and he trusted that many were praying for him. He became much encouraged—giving his fears to the wind, and unfurling his flag fearlessly, and looking aloft to the hills from whence his help came. He then turned once more to that fashionable party, and had much cause for gratitude; for a great change had come over that group. He now saw grave, serious persons before him, who were listening very respectfully. There was one face more serious than the others; and he hoped tears would soon be seen falling from those lovely eyes. Becoming still more encouraged, he went on with his sermon, at the close of which many mourners came to the altar; and among the young ladies bowed humbly before the Lord, was one who belonged to that laughing group, which had anticipated so much fun when they came so near as not to lose a word. If the whole truth was known, I suspect that party of fashionables from W——, felt that a great change had come over the spirit of their dream. If the tempter had known what was going to happen, he would have persuaded them, if possible, not to go so near the altar. I would not be surprised if some of them, if yet alive, still remember that scene. That young lady was so much affected that she could not walk alone; but had to be assisted to one of the tents.

During the evening, I was at Brother S.'s tent, to which that young lady had been taken; and there she was afterwards happily converted. That happy young convert had come with an aunt, who professed to be much hurt at what had happened. She was very angry with her neice for having gone to that Methodist altar, and knelt down to be prayed for on the straw. It was too bad; and she regretted having come. She resolved to carry her neice home at once; for it was mortifying to think she was convicted among those shouting Methodists. And then, the greatest offence of all was, that she went to the altar after that singular preacher had called up mourners—the very man, too, of whom they had made such sport! It was too bad! The party left. The aunt took her neice away; but not till she was made happy in her Saviour's love, and rejoiced in the hope of heaven.

The glorious meeting still went on; and Brother S., at last, had his long-prayed-for wish granted—his father became a member of the church; but he had not yet found his Saviour in the forgiveness of his sins, though he was deeply in earnest resolved to seek him to the last.

Some distressing news was brought by some persons returning to night-meeting, from the party who had left for W——. It seems, that after the aunt left with her neice, she began to scold and abuse her for what had happened; and said, she was so enraged, that she never expected to forget it. The young lady took it all very mildly; but the aunt finally became so angry, that she requested some of the party to let her neice ride with them. The exchange was made, and the aunt rode on alone; when, soon after, her horses took fright and ran off. The carriage was broken, and she was thrown out, and so hurt as to be insensible. Some persons passing by, saw her friends trying to restore her, and were told how it had happened. What sad news! What a happy deliverance to the happy young convert! Surely the Lord watcheth over his children.

The blessed meeting was closed at the camp-ground, to be continued at Sparta. I went home with Brother S.'s father, to stay a day or so with him, and then go to another meeting, at Dr. Pierce's request. The old gentleman was much distressed. I prayed for, and tried to encourage, him; but he seemed to fear that his day of grace was gone for ever; and he told me he thought he had committed the unpardonable sin. I was very sorry for him; but told him I expected, after I left, to hear he had found the Lord. We were sitting at dinner, when he got up in great agony of mind, and went weeping into another room. After praying with him again, and telling him I expected soon to hear he had found the pearl of great price, I left him, and went on my way. On Monday, Dr. P. came down, and told me they had had glorious times in Sparta; and that the old gentleman had been powerfully converted in love-feast, on Sunday, and had requested him to tell me the good news. To the Lord alone be all the glory.

## LEAF THE NINETEENTH.

MEETINGS AT OLD SPRINGTOWN; OR, THE PREACHER WHO, WHILE WORKING FOR OTHERS, ENJOYED HIMSELF VERY MUCH.

Perhaps more than sixty years ago, there was a famous place of summer resort for many families from the low-country, a few miles from Odum's bridge on the Salkahatchie, called Springtown, which I suppose gave name to the surrounding neighborhood, and to a church of our Baptist brethren, with which my first recollections of the preaching of the gospel are connected. It is the most beautiful place for a church, that I now remember ever having seen. The thoughts of my boyhood were associated with Springtown; and now, in the decline of life, they still linger around the old place. I went there oftener than anywhere else, until I left the camps of sin, and started for a better world. All hail! to the old church, and the happy hours I spent there in the olden time. For years, I generally fastened my horse to the same tree; and often sat on the same bench, near one of the posts behind which I would hide my face when I did not wish the preacher to see me.

I remember the Rev. Mr. Duncan well. I see him now, as I used to see him more than forty years ago. I sometimes found his eyes fastened on me with a marked expression. I have more than once got behind that post, while he, with earnest voice, was entreating sinners to flee the wrath to come. It was Brother Duncan, who more than once, as I have elsewhere mentioned, said he believed I would have to preach, and that he would live to hear me. And so it came to pass; though I had been preaching many years before he heard me. He asked me, with strong emotion, if I had forgotten what he used to tell me? With tears almost falling from my eyes, I told him I had not.

In the olden days, Springtown was a famous place for a

large turn-out, and many came there from a distance. All classes met there, from the different ranks of society in Barnwell District. The grave, the sedate, and the pious were there; those who were seeking the salvation of their souls, who were wounded by the shafts of the Spirit, and who were mourning the love of the Lord to know, were there; those who had once tasted that the Lord was precious, who had been valiant for the truth, who had endured hardness as good soldiers of the cross, who ran well for a while, but, alas! had now gone back to the world, and the brethren with sorrow of heart had dismissed them from their communion, were there—some of them were trying to find again the good old paths, that they might walk in them to the joy of their hearts; others of them were even more careless, more hardened in sin than ever before. Gay, careless, wicked young men were there, who made sport of holy things, and said plainly, by their actions, "as for the man, Christ Jesus, he shall not rule over us." Beautiful ladies were there, who loved the fashions and pleasures of this life much more than they did the blessed Saviour of the world and his church. Some were there, who with care read the holy Book by day and night, and who prized it far above all the books of this world; while others were there who scarcely ever opened the holy Bible, had no desire to read its inspired pages, and who professed not to believe its sacred truths. Children of poverty and sorrow were there, whose parents were compelled to labor for their daily bread. Boys and girls were there, living in the enjoyment of every earthly blessing, having no wish ungratified. Husbands and wives were there, who were living happy in the possession of wedded love, which, we are told, "is the only bliss that escaped the fall." Husbands and wives were there, whose love did not long survive the days of their courtship, and whose hearts were now separated from each other. Happy lovers were there, with the day of their espousals near at hand, mutually longing for that hour which would make them one for life. Others were there, who had once rejoiced in each other's love, but were now divided in feeling as far as the east is from the west. Young men were there, the pride and delight of all who knew them—the hope, the defence of their country. Young men were there, the shame, the sorrow of their relatives, for they feared not the Lord, nor regarded man.

And Springtown had another famous place of resort for all kinds of spectators—Odum's bridge, the public place for baptizing those who had left the world, and had come out on the side of the Lord. Imagine yourself there on some holy Sabbath, when a large crowd had collected, to witness a baptism by immersion. Let us stand on the bridge, with the waiting throng. Be careful that you do not lean too much against the railing; there may be some danger, for others are leaning against it as well as yourself. Now, before the preacher enters the water, with those standing near him dressed in white, with serious faces and downcast eyes—thinking, I hope, of the white robes and the palms of victory on the other side of the flood, in the green fields of Eden—let us overlook the general crowd, both on the bridge and on each side of the creek, in carriages, buggies, and gigs; on horses and on foot. Do you think all those in that crowd are thinking on religious subjects? If you do you are greatly mistaken. Look again; do you not see several persons laughing and talking; paying no more respect to the solemn sight before them than they do to the preaching of the gospel in the house of the Lord. Some are there who do not wish to see the work of the Lord reviving, and sinners returning from the error of their ways, but would prefer that Zion should languish and iniquity abound. Many a gay and trifling son and daughter of fashion is in that throng, sporting with the golden moments of this short life, at the risk of the loss of their immortal souls. What do they care about religion, or the church, or the Saviour of men? They say, they are as good as they wish to be, that there is no use in talking so much of coming out on the Lord's side, and starting for heaven. Others are present whose hearts are full of wicked thoughts—anger, envy, and revenge possess their entire hearts.

But now look at the other side of the picture; there are many beautiful sights to be seen, at which angels and holy spirits love to look. Notice that aged man and the woman at his side; their eyes are filled with tears; and they, perhaps, are thinking of the time long gone by, when they were first made to dread the wrath to come; when after drinking the wormwood and the gall, they at last passed from death unto life, and were in that very stream baptized in the Lord. They feel very thankful for the grace that has brought them safe thus far, and hope to be in a better world. Look at those young ladies, with tears streaming from their eyes; they are sorry they have not yet found the pearl of great price, and are praying now that they may soon be ready to give their hearts to the Saviour, and their hands to the church. Notice those young men near the centre of the bridge, who look so serious, so sad. The blessed Spirit is at work in their hearts—reproving them "of sin, of rightousness, and of a judgment to come." How the tears fall from their eyes into the water that flows beneath them. Devils are disappointed, while angels are rejoicing; for those young men will soon embrace the faith, following their Saviour and the example set before them. Perhaps one of them, in years to come, will preach the blessed gospel. Observe that strong man mounted on that fine horse near the water: he is much distressed, for he once loved the Saviour, but has gone back to the world; the sight before him reminds him of all he has lost; and he is now resolved to return to the blessed Shepherd. See that man on your left, dressed in deep mourning, with crape on his hat and arm; now his face is cast down; now his eyes are lifted to heaven. He seems to notice very little of what is going on around him. He has lately lost his much loved wife—the mother of that little boy at his side. When she kissed him the last time he promised her to meet her in heaven; and he is trying to keep his word. He has been up more than once for the prayers of the church.

But let us stop looking about now, for the solemn service has begun. Listen to that holy song. Now the minister with those around him enter the stream; and one by one they are baptized in the name of the Lord of hosts. We will leave the place now and return to the church, hoping the Lord will save us all in his heavenly kingdom.

Before I tell you of some of those good meetings they used to have there in olden times, let me tell you of some of the old members of the church. Close by one of the windows, not far from the pulpit, is an aged man, trembling beneath the weight of many years. He is quite deaf, and you have to speak very loud to him. He loves the church, and has been a long time traveling the road to heaven. That is Brother Daniel Odum. That man who sits not far off, and who looks like him, is his son. Captain Odum is one of the old members whose faith is firmly fixed on the Rock of Ages. See that man in front of the pulpit with a serious, grave face, and with his eyes fixed on the preacher as if he wished to hear every word; and near by you will see a man who resembles him much, and who, if possible, pays more attention to the sermon—bending slightly forward, with his large eyes opened wide. Those are two brothers, by the name of Rice, good men and true. See that thin, spare man, with a modest, quiet face, sitting near the end of that bench; that is Brother P. S. These, with many others, worshipped the Holy One of Israel at the memorable Springtown church, where I often went when quite a young man. After I joined the church, of course I did not go as frequently as before; but I did so once in awhile, for the sake of "auld lang syne." In after years, when I had been called to the ministry, I was sometimes requested to preach there. I have been to many good meetings there since I started for heaven.

I was there once on the holy Sabbath, and was in the pulpit, when I unfortunately threw down the Bible, which, being a large one, got quite a heavy fall. I was much confused—hardly knowing what to do.* I sat down much distressed; but a good Brother, John Odum, whom I expect is

---

*I was once present at a Methodist meeting of some interest, where I was to exhort after the sermon; and when I rose, by some unlucky move of my hand, I turned over a tumbler of water into a friend's hat. I at once sat down; for some time much confused. There was a brother present who had witnessed the fall of the Bible, and who observed afterwards that he said to himself, Brother B. will not say another word, or else will give us one of his Springtown efforts again. After awhile I got up and began to exhort, and by the aid of the Holy Spirit, made quite an impression on the congregation.

in heaven to-day, handed it to me. I arose at once, and after thanking him, began, with the help of the Lord, to exhort; and with such effect that some of the friends thought it was done intentionally. But those who know me well, will believe me when tell them I only spoke on the impulse of the moment.

I was once present at a blessed meeting at old Springtown, with that pious and venerable minister of the Lord, Brother Brooker, one of the good men of old, of strong faith, and full of the Holy Ghost and of power, in whom saint and sinner believed. The good old man and myself were alone for several days. The members of the church seemed to rejoice in the anticipation of the joys of heaven, when the warfare of life is over. I generally preached, and he exhorted, and the Strength of Israel was with us. I see him before me now, as he stood in the olden days, full of zeal, and hope, and trust in the Lord, and, with tears flowing down his aged face, told us of the blessed hope he had, through grace, of one day getting to heaven, where he hoped his old friends would gladly welcome him, and where he expected to spend a happy eternity in praising the Lord; and as he turned to sinners and implored them to flee the wrath to come. Then he would sing a holy song, and young and old would come up for prayer, when some one would experience a change of heart; and then he would pass through the crowd, and shake hands with the brethren—Odum, Rice, Matheny, and others—telling us he hoped to meet us all in heaven by and bye. Thus, day after day, I would preach, and he exhort, and the blessed Spirit would descend. O! it was a holy, happy meeting.

I love to think of those glorious times at old Springtown. "Some men never sell for what they are worth," while others do for more; that is, some persons are thought more of than they deserve to be, while others never occupy their proper position, and are not properly valued by the church and the world. I have seen more than one member of our church standing where I thought he ought not to be—the place being either too high or too low. Now, the good Book tells us, that the man who went up too high was made to descend; and the man who took the low seat was requested to go up higher. But in these days, we see some persons are permitted to fill positions too exalted for them; and, strange to say, instead of being made to come lower, they are allowed to continue to climb still higher: while on the other hand, you will see a man, who is thought much more of by the Holy Spirit, yet is made during his laborious, useful life, to sit in some humble, obscure place. But I think in eternity another change will take place. I hope so, at least. And many will be quite surprised, when they see many Methodist and Baptist preachers, who never had LL.D., or D.D., or P.E. attached to their names, filling a more exalted place in heaven, and much more respected and esteemed by the inhabitants of the better world than they were while here upon earth. Now, in my mind, that good man, Brother Brooker, never "sold for what he was worth;" he was permitted to occupy too low a position. But that earnest and zealous preacher has long since gone to the green fields of Eden, on the other side of the flood, where I expect the blessed spirits of glory respect him much more than the sons of men did upon earth. He did not enter into the rest that remains for the people of God as soon as he expected—as soon as he hoped to; but his happy soul has been for many years rejoicing in the realms above, close by the eternal throne. All hail! departed brother; thou hast fought the good fight; thou hast kept the faith; thou hast finished thy course. Thy warfare is over; thou hast long since entered into the joy of thy Lord.

I had had a two days' meeting at one of our churches, which closed on Sunday evening; and on Monday morning, one of the neighbors asked me to come and help them at Springtown, for they had been there two days without a preacher, saying that Brother Dowling said, unless a minister came that day he would have to close the meeting. I went, and was there alone for two days, when other brethren came, and the meeting was kept up for nearly a fortnight. It was a most glorious season of refreshing from the Lord. When I first got there, Brother D. requested me to take charge of the meeting, and conduct the service as I would a Methodist meeting. The friends generally seemed pleased that I had come. I tried to labor as faithfully for them, as if I had been in my own church. There was a great outpouring of the Spirit; and the Strange Preacher enjoyed that blessed meeting, and his soul exulted in the Holy One of Israel. That was as good a meeting as I ever took part in at that holy place. Brother D. came to me one day, and said, he wished, after I had finished preaching, to address those present, and to advise them to pray for a deeper work of grace; and then to invite all who felt like meeting me in heaven to come and join their hands. O, my soul! what a crowd came up! We wept and rejoiced together. Sinners were then requested to kneel at their seats; and every person in the house bowed before the Lord. What a solemn time! We prayed together; and then some sweet songs of Zion were heard; and the Strange Preacher clapped his hands, and shouted, "Farewell, world! I am bound for the kingdom." And Brothers D., and R., and K., and C., and others, looked as if, were it the Lord's will, they were then willing to leave this world, and go home to rest for evermore, on the other side of the flood, in the sweet fields of Eden; there was "rejoicing in the tabernacles of the righteous, for the right hand of the Lord did valiantly." It seems that I can even now feel the pressure of the hand of more than one happy servant of the Lord, as I went among them, praising the Lord, "for his goodness, and for his wonderful works to the children of men." A stranger passing by, and seeing how we were enjoying that gracious outpouring of the Holy Spirit, might have said to himself, "this is a very fine time our Methodist friends are having here." But it was a Baptist meeting at Springtown in the olden days. After a while Brother Sanders, the pastor, came and others with him. The blessed work continued to increase in interest; the Lord was in his holy temple—"his stately steps were heard amid the golden candlesticks." What a beautiful sight it must have been to the Great Head of the church, to see his servants agreeing together in love, and travelling along side by side, to "Immanuel's land, where the waters flow so sweetly!" What pleasant prayer-meetings were held in those days, before preaching; and how the sweet songs, which Brother C. and others sung, would help to encourage the heart of the minister, when he stood up to proclaim the gospel to a lost world!

The meeting was well attended every day, and the interest manifested continued to increase rather than abate. The preacher was requested by his Baptist brethren to remain with them to the end; for as the Lord had begun the good work with him, they wished him to remain to the close. I had to preach, and to leave them on Friday, to go to Binnakers camp-meeting. What an affecting scene it was to see the Strange Preacher parting with his friends on that memorable evening! Some of them said, as he was going to leave, they would go too; so they left their meeting, and went with him. It closed on Sunday evening; and many concluded it was one of the best times they had ever had at that church.

Many of the old heroes of Springtown have long since gone home to that happy place, where the "wicked cease from troubling, and the weary are at rest." They served the Lord in their day and generation; they held out faithful to the end; and they now rest from their labors in the paradise above.

## LEAF THE TWENTIETH.

"IN UNION THERE IS STRENGTH;" OR, THE TWO FLAGS WAVING TOGETHER; OR, JUDAH AND SIMEON TOGETHER, WITH LOCKED SHIELDS, PRESSING THE BATTLE TO THE GATE.

I have often said, I regarded it as a blessing, that there were several branches of the one true church of our blessed Lord and Saviour Jesus Christ; for by this, I think, all men are left without excuse. I have always, as thousands can testify, told the people to join whatever branch they preferred; and I have often felt very sorry that there was so little love and good feeling, as there seems to be in some places; because of which, I am afraid, there has been untold injury done to the cause of truth. I believe in every person living in the church of one's choice; but I think all children of the Lord should comfort and strengthen each other in their labors of love, and in advancing the kingdom of our Lord upon earth. I know there are some persons, for I have seen them at their low calling, whose whole hearts are employed in proselyting. Never mind how contented a man may be, some of these birds of evil omen will gather around, and try to make him discontented where he has long enjoyed himself.* And should they succeed in bringing him over, they will wave flags, and blow trumpets, and publish it from the house-tops, that a great victory has been won. I suspect angels are sorry, and devils glad, to see such men at their foul work.

But, O, my soul! what a beautiful sight it is, to see members of the various churches helping at each other's meetings to press the battle to the gate, by preaching, exhorting, and praying together—making united efforts to advance their Master's cause! I believe, that in some places, one branch of the church will do more good than another; and think it is the direct will of the Lord; for in Judges i. 3, it is said, 'Now, after the death of Joshua, it came to pass, that the children of Israel asked the Lord, saying, who shall go up for us first against the Canaanites, first to fight against them? And the Lord said, Judah shall go up; behold, I have delivered the land into his hand. And Judah said unto Simeon, his brother, Come up with me unto my lot, that we may fight against the Canaanites; and I likewise will go with thee into thy lot. So Simeon went with him." Now, I think there is more spiritual truth in that passage than most persons suspect.

More than twenty-five years ago, one night just before daylight, I was aroused from my slumbers with the glad news that the Lord had favored his Zion, at Barnwell courthouse, with a most gracious revival—that the Baptists and Methodists were united in the meeting, and that the two flags were waving together; that Judah and Simeon, with locked shields, were "pressing the battle to the gate." Among the mourners were two of my nearest relatives; and I was requested to hasten to the help of the Lord against the mighty. After finishing his task the evening before, a faithful servant got a horse, and brought me the letter. He could not be persuaded to remain till morning, but started at once on his return. I could not sleep any more that night, because of joy and expectation—joy for the glad news I had heard, and strong hope and expectation of still greater manifestations of power. I hastened on, and found there a blessed state of things. It had begun in our church, and the Baptist brethren had united heartily in the good work. Brothers Townsend and Green, of our church, were on that circuit at the time, and Brothers Duncan, Brown, and Peoples, of the Baptist church, were with them. They had their war harness on, while the banner of Calvary waved over them. In some respects, that religious occasion excelled all that I have ever seen in my roving life. I never saw at any other place the two flags waving so fearlessly, harmoniously together; where Judah and Simeon fought so gallantly, with locked shields, and bore down all opposition.

The meeting had been kept up alternately in each church; and I suspect, such times had never before been seen in the place. While thinking of that blessed meeting, the battle of Mount Tabor rises before me, with all its unfading glory, with all its immortal surroundings—"that Zebulon and Napthali were a people that jeoparded their lives unto the death, in the high places of the field. They fought from heaven; the stars in their course fought against Sisera." Brothers Duncan and Townsend were the two great chiefs of Judah and Simeon, who led the hosts of the Lord in that famous passage of arms with hell. The Holy Ghost was present, reproving of sin, of righteousness, and of a judgment to come; sinners were convicted; mourners were weeping; and Christians were rejoicing in the Lord. And angels carried the glad news to heaven, that prodigals were coming home to their father; while devils lamented the loss of their victims.

My Baptist brethren, you who knew Brother Duncan, twenty years ago, remember with what power he exhorted, when the Holy Spirit was with him, and when he had the pleasure of seeing his relatives and friends seeking their Saviour. And you, my Methodist brothers, who remember Brother Joel Townsend, the good man and true, know what a great man he was for protracted meetings, when the Strength of Israel was with him. All hail! to those veterans of Prince Immanuel.

The meeting continued to increase in interest. Many hardened sinners trembled beneath the preached word, and, throwing down the arms of their rebellion, fled to the Saviour for mercy. Many precious souls were happily converted, and "told to all around, what a dear Saviour they had found;" and the membership of both churches were very much comforted, and were bravely coming up to the help of the Lord. O! how the Saviour and the happy saints must have rejoiced, when they beheld those two flags waving together—Judah and Simeon, with locked shields, charging the powers of hell, and winning the hard-fought battle. What gracious seasons of refreshing we had from the Lord of Hosts! We had good congregations, particularly at night; and they were generally attentive and respectful; and sometimes a very strong impression would rest upon the entire throng. At times, the prayer-meetings were honored by such displays of the Holy Ghost, that all who were there might well say, we are sitting in heavenly places in Christ Jesus. How much I enjoyed myself at that never-to-be-forgotten meeting! I have thought, that those who pass through great revivals, without embracing the terms of salvation, will be hard to be impressed in after life, and may never forsake their sins; and that the gospel seldom reaches their hearts. I have never been much surprised, that some persons who passed through that revival without experiencing a change, still remain in the broad road to ruin. More than once during the services, some persons were so deeply convicted, that they seemed to have lost all power of motion. I remember one day, when about leaving, some man was found lying between two benches, perfectly helpless. Some persons became quite alarmed for him, as it was a sight they were not used to. Brother Townsend, the old hero of the cross, who had witnessed many such scenes, told them not to be frightened, as he was under strong conviction, and it would yet be all right with him. Nothing took him by surprise.

The meeting was carried on for several days, without the door of the church being opened. But several had been converted, and were waiting to join. So one night, we opened the door to both churches: those wishing to unite with the Baptist church were to give their hand to Brother Duncan; and those wanting to join our church were to go to Brother Townsend. I thought this would be a scene on which angels would love to dwell. When the moment arrived, there was much interest manifested, and the preachers took their stand, to receive those who might come. We got four members, but our Baptist brother got none; and I was so sorry to see it, that I could hardly refrain from weeping; for I thought, had it been otherwise, that our Saviour would have been better pleased. But so it was, and I was quite sad.

The meeting continued for some time with unabated interest, and many united with both branches; and before the final close more joined the Baptist, than the Methodist, church. Prayer-meetings were held in private houses; and the whole place seemed under religious influence. Old Barnwell has never had such a time of holy visitation, at least as far as I remember. I suspect the fallen spirits more than once looked on astonished—more than once smote upon their breasts, as they saw those two flags waving so gloriously together, while Judah and Simeon fought so gallantly together, pressing the battle to the gate.

The holy Sabbath, the great day of the feast drew near. The report of the revival had spread far and near; and many came from the country. What a memorable Sunday was that! The power of the Highest descended upon the church and the world, and a deep impression rested upon all present; and the great work was still more enlarged. As those who united with us preferred to be immersed, we concluded to baptize all together.

It was Monday morning, and a crowd had gathered at the water side. It was sale day at Barnwell, which fact caused it to be greater. What a sight for hell and heaven! There stood Brother Duncan, and those who were going with him; and there, too, Brother Townsend and his members. Look at the throng, in carriages and buggies, on horseback and on foot. See how crowded is the bridge. About the middle, near the water's edge, holding on to the railing, seated down, was seen the Strange Preacher, regarding, with much emotion, all that passed around him. Among those now confessing their Saviour to the world, are two very near to him —the father with Brother D., and the son with Brother T. The two preachers with their converts—the chiefs of Judah and Simeon, entered the water side by side, and then separated, and formed two lines fronting each other. What a moment of interest! All were looking at the ministers and those around them. Brother T. requested Brother D. to begin; but Brother D. wanted him to lead; and then Brother T. baptized one, in the name of the Father, of the Son, and of the Holy Ghost; and Brother D. said "Amen;" and then Brother D. baptized one, and Brother T. responded "Amen." And so the solemn services were conducted to the close. Brother D. said to his own brother, as he took his hand, "brother, my brother." And the father and son now embraced each other in the water; and the Strange Preacher could not bear that sight, but shouted out aloud, and gave glory to the Highest. The benediction was pronounced, and the crowd retired.

My friends, let me try to draw another picture for you. I was once travelling alone, and had crossed safely over a deep, broad river, and was passing through a swamp on the other side. It was a hot day; and the sun was shining very brightly, when I came to a large field near the roadside, filled with golden-headed wheat, ripe for the harvest. I stopped, and said to myself, "What a picture! Can I not make use of it in my Master's cause? Suppose, this very hot day, some few reapers were appointed to cut that wheat down in an allotted time, which would soon transpire, and were to be well rewarded by the owner when the work was done." I said to myself, "they would not quarrel with each other, but go regularly to work; for the sooner that field is reaped, the sooner would the resting time and the bounty come." I said again to myself, "now, the world is a great spiritual field, filled with immortal souls, ripe for the harvest; and the different branches of the one true church, and all the preachers, have been appointed by the Master to gather that great harvest field. Why should they dispute with each other—the world is large enough for them all to work in, and win souls for their Master. The day of judgment is hastening on, when we will have to stand before the great Eternal; and, O! that the friends of the Saviour would go to work to gather in that mighty harvest. If we are faithful to the end, that blessed time of rest and of bounty money will come at last; and then, when the great field of the world is reaped, the angels will sing the harvest home." O! friends of Jesus, in the one true church, in all the sincerity of my heart, I entreat you to be more united in love and friendship. We all serve the same Lord, and are all bound for the same place. I believe, with all my soul, that we would please our Saviour better, and would better advance his kingdom among men, if we were more strongly united in the bonds of Christian affection.

I think it is still remembered in heaven and hell, that there was once a time, at Barnwell court-house, when the two flags waved harmoniously together; and that Judah and Simeon, with locked shields, pressed the battle to the gate.

## LEAF THE TWENTY-FIRST.

### MEETINGS IN ALABAMA.

Well, my friends, let me tell you of some interesting meetings I attended in Alabama, some twenty years ago. I went to visit a friend, who lived near Montgomery, and to attend some meetings in the vicinity. I took the cars at Bamberg. I enjoy a railroad ride very much, when there are not too many on board, and when there is no smoking or drinking. Now, let us suppose this trip to be at times pleasant, and at times otherwise. Observe those young men seated together. For a while they were rather silent; and I thought one of them seemed a little serious—evidently more so than his companions. The Strange Preacher said to himself, "I suspect he is a member of the church; and I hope the rest wish well to the cause; I will sit near them, and if I see an opportunity, speak to them on religious matters." But you must not always judge by appearances. The young men were whispering together; then he whom I thought looked rather serious, took out a bottle, and passed it round. The Strange Preacher was much surprised, and was soon to be more so. They had finished drinking, and the same young man whom he imagined pious, with a polite bow, offered the bottle to him; after which the Wandering Arab kept as far from them as possible.

At the end of the journey I found my friend, the Doctor, waiting for me. He welcomed me, was much delighted to see me, and said that he had given out several appointments for me and that the friends were looking forward to them with some interest. My friend had been married some time, and had several children. Both he and his wife were church members, and she appeared to enjoy religion—was happy in her Saviour's love; but he confessed himself a backslider, and rather cold. While conversing with him, my feelings were much moved when I found out how indifferent he was. I had some time to rest before the first meeting began, every thing being done to make me feel at home. The Doctor observed to me, several times, that I must not expect a good meeting; for the people generally were indifferent, and they had not had one there for several years; that the services would not be protracted, as we would be perfectly willing to close on Sunday, for it would be a heavy drag throughout. The circuit preacher was to be there, but notwithstanding our united efforts, he was afraid it would prove a failure. This intelligence caused me to feel cast down, and I began to regret having come; but it was too late, and I resolved to do the best I could. I prayed to God and placed my trust in the Rock of ages. The time was near, and the Doctor repeated his warning. I asked him not to mention it again, as it discouraged me, but he said he did it purposely; for he saw how high my hopes were, and he wanted me to know the true state of the case. One day I became so disheartened that I told him I would retire to my room awhile. He gave me the last Southern Christian Advocate: I took it, but did not expect to read many lines. When I was alone I looked to the Lord for help. After a while I opened the paper carelessly, but my attention soon became fixed. I saw a piece entitled, "A Minister's Dream of meeting his Mother in Heaven;" which I read and found that it was a dream of my own. I became roused up, and again knelt down and thanked my Lord. I exulted in the hope of meeting that mother in the green fields of Eden. Some time before, I had told that beautiful dream for the first time, while preaching at Summerton, in Sumter District, and I was told afterwards that Miss E. S., the sweet muse of Clarendon, was present and wrote those beautiful lines, which I saw for the first time while in Alabama. I was much comforted and strengthened, and when I left my room, my feelings were entirely different from those with which I entered it.

The church was called Oak Grove, and when we started to the meeting the Doctor still continued to warn me not to expect too much. I took it much better than before, and prayed with more faith to the Saviour of my dear mother, long gone to heaven. My trust was firmly fixed on the Eternal Rock, and I claimed the promise and had hold on the horns of the altar. I cannot remember my text. Before I got through, Brother Duncan, the minister in charge, came in. I was afterwards introduced to him, and he preached in the evening. I was much pleased with him. The meeting had begun under happy auspices, and I praised the Lord for that gracious time. The members of the church enjoyed themselves very much—my hopes were high—my flag was waving. The Doctor came to me much excited and observed that he had made a great mistake, and wished to recall what he had said. He was convinced that we would have a revival; and did not know when we would close. Sunday came, and O, what a happy day it was for the entire church. I hope the friends in that community have not forgotten that gracious time. Our love feast was a season of refreshing from the presence of the Lord. The church could not accommodate the large crowd. We had two sermons, and Brother D. made a still stronger impression on me, and there was a blessed manifestation of the power of the Highest. I was told that such scenes had not been witnessed there for years. Several mourners came to the altar, and among them I had the pleasure of seeing the Doctor and a friend of his come to the altar. Both were members, but had grown cold and wished to be restored to their first love. The church felt much and prayed earnestly for them. We had some conversions and several additions to the church. The meeting continued and the Doctor came to me again and spoke of the happy time we were having, and said he had no idea when we would close. The meeting increased in interest, I think, until the next Sabbath. I have forgotten several things connected therewith, but one circumstance I hope never to forget.

One day during the meeting Doctor Hamilton, the Presiding Elder, came to help us, and I think preached twice. The first sermon I have never forgotten—particularly the introduction. His text was Psalms lx, 1-3. The sermon made a life-time impression on the Strange Preacher—having heard hundreds since which I have entirely forgotten, and having preached many myself, of which I have no recollection. But that of Doctor H. is still remembered. His face would interest you before he said anything. He represented to us the

Eternal Jehovah, seated on his throne, surrounded by all the glories of the better world. The great princes stood all around the immortal King. The six winged seraphim stood and cried, one to another, "Holy, holy, holy, is the Lord of hosts—the whole earth is full of his glory." And you might have imagined you saw the holy angels fall before the throne on their faces as they worshipped the Eternal, saying, "Amen; blessing, and glory, and wisdom, and thanksgiving, and power, and honor, and might be unto our God forever and ever, amen." He then spoke of the distressed state in which the man was, who was represented in the text. He enlarged upon the awful pit as he saw it represented. There the poor prisoner raised his plaintive cry for help, but was not lifted up. He did not stop, but still continued his cry. What he said about waiting patiently for the Lord was a sermon itself. Imagine again that you behold the King on His eternal throne. What is that which seems to impress the Monarch? He seemed like one listening to a distant sound. He raises his hand; there is a great silence in heaven. The King leans forward and listens again. He descends from his throne, and goes to the golden walls and bends over, and signs to the angels again, and there is still a greater silence. The blessed spirits hold their breath and the holy winds are hushed. The King inclines still more—the holy land is just beneath. He has found out from whence proceeded that cry. It is from the man in the horrible pit; he hastens to his help and delivers him, "placing his foot upon a rock and establishing his going." Thus is the sinner saved from the awful pit by the Saviour of the world.

The meeting closed, and I went on to other appointments. On my way to Robinson Springs I spent some time in Montgomery. Come, friends, and stand with me on the banks of the Alabama river, and listen with me when I hear, for the first time, that beautiful story of "Here we rest." The Doctor asked me, if I knew the meaning of the Indian word "Alabama." He told me, that long before the days of '76 there was a tribe of roving Indians, flying before the advance of the pale face, who was driving them off and taking their lands; and that after a long and dreary journey they came at last, tired and faint, to a noble river, teeming with fish. The woods were filled with game, and this seemed to them an earthly paradise, and here their chief told them to stop; that they had at last found their "Alabama," meaning "here we rest;" that their roving life was ended, and that the pale face would follow them no more, as he would be content with what he had got. The tribe believed him, and sang, "Trouble's over, trouble's over," and enjoyed themselves in peace for many years. One summer's evening, near sundown, the young men had returned from the hunt, loaded with game, and many fish had been caught; the children were playing under the noble trees; the old men were seated round, smoking the pipe of peace; and the aged chief was standing apart from the others, well pleased with what he saw. Suddenly he started, looked up, and listened! His face had a sad expression—he gave the sign—there was silence all around. A tear fell from his eye; he smote his breast, and said aloud, "I hear the hum of the honey bee— the pale face is coming. Yes, he is coming—this is no longer an Alabama for us—we must again begin our wandering!"

The Doctor said that he was present, several years before, when the last of the Creek Indians were removed to the lands in the West, which had been given to them, when two warriors, who said they would not go, had to be bound; and while waiting at the river, they, by a mighty effort, burst their bands and tried to escape, but were soon killed by the soldiers; whereupon the Indian maidens rushed up, tearing their hair and lamenting the death of their leaders and frequently kissing their wounds. My friend told me how sadly he felt as he looked on. And while I listened, with tears in my eyes, a cloud gathered overhead and several large drops fell slowly, when the Wandering Arab said to himself, "perhaps some departed spirits of the Indian braves are hovering over us, weeping with me as I listen to the sad tale of the Alabama—here we rest." No where will we rest safely but in heaven.

I was at more than one meeting at Robinson's Springs, but I have forgotten most things connected with them. There, I formed the acquaintance of a Brother Whetstone, a local preacher, who had removed from South Carolina—and an uncle of Captain Whetstone, of our neighborhood. He was in the decline of life; but full of faith and hope—bound for glory and heaven. I was treated with much kindness by that aged servant of the Lord, and all his family.

The lands in this portion of Alabama were not so rich as those around Oak Grove; but my first impression was, that my friends there enjoyed more heartfelt religion, and were living nearer the throne of grace. And, after all, pure religion is much to be preferred to the riches of this world. One good Heaven-blessed meeting, where the church is refreshed, where backsliders are reclaimed, where immortal souls pass from death unto life, where some are called to preach—is worth far more than all the cotton and lumber that was ever floated down the Alabama and Edisto rivers—yes, a thousand times more.

There was preaching at Dr. W.'s house one night. We had a season of rejoicing—one of those old-time meetings, which the Strange Preacher loves to attend, as he passes through life, calling for volunteers for glory and heaven. It was a season of general enjoyment among God's people. How happy I felt, while listening to those heavenly songs; one of which I remembered having heard once before. The chorus was,

" We have but one more river to cross,
And then we'll sing Hosannah ! "

During my trip, the best meeting I attended was near the Springs, at a church called Tabernacle. It was a very interesting time. With the exception of one blessed sight, I now have but a faint recollection of that meeting. All else has passed away, leaving scarcely a trace behind. My text for that day was one I used often in the olden time. It was II Kings vii. 3, 4. Twenty years ago, it was a favorite passage with me. There was a large crowd out; the singing was thrilling, and the walls were made to ring; the power of the Highest came down, and many mourners came up. The doors of the church were opened, and among others came a very old man, over eighty years old. He had two sons, class-leaders—good, pious men. The walls of that venerable house, and the grand old woods around, seemed to cry out, " Glory in the Highest!" we, too, joining in the cry. Brother W., and several others, seemed ready for that happy land; and the Wandering Arab clapped his hands, and shouted, " Farewell, world!" He passed through the throng, exhorting and entreating sinners to give their hearts to their Saviour. But no words could tell the joy of the wife of that old man. She was completely overpowered, and remained for some time insensible—seemingly hovering between the two worlds—wishing at once to be in heaven to thank the Lord personally for her husband's conversion, and to praise him for ever; and then again, if it was the Lord's will, she would gladly remain on earth, to help, and to rejoice with, the father of her Christian sons on his way to glory. Some persons became alarmed, and sent for Dr. W. When she recovered, she said, with a heavenly smile on her face, and a tear of bliss in her eye, that she was only overpowered by the unexpected pleasure of seeing her husband, for whom she had been praying for more than forty years, profess religion and join the church. The tide of feeling was very strong in our midst. The old lady said she wanted to see me; and I can almost now feel the pressure with which she grasped my hand. She told me that she would never forget me; for that, by the help of the Lord, I had saved her husband.

Farewell to Alabama!

## LEAF THE TWENTY-SECOND.

A MEMENTO TO MY DEPARTED FRIEND, REV. H. H. DURANT; OR,
A VISIT TO SANDY SPRING CAMP-GROUND, SOUTH CAROLINA.

I met Brother Durant first when on the Walterboro circuit. He was then quite young, and I soon felt a strong attachment for the youthful preacher. I saw him for the last time at Binnakers, not long before his death. I loved him as a brother in Christ, all through our long acquaintance. Farewell! dear departed brother; we have spent many happy hours together in this vale of tears; I trust through grace to meet you, to use one of your favorite sayings, far "above the blue-throned stars," where sickness and death are felt and feared no more.

Some years ago, I had the pleasure of attending a meeting at Sandy Spring camp-ground, with other preachers. I cannot be minute in describing the journey; but we arrived there after night, and found the friends glad to see us. The next day, it was not long before I saw some signs of the Lord among his people. Occasionally, there was a shout heard in the camp, and some mourning soul would be blessed by the Lord. To make use of a figure, the friends generally might be said to be sailing along pleasantly, not far from the shore, but in full view of land all the time—near enough to converse with their friends on the beach, and to send messages of love to the dear ones at home. And now and then, a vessel returning from a long voyage, would say to those sailing near the shore, "better not go too far, for the sea is very rough over the bar."

Now, let me tell you of the great hero of camp-meetings. We were called to the stand by the loud-sounding horn, and the man that everybody loved to see was in the pulpit—the right man was in the right place. The hymn had been sung, and the great crowd was bowed in humble prayer. Those of you who have heard Brother Durant pray, remember with what power and unction he seemed at times to be blessed—how he at times bore his congregation away from earth almost to the eternal throne. He gave out his text. Well, says one of those who have often heard him, I can guess what it was—"As the hart panteth after the waterbrooks, so panteth my soul after thee, O, God!" No; that was not it. "Who is he that cometh from Edom, with dyed garments from Bozrah?" No. "Thy eyes shall see Jerusalem a quiet habitation." Not that. "A king shall rule in righteousness." Try again. "The time is short." That's not it. Well, it must have been that great favorite of his—"As Moses lifted up the serpent in the wilderness." That's it; you are right now. Those of his friends who have often heard him on that passage, I hope will now be reminded, both of his appearance in the pulpit, and of his style. When he first got up, there was a very careless air about his person and manner. One who had not heard him before, might have thought that he was either very sleepy or very tired; and he might have said, "I won't be much surprised if that preacher should finish his sermon seated." But let the stranger wait—a change was sure to come over the preacher in time. Though Brother Durant generally begun as above described, he usually became more interested himself, and so would interest his congregation. As he went on, he began to warm up a little—became more erect; his hands no longer hung heavily by his side. He was telling us how the Lord punished the children of Israel with various plagues for their sins; and spoke of the fiery serpents, and of many being bitten by them; and of the sudden awful deaths therefrom. He dwelt upon the general terror and distress throughout all the hosts, and told that the great Jehovah, remembering the covenant he had made with Abraham, Isaac, and Jacob, became sorry for his people, and told Moses of the remedy.

A brazen serpent was made, and put on the top of a high pole; and a proclamation was made throughout the camp, that all who had been bitten could be cured by looking on the serpent. The heralds were not sent out to spread the news to a few favorite tribes; but to publish it to the entire host. You might have imagined you saw the messengers passing through Benjamin and Manasseh alike—through

Reuben and Judah, and all the tribes. Some who had been bitten, were but little moved by the news. Having no faith in the remedy, they perished without an effort; but the general alarm was very great. At last, some of their own accord, and others by persuasion, looked and were saved. The glad news now spread rapidly everywhere; but still some remained incredulous—they had no faith. Others were running about, hunting their friends, and entreating them to come and be cured; but hundreds were still perishing, though the serpent was placed in their midst. Preacher and congregation were alike very much excited; and he roused himself for a mighty effort, and the crowd looked expectant; ministers, exhorters, and others were much moved, and were all attentive; but perhaps the Strange Preacher was more affected than all others. He could not sit quietly.

Brother D. paused, and looked up, as if asking Divine help, and then requested the church to pray for him, and paused again, as if to gather all his strength for the great attempt. He then drew a picture, which I hope many will remember in blessed eternity. He presented to them a very old man, father of children and grandchildren, who was much respected throughout all the host, who had been bitten by a fiery serpent, and was in the last extremity, his wife was weeping over him. She had been the partner of his many griefs and his few pleasures, all through life. She hung over him, overwhelmed with sorrow; for she remembered how faithful he had been, and thought of the many times in Egypt, when he had worked hard to finish his heavy task, and then come and help her with hers; and had often saved her from the whip of the cruel taskmaster; and now he was almost dead before her eyes. She entreated him to look; but he had no faith. She remembered the birth of their first child; and felt even then the kiss he gave her when he saw the first pledge of their love. Oh! if he would only turn his eyes to the brazen serpent; but no, he would not. She thought of the time when there was no straw given them to mix with their mortar; when he would rise much sooner than usual, and go all about to gather some; and would work hard to finish his task, and would then assist her. She remembered, too, the time when the arm of the taskmaster was made bare for the blow, but it fell not, for he helped her through in time. And there he lay, almost dead before her eyes. His relatives were all weeping around him, and implored him to look; but all in vain. He seemed almost to pass away; but some one now came up, who had long known the old man in Egypt, and respected him much, and told him, that just a short time ago, an aged man, who was almost as bad off as he was, looked, and was cured. He had no faith, and would not comply. Both preacher and people had now become still more excited; and the Strange Preacher said to himself, "I am afraid he will die, before he can be persuaded to look!"

The preacher then told of some happy ones, running about almost wild with pleasure, telling of those who had been saved. One who knew the old man, and had worked with him in Egypt, came and told him of one who was much worse off than he, and who raised his expiring eyes and looked, and was cured. This seemed to arouse him a little. Every now and then, some one would pass them, bearing their almost dying friends in their arms, to the foot of the pole, that they might be saved. The old man's wife then made one last effort; she stooped down, and whispered in his almost closed ear; she kissed his cold lips, and told him of their sorrows and joys in Egypt; and entreated him, for her sake, to look and live. The old man faintly returned her kiss; and then, with a smile of love true till death, she told her sons to take their father, and gently carry him to the foot of the pole. They carefully raised him up; but some who were passing by, advised them to lay him quietly down, and let him pass away, for it was too late. But another said, there was yet hope; for a man who was apparently dead, opened his eyes, and looked, and was cured. The group slowly moved on; the wife walking by his side, praying to the God of Israel to save her husband. The Wandering Arab became so moved, that he whispered to a brother, "The old man is almost gone; he has only three breaths to draw; and he will die before he gets to the pole." The group slowly moved on, with their nearly lifeless burden; the old man drew one more breath gaspingly, and then another, which lasted him to the foot of the pole, when he remained without moving, in the arms of his weeping sons. The Strange Preacher said to his friend, almost loud enough to be heard by others, "What a great pity; it is all over with the old man; he is dead; he is dead." But no; he had one more breath to draw. His wife kissed him again, and he opened his eyes very feebly; she pointed him to the serpent; he looked, and was saved. O, my soul! who can describe what followed? He was cured at once; and sprang to his feet, clapping his hands, and praising God aloud. He threw his arms around the neck of his wife, and kissed her. He laughed and cried aloud; and taking up the bed on which he had been borne, ran off like an antelope, through the camp, praising the God of Israel.

My friends, you must excuse me for not telling you the effect this produced on the congregation, for I cannot. The Strange Preacher shook hands with some in the altar, and shouted out, "Farewell world, I'm bound for the kingdom."

One more picture connected with that sermon, and I will, for a while, be done with the great revivalist. He told us of the great change which takes place in the sinner, who has long been dead in transgression and sin, when he looks with faith to his Saviour, and is saved. He spoke of an old gray-headed sinner who lived in the District in which he was born, who had lived nearly to the close of a long life without hope and without Christ in the world. His wife and son were God-fearing Christians; but he was very wicked, and all hope of his salvation was nearly gone. At last he became powerfully convicted, and awful horror took possession of his soul; then he cried aloud in his agony and asked all to pray for him; that he knew there was no salvation for him, that his day of grace was forever gone, for he had committed the unpardonable sin, and God never would forgive him. He was encouraged to look to the Saviour and be saved; but he would not be comforted, but continued to ask others to pray for him, saying he knew there was no mercy for him—God would never forgive so great a sinner. He said, if he ever got religion he would never tell any one about it, for he had been so great a sinner he knew none would believe him. He continued in that state a long time, having a certain place to which he often went to pray. On a bright moonlight night—after midnight—feeling worse than usual, and being afraid to go to sleep, lest he should be lost before morning, he got up and went to the old place to pray once more, ere he should die and go to hell, where he expected to be before sunrise. He was all alone; he fell upon his knees and told the Lord he was come to offer his last prayer before being forever lost; he knew his sins were too great ever to be forgiven; but he prayed God, for the Saviour's sake, to have mercy on him, and he would give him all the glory—keeping back none—that even then at that honr, he would go and tell his neighbors—the Major, the Squire, cousin Mary, and all. As soon as the last promise was made, his Saviour's intercessions prevailed, and light broke in upon his despairing soul; his sins were forgiven and he was happy in his Saviour's love. He sprang up and laughed aloud for joy, and cried aloud, "I have found the Lord," and ran to the house and awoke his wife and son, and told them the glad news, and of the promise which he had made. They begged him to wait till morning, but he would not. They told him there was a heavy cloud gathering, and they expected a storm. But he said he was resolved to tell the neighbors that night, that the Lord had pardoned his sins. So he told his son to saddle the horse. His son told him the saddle was not at home—he would have to wait—but he had a sheepskin thrown across the horse and was off.

In imagination the Strange Preacher saw the scene pass before him. The old man rode off, giving vent to his feelings in loud praise, and went over to the Doctor's and awoke the family and asked if all were present, but was told there was one still up stairs; he wanted him present too. He then told them that he had found the Lord, and requested them to rejoice with him, after which he rode off, clapping his hands and shouting. He then went to the Major's, over the creek, and aroused the whole house. The circuit preacher was there, but though sick, he had to rise too. He told them the glorious news and begged them to exult with him. He then proceeded to the Squire's, and called up the whole family—the old grandmother and all, and clapped his hands and shouted until the woods rang. He rode off bare-headed, and went on to the last place, which was cousin Mary's. The old horse was very tired, but he got there at last. There were many young folks there who had set up very late, but were then fast asleep, and it was some time before he could awake them; but he continued to call, and at last roused them up, told them who he was and what had brought him at that late hour; that he had been throughout the neighborhood to tell the good news. All were present; even the servants had come to find out the cause of so much excitement—even old Cudjo and Maum Hannah were there. He told them the joyful tidings and begged them to rejoice with him, and they rejoiced with him.

Brother Durant was through, and such a shout was never before heard—such a sight never seen at that camp-ground. Some were prostrate in and around the altar, praising the Lord aloud. Mourners came up by hundreds; scores were converted; and the Strange Preacher was passing through the crowd trying to sing—

"I want to live a Christian here, I want to die a shouting,
  I want to see my Saviour near, when soul and body are parting.

"But you have forgotten to tell us anything more about those persons in their little vessels, hugging the shore—keeping always in sight of land—near enough to speak to friends on the beach, and by them to send messages of love to those at home. Do tell us what became of them." I am glad you reminded me of them, for I had almost forgotten them. For a while every thing went on very pleasantly; the sky was cloudless and the water beneath bright and smooth; in fact more than one of the party was seen to look in nature's mirror below. Brothers C., and H., and R., and S. were among those who were more daring, and ventured farther from land than the rest. As time passed on there would be a little ripple on the deep—a slight agitation in the water—nothing, however, to alarm the most faint-hearted. Occasionally you might notice that the wind was a little strong, and then the vessels would be driven a little farther from land; and then those who were more daring would appear to enjoy it very much. But soon the blast would subside, and all become calm. I noticed, however, that when Brother D. had got some distance into his sermon, that the Storm King —to use a remark of his—had begun to rouse himself, and those nearest the shore seemed a little uneasy; but as all was right I thought no danger need be apprehended. The wind, however, continued to rise, and when Brother D. was telling us of the aged man who had been bitten by the serpent, and who, when about to draw his last breath, turned and looked, and was cured. I felt that the Storm King had unfurled his banner and was riding triumphantly on the wind. As soon as I had recovered somewhat from my excitement, I raised my spy-glass and looked towards the shore— all was confusion on the little vessels. I merely caught sight of Brother C., leading the way, with R., and S., and H. close behind him, under the influence of a very strong wind that was hurrying them on to the bar at the rate of thirty miles to the hour. The other little barks were overturned, and the friends, with their life-preservers on, were making desperate efforts to reach the beach. But when we were told of the old man who was so happily converted, and who had rode bare-headed, without a saddle, to let his friends know the glad tidings; and when he had reached the last house, and cousin Mary and Maum Hannah were rejoicing with him, I took my glass and turned it again to the shore; and the little barks, with C., and R., and H., and S., were seen far over the bar, still under the influence of a tremendous pressure. Some time after, a vessel returning said the little vessels had passed them, and the passengers had requested them to say to their friends at home, that they were well provisioned and all was right, though it would be many days before they could return.

Farewell, for a while to H. H. Durant, the great revivalist of the South Carolina Conference—the famous man for protracted and camp-meetings—who did so much good in his day and time, and who was said, in one year of his ministry, to have taken more than a thousand persons into the church. Farewell, dear brother of my soul. May we meet in heaven.

## LEAF THE TWENTY-THIRD.

A MEMENTO TO MY DEAR DEPARTED BROTHER IN CHRIST, REV. W. C. KIRKLAND—THE MAN WHOM THE CHURCH AND THE WORLD LOVED.

Art thou gone to the Jerusalem above, thou long-tried and ever-true friend of my soul? If I should neglect to say something of thee, while dwelling on the scenes of my past life, I would feel that I had done wrong to thy memory, and to the very strong affection that existed between us. Never can I forget W. C. Kirkland, one of the most upright of men —one of the purest of Christians. To know him well was to love him much. I remember him even before he began to preach. I remember so well when I saw him for the last time—I went with him to Bamberg, where he took the train for Spartanburg. We never met again; for he was called soon after, to enter the rest which remaineth for the people of God. We had, for many years, called each other, David and Jonathan—and truly was he the Jonathan of my soul.

He was born in Barnwell District, near Buford's Bridge, where many of his relatives and friends still live. His manner was so kind and prepossessing, that you always felt at home while with him. To a member of the church, who knew him well—if cast down and depressed—a friendly shake of Brother K.'s hand, was like water to the thirsty traveller. But the true friend, the pure Christian, the good preacher, the brave knight of the cross, has gone "where the wicked cease from troubling, and the weary are at rest."

He did much service to the church and the world; he bore the heat of many summer, and the cold of many winter, days—preaching to all of religion and of heaven. He did much good by his ministry, but more by his private walk and conversation. I suspect few ever did as much service to the cause, out of the pulpit, as he did; for the Holy Spirit seemed to be always present with him. His whole life was as "sweet ointment poured out." He was also much respected and loved by members of other branches of the church. In some places, I suppose, he had as many Baptist as Methodist friends; and his name will long be remembered by hundreds on the many circuits which he travelled, from the mountain to the sea-shore. He was ready always "to rejoice with those who rejoiced, and to weep with those who wept." But why should I attempt to say more of him who was so well known and loved in these lands?

Years ago, while he was travelling the long and laborious Barnwell circuit, by his urgent request, I went to help him hold a two days' meeting at a place called Concord, where those true friends of the church lived—Brothers Spann, Barr, and Smith, and others. It was my first visit to the place; and the road was a long, weary one. Did any of you, my friends, ever pass that route, and feel like saying to yourself, "somewhat like this is the way to glory; for they say, 'Jordan is a hard road to travel?'" I acknowledge that I more than once had such thoughts; but brother "Jonathan" had charged me to be there, and had promised me a large congregation. It was very unpleasant travelling; for it was just after a heavy rain, and the weather was very warm. The road was filled with water, and was in places even boggy. I crossed the Edisto at Gunter's Bridge; but the church was many miles from the river. Late in the evening, I got to a brother's house—a small affair. I soon found out with regret that there was no shed-room to it for the preacher. I had been expected by the family, and was told I had to preach that night—that Brother K. had appointed the meeting, and that he had told them I was fond of night meetings, and would not disappoint them. The Wandering Arab will never forget that time; but not for the great outpouring of the Spirit—not because he fired off a big gun, and swung clear—not for the conviction of sinners, for the reclaiming of backsliders, or for the conversion of mourners. "For what,' say you. I will tell you presently—only hold on a little. I will not now say unto you, as Antony did over the body of the great Cæsar—"If you have tears, prepare to shed them now;" but I will say, if you ever did enjoy a joke on the War Preacher, prepare to do so now.

The night came—that short summer night—but, O! how I wished it shorter than it was. The small congregation had assembled. Friends, are any of you fond of smoking? Do you love the smell of a strong old pipe, which has often been used, but not often cleaned? Now, between you and me, I am well acquainted with a preacher who cannot endure it, but who would almost prefer taking a dose of salts any time, than have to smell for ten minutes a strong old pipe. So you may form some faint idea how the parson felt, when he found out he would have to bear the scent of at least twenty pipes at once. But so it was; for as soon as the little crowd got into the house and sat down, each one pulled out his old pipe, got ready, and went to work. It was then all over with the Strange Preacher. He had been thinking what he should preach from, and had selected one of his favorite subjects; and he had prepared some pictures with which he thought some of his friends would be pleased. But when he found he had to face the fire and the smell of twenty pipes, he struck his flag at once; there was no preaching in him. Have any of you ever heard what may be called a ten cents' sermon? There was one preached that night, and no mistake. The parson waited for the smokers to stop, that he might begin; but no, they smoked on. He opened and closed his hymn book and Bible; but they smoked on. He then moved, and drew up his feet, as if ready to rise; but all in vain, they smoked on. He cleared his throat, and spat on the floor; but they smoked on. The Strange Preacher was almost in despair. He drew out his watch once or twice, with a quick, sudden jerk, as if the last moment had come; but all to no purpose, the twenty old pipes smoked on, as if for life and death. The parson then made another pretence, as if going to rise—he pushed the table a little from him, and holding the open book in one hand, rose almost half from his seat, and then turned his despairing eyes; but out rolled the smoke from those twenty old pipes, as if from as many little furnaces; and the smokers smoked on, as if the ransom of a captive prince depended on their doing their best. Alas, for the Wandering Arab! he felt that it was all over with him, and he said to himself, "If I ever preach again, it shall not be from any of my favorites; I will draw no pictures to-night." He resumed his seat, and felt sad at heart; and he was well satisfied that if his Brother "Jonathan" had only known how the case was to be, he would not have left an appointment for his "David," at that place. He then beckoned a brother, and asked him, in a whisper, if those smokers would smoke on during preaching. "No," said he, "but they will go on till you commence." The parson then sprang to his feet, gave out the hymn, and the twenty smokers stopped as if moved by the same impulse; and a very short sermon was then preached; and, even in those days, when money was so plentiful, I doubt if it was worth more than ten cents. The benediction was pronounced, and soon the smokers were at it again.

But it is bed-time now; and there is no little shed-room for the parson; and some few of the smokers still remained. The long ride, and those twenty pipes, had worn me out entirely; so I thought I must go to bed—shed-room or no shed-room. I whispered to the brother, and asked him, how I should proceed. "O!" said he, "the old woman is in the kitchen now, that's your chance; but you had better be in a hurry, or she'll be back before you are through." The preacher partly undressed. He had not time to wind his watch; and he offered up a little five cents' prayer, and sprang into bed. His head had hardly touched the little pillow, before back came the old woman. It was some time before he could sleep; and he said to himself, "I love Brother 'Jonathan' too much, not to make an effort at improvement here, for his sake."

Morning came; there was a long ride yet before the parson; he therefore made an early start. The sun had just risen; and Gunter's Bridge and the Edisto were not far off. The brother went a short way, to give the preacher the right direction; and when about to separate, the preacher asked to be permitted to give a little advice. He entreated him to endeavor to lay hold on eternal life; and spoke of the joys of heaven, and said he hoped he would meet him there. The brother wept, and gave the parson a parting grasp. And the preacher, as if he had just thought of it, said, "Brother, we have not yet got to glory, but are still in this vale of tears; so we should attempt to make our friends comfortable when they come to see us. If I ever pass by here again, I hope I will have the pleasure of seeing another room to your house. Farewell; let us meet in heaven." I then rode off a little way, when I stopped, and looked back. The early sun was not far above the forest trees, and Gunter's Bridge and the Edisto not far off. But there still stood the good brother, gazing at the Strange Preacher, with a look that, even at that distance, seemed to say, "while life lasts, I will not forget you; and if you ever pass here again, you shall see the room." Once again, in my roving life, I crossed at Gunter's Bridge; and when I came in sight of the house, there was the shed-room.

I reached Concord, and felt more than repaid for my long ride, and for having to face the twenty smokers, when I felt Brother "Jonathan's" warm grasp, and heard him say, "My dear Brother 'David,' I am so glad to see you;" and then to have been introduced to such good men as Brothers Spann, Barr, Smith, and others; and to have enjoyed with them a good meeting.

Another meeting I attended with Brother Kirkland, was at Buford's Bridge, where there was a time of refreshing from the presence of the Lord. I expect always to remember how Brother K. preached, and prayed, and sung—how he seemed full of heavenly thoughts when he told us of the Saviour's love for a lost, ruined world. Never mind what the text was, whether, "Moses said unto Hobab, come thou and go with us;" or, "With one accord, in one place;" or, Moses to the Lord, "We will not go hence unless thy presence go with us;" or, about the old and the young prophet—the Spirit of the Lord was always present with him; and he preached from the heart to the heart. He sometimes looked, as if his gaze was on the other side of the flood, in the sweet fields of Eden. I have seen three preachers in my life, whose faces, while in the pulpit, excited me more than all others; and if those men stood before me, even if they remained silent,

I would enjoy myself more than while listening to well-arranged sermons from some men I have heard. Those preachers were—Bishop Capers, Brother McPhail, and W. C. Kirkland. I could never look at them long, without wishing that I was as well prepared for heaven through grace, as I thought they were. Brother K. told us of his boyhood, of the days spent with his relatives and friends in that neighborhood; and of his dear departed father, whom he knew would welcome him to heaven. At times, he would clap his hands, and cry out "glory!" making you think, while looking at him, that you almost saw the face of an angel.

I remember Sunday night as being the best time we had. Then the holy man was transported with delight, for he saw some dear ones coming up for his prayers, and he prayed as if he had hold of the horns of the altar; and when he arose from his knees, he began to sing, "I feel the work reviving, reviving in my soul;" or, "Our bondage it will end, by and bye;" or, "Where now are the Hebrew children." I have often enjoyed myself very much at Mizpah; but never as much as when I worshipped the Lord there, with the Jonathan of my soul—the pure, the heavenly-minded W. C. Kirkland.

Another meeting I attended with him, at Barnwell courthouse. "There!" do you say, "where you have no church?" Yes, there it was. Did you know that holy woman, one of the sweet singers of Israel—sister T.? I met Brother K. there many years ago; but that good woman has since gone to heaven. It was the hour of private prayer, and we retired to our room, and bowed our knees before the throne of grace, and spent some time in silent devotion. We arose; one said to the other, "Brother, it has just occurred to me, that we ought to have a protracted meeting here." The other replied, that he had been thinking of the same thing. So it was agreed upon. We had no hope of having any addition to our church; but thought it would help our Baptist and Presbyterian friends. One of us remarked, that we would preach and pray; but would not open the door, as we did not expect any members. We left our room, feeling happy in our souls. Sister T. looked as if she could almost guess what we had been talking about. We told her, and requested her to announce the meeting for us. She asked if we expected to get any members there. We replied, no; but we thought it would help the other churches. She said, she expected it would.

The time for our meeting came; and the ministers were there ready to begin the good work. We did not expect any members, but hoped we would help others—that shows you, friends, what kind of a spirit possessed W. C. Kirkland. I never knew him lto abor more diligently, or pray with greater power, or preach with more unction—not expecting one member. He still continued to work, not for himself, but others; while devils were no doubt astonished, and the holy angels regarded him approvingly, because they had seen few such men. O, my soul! what a gracious meeting we had; and how much Brothers D., B., and A. enjoyed themselves. And sisters T. and A. looked, at times, as if they were listening to the harps of heaven. The Holy One of Israel was graciously present; and Brother K. shouted aloud "glory;" and the Strange Preacher shook hands with his Baptist and Presbyterian brethren, and requested them to meet him in heaven. Our Baptist Brother B. asked why we did not open the door; and said he thought we would like to do so. Brother K. replied, that "we would do so every day, if we expected any members; but we will not open the door here, as this meeting is for you and the Presbyterians;" and Brother B., with a smile I can never forget, said, "we are very much obliged to you; but I would like to see you get some help for your own church." "O! never mind," said Brother K., "we are working for the Lord." And the Strange Preacher then thought to himself, that he could almost hear the Saviour say to the angels, "that is a man after my own heart."

The meeting continued for two weeks—Brother B. every now and then asking us to open the door of our church; and to please him, Brother K. consented to do so, telling him what would be the result. No one joined.

Such a preacher was W. C. Kirkland. Where can we find

another like him? Farewell! dear brother of my soul; if I ever felt glad to see you on earth, how much more will I rejoice to meet you in heaven! From my heart, I believe I would have loved my Saviour more truly, more devotedly, and that I would have served him more faithfully than I have done, if I could have been blessed with that good man's prayers and advice more than I was. I have often done and said things, for which I have been sorry afterwards, which I think never would have happened, if I could have always been with him. I believe I would enjoy more of heaven than I now expect to when I get there, if the Jonathan of my soul had been with me more. Farewell! much-loved brother; heaven gained all of what earth lost, when you left us. I was much benefitted by being so often with you. Alas! for me; I am afraid I sometimes grieved the blessed Spirit, and made my guardian angel almost weep, because thou wast not always with me. Farewell! dear brother; I have missed thee much, and think of thee often. Through grace, I hope to meet you at last, in the green fields of Eden, on the other side of the flood.

" Thou art gone to the grave—but we will not deplore thee;
   Though sorrow and darkness encompass the tomb;
   Thy Saviour has passed through its portals before thee,
    And the lamp of his love is thy guide through the gloom.

" Thou art gone to the grave—we no longer behold thee,
   Nor tread the rough paths of the world by thy side;
   But the wide arms of mercy are spread to enfold thee,
    And sinners may hope, since the sinless have died."

# LEAF THE TWENTY-FOURTH.

#### REMARKABLE DREAMS.

From these Stray Leaves my friends must have learned that the Strange Preacher puts more faith in dreams than some people do. I know that many nightly visions are vain and foolish, and some of them I know are very wicked; but I do believe there are others direct from heaven. How do you account for the one in which I was told that Dr. S. should join the church; and the one about the black-eyed young man on my first visit to Rock Springs? Both came to pass. And I pledge my word for them, and any others I may relate. Why should not dreams and visions be direct from the Lord in these days as well as in olden times, when the New Testament spoke of such things? We are told that in the last days we shall see visions and dream dreams.

When I was almost of age, I became very much cast down and depressed, and was possessed with the thought that I had not long to live; that I would soon pass from earth to great eternity. I knew I was not prepared, which conviction added to my distress, and my feelings were indescribable. One night, during this time, I had the following dream, one which I think was from the Lord. I saw the Saviour of the world, who stood near me, and said to me, "You expect to die soon, but you will not; you will join the Methodist church before you die. Be thou faithful till death, and thou shalt have a crown of life." I became quite alarmed and was in great distress, and thought my last hour had come. I remained thus for awhile, but alas! for poor human nature, my sad thoughts soon left me; I went on in my wicked course.

Now, some persons may say, that was the reason you joined the Methodist church; but I assure you I did not think of the dream until some time afterwards. I suspect if I had thought of it at that time I would have joined more willingly, if possible, than 1 did. This dream seems to me very strange, unless we consider it as coming directly from God.

Many years ago, the summer my father died, I had ruptured a blood vessel, and was quite weak for some time. While in that condition I often felt the Lord precious to my soul. But let me tell you first of something which happened years before this, that might have had something to do in bringing about the sweet vision I had at that time.

When I first joined the church some of my relatives were much surprised and mortified. There was one who appeared more so than the others; who once told me, in the presence of several others, that I had acted shamefully, disgracing the whole family; that if I ever got to heaven, where my mother was, she would not recognize or acknowledge me as her son. This distressed me very much, more than language can tell.

Many years after, I had the following dream: My hour of death had come—the last hour of my stay upon earth. I bade farewell to all present, wife and children, and others, and I thought my happy spirit took its flight for the eternal world. At last I thought I entered the Jerusalem above—the eternal home of the ransomed of the Lord. The golden gates being thrown open, I saw the Everlasting Father on the throne with the Son and Holy Spirit. I fell prostrate, and after a while I heard a voice from the throne, which said, "Show him his name;" and I saw written in golden letters, "LUCIUS BELLINGER, a sinner saved by grace." Then I heard a holy song in the palace of the Eternal, "glory be to God! the dead is alive, the lost is found, and the prodigal has come home to his Father. Welcome home to heaven, brother." And then I heard a voice from the throne again! "go, crown him now;" and then a spirit came and bound my head with a wreath of glory. And still the song went on, "glory to the Lord! the dead is alive and the lost is found, and the prodigal has returned. Welcome home to heaven! brother." And on the left hand, I heard the rustling of wings; the sound came nearer still—it came up to me. The wings were folded upon the breast, and the spirit stooped down and kissed me on the left cheek, and a voice spoke, "Welcome home to heaven! my Methodist son; I am so glad to see you. I was your mother, my son, in yonder world; I have been your guardian angel ever since I died. Welcome home! my son." And once again that holy song was heard, "glory be to God! the dead is alive, the lost is found, and the prodigal has come home to his Father. Welcome home to heaven! brother."

I woke up transported with pleasure, and I wished for awhile, very much to go to heaven, to see that mother at once. I love to think of that dream more than all the many I have had. O, my blessed Saviour, I thank thee even to this day for that blessed vision of the night. O, that my mother may be the first of the ransomed of earth to welcome me upon the banks of eternal deliverance.

Some sixteen years ago last fall, I think, my wife paid a visit to some of her relatives in Georgia, and was absent several weeks. Before she told me "good-bye," she said she had a request to make, and I must grant it before I knew what it was. I had no idea what it could be, but I told her I would do so. She then told me that she wished me to stay at home until her return; I must have no appointments, and must not visit my neighbors. I told her I had appointments out already. She said I must not fill them. She wanted me to do this, that I might form some idea of how she felt during my absence; she wanted me to be situated only once, as she was so very often. My word was out, and I had to stand to it. I faced the fire, but O, what a cross I found that promise. It was a time never to be forgotten. The War Preacher at home, and good meetings going on within reach, none of which he could attend. The sound of the raging battle, the shouting of the captives, the waving of the flags not far off, and the preacher at home, like the war horse tied to the stake, while the great battle is being fought before him! The preacher, kept at home by his promise, longed for one day of freedom, that he might strike one brave blow by the side of Brothers Kirkland, Mouzon, Raysor, Varn and others; but it could not be. I hope I may never be so situated again. When my wife returned, and found out what a cross it had been, she said she was sorry she had made the request.

While I was passing through that great trial I became cast down and depressed; I was in the depth of the valley. One night I had the following dream: Two very beautiful golden winged spirits, in the bright robes of immortality, stood by my side. One of them touched me and roused me up, and said, "Brother, I have come to show you your resurrection body." I looked, and very near me was one of the most noble and sublime forms that the eye of imagination had ever witnessed. I was transported with delight. I was told that when I rose from the grave that was to be the body I was to have. I asked one of the spirits who he was. He said he was my brother William, who died when he was a little boy. He smiled on me so kindly, and told me that my Father in heaven had sent him to comfort me, and to show me my resurrection body. I asked him if he meant my earthly father. He said no, he did not mean him, though he left him in heaven; that he meant my Heavenly Father. During all this time the other spirit said nothing; but every now and then she smiled sweetly, and shook her golden locks, and looked on me lovingly with her blue eyes. I said, "Brother, who is that by your side?" He said it was my sister Rebecca. I thought she looked a little sad, as she said, "O, brother Lucius, have you forgotten me?" I replied, "O, no, I have never forgotten you." She then bent over and gave me a sweet kiss; and both said that my Heavenly Father had sent them to comfort me, and that my earthly father, too, was in heaven.

Many years ago I was at a meeting in the bounds of the Barnwell circuit. We had a gracious time. On Sunday night I stayed at a good brother's house. Some time after I had lain down, 1 dreamed that we had a very fine time the next day; that a gentleman whom I thought much of, had knelt for prayer, and before I got through preaching, (I remembered what I was speaking about) a voice near by my side said, "Mind you, that is for the Major." I got very happy, and shouted aloud in my sleep, and was roused up by the brother, in the next room, calling to me and requesting me to stop, as I was making a great noise and disturbing him and his wife. I told them in the morning why I had rejoiced so, and that I believed firmly it would come to pass. I told them I remembered how I finished my sermon, and the voice said, "Mind, that's for the Major;" and I expected him to come up. The good brother looked as if he did not place much confidence in it. We went to the church and we had a gracious season in prayer meeting, at the close of which he came to me and remarked, he believed then it would come to pass. What say you to that, friends? Our faith had now united in the same thing.

Before leaving the house I told him, that the night before I was standing on a step when the man knelt down. I preached the sermon. The good Spirit was present, and mourners were called up. I was standing in the altar waiting for them; the man had not yet come up, but I was expecting him. I turned and went and stood on the steps of the pulpit as if going in; my hand was on the door. I turned round and looked at the man I had seen the night before. The Major then came up and knelt for prayer—his wife with him. The preacher was cut loose from his moorings, and lost all self-control. I wish brother James Hutto and his wife were now alive to tell you that it was at their house I had the dream.

My father never heard me preach but once, and that sermon I had preached to him years before, while asleep. I once dreamed that my father came to me as I was going in, or coming out of the pulpit, and said to me, "My son, from what are you going to preach," or "what have you preached from?" I replied, from Psalm xciv, 16. He asked me how I had managed, or how I was going to do it. I told him how, and he replied, it was better than he had expected, and that he would like to hear it again. Some years after I preached my first and only sermon before him—using the same text.

Perhaps there are few persons who are more fond of singing than I am, yet I cannot raise a tune myself. I try very often, though I do not know long, from short, metre. My wife told me, that one night she heard me calling up mourners; I would exhort awhile, and sing awhile, and then speak as if some persons were present, telling them I was glad to to see them, that I had been praying for them a long time;

and speaking to others, would say, "you had better not strive against the Spirit—he may not always bear with you." She said she thought I was making the song as I went along, and was singing correctly to the tune of, "I want my friends to go with me."

Some very amusing things have happened in connection with the parson's preaching and becoming very happy while asleep. I dreamed once I was holding forth from Psalm xlii, 11, to about thirty persons. I must have got along better than when awake, for there was a great impression made. I was much excited, and praised the Lord aloud. My wife woke me up and said it was time to stop, that I ought to be ashamed of myself, for I had shouted and clapped my hands and made so great a noise that I had brought the dogs from the servants' quarter; and they were barking and running around the house in full cry, and had come to the back door and were trying to get in. I then had a hearty laugh at it myself.

Please bear with me till I tell you of one more amusing circumstance. The Strange Preacher, I am told, before beginning to hold forth when asleep, seems to be in great pain, groaning out aloud, and not long after begins to shout and clap his hands. When at a house for the first time I generally tell the friends not to be alarmed, should they hear a noise in my room. Some years ago, on the Cooper river circuit, I was at a friend's house, where I was told next morning, by some persons who occupied a room near mine, that some time after midnight they were aroused up by a noise in my room; that I groaned aloud and appeared to be in great pain—causing them to think I was sick. They opened the door and listened; the distressing sounds were still heard and they became very much alarmed, and were going to wake the others and send for a doctor, as they thought I was in the last extremity. But suddenly a great change came. I began to clap my hands and cry out, "Farewell world, I'm bound for the kingdom;" and then to sing "I want to live a Christian here, I want to die a-shouting." They then concluded to let the War Preacher alone.

# LEAF THE TWENTY-FIFTH.

## REMARKABLE PRESENTIMENTS WHICH CAME TO PASS.

What do you think, my friends, of those strong impressions which some persons have, and which come to pass? From what source do they come? I believe, at times, they are direct from the Lord, who thus gives us a warning of what is to take place. Let me mention some of the impressions I have had, which afterwards came to pass.

What I am now going to relate, happened some forty years ago. It was in my most reckless days—when madly rushing to ruin, as the war-horse does into battle, without believing it when told of it by others. I became suddenly impressed that I had to preach before I died. The feeling was strong upon me. A member of our church was then with me; and I expect, if still alive, he would testify to what I am going to tell. I took a pen and ink, and, as seriously as if I was making my last will, wrote down that I would have to preach in after-life—there was no mistake of it. I mentioned the name of one church particularly—Hephzibah. I also stated that I would often hold prayer-meeting in Pine Grove church, and signed my name, and wrote the date. I then gave it to him, and charged him to keep it; that we would live to see it come to pass. He seemed much struck, and would often allude to it. The paper was lost; but it all came to pass more than thirty years ago.

I sometimes think, when the thought of religion is farthest from our minds, serious thoughts will suddenly possess us; and the Lord will impress us with a picture of our future lives, which will be sure to come to pass. When I was a wicked young man, I was once writing to a person for whom I had a high regard, and concluded the letter with this solemn remark—I had not thought of it before; "If we ever meet again in this world, you will find me in the pulpit, preaching the gospel, and on my way to heaven." Some twenty years after, and while I was in the pulpit preaching, that person came into the church. These things seem remarkable to me. What do you think of them? From whence do they come? Has the Lord nothing to do with them?

You must have noticed in these Stray Leaves, that sometimes I have been so strongly convinced of some things, as to speak of them beforehand. I have asserted that I believed such a person would join the church, or get religion, and it came to pass afterwards. After I had been preaching several years, I was once present at a Baptist meeting, not fifty miles from my home. It was Saturday. I exhorted for them; and I became convinced that there was one person present in the small assembly, who had heard a sermon for the last time in that church—that before the preacher returned that day four weeks, that individual would be dead, and the preacher would preach the funeral sermon. I spoke of it in the pulpit, and called on the friends to bear testimony. A member of the the church then present died, and the funeral sermon was preached at the next appointment.

At a protracted meeting on the Barnwell circuit, was an old gentleman whom I had long known, who seemed to be interested in the services. I went to him, and offered to pray with him; and he knelt at his seat. I was afterwards convinced that we would never meet again on earth; and that he had attended his last meeting at that place. I bade him farewell; and told him it was our last meeting in this life. I never saw him again; for in a few weeks he was called to eternity.

I will mention one more event, which I think very remarkable. I do not know how to account for it, unless it was a visitation from the Holy One of Israel. I was once preaching, and when near the close, became suddenly impressed with a sad thought. I told the congregation, if any wished to, they might write down what I was about to tell them, so as to refer to it if they desired. I then remarked, that there was a person present who would never hear me again; and that the Spirit was then striving with that person for the last time; that the person expected to attend such a camp-meeting, but would not go; but would be soon called to die, and would send for either myself or another preacher. I recalled those words; but said that the friends would send for me without that person knowing it; that I would set out, but the person would die before I got there. That person was resolved to go to the camp-meeting, that it might be proved that the Strange Preacher had made a mistake for once; but, alas! sickness and death soon came. The sands of life had nearly run out; but the person told a relative not to send for me. I was sent for, however, without the dying one knowing it; and I started—but on my way I met a gentleman, who told me it was too late. I turned back. How solemn and sad! Thus I feel now, while thinking of that remarkable occurrence.

Some weeks after this, a member of another church told me, he was present that day when I made the prediction, and that it had come to pass; and that it had made quite an impression—persons were speaking of it. He expected there would be a revival at the meeting which was soon to take place. It was so, and it was perhaps the best time we ever had at that church.

These presentiments seem very remarkable to me; and I believe they were from the Lord. What do you think?

## LEAF THE TWENTY-SIXTH.

#### THE STRANGE PREACHER TRYING HIS BOB.

Brother preacher, did you ever fish for an old trout? You often saw him playing around your hook, coming quite near, but he would not take hold. He was a large one; and you tried him often and long—in hot and cool weather—when the sun was very bright, and when it was behind a cloud—when the wind was blowing, and when everything was calm. But all in vain; you never got a bite, and became very much discouraged—quite worn out. You then changed your bait, and tried first one kind, and then another; but still all in vain. You were then at your wit's end, and thought you might as well strike your flag and quit, and never try the old trout again. One day, you spoke of your bad luck to a friend, who asked if you had ever tried your bob. You replied, no. He said, that sometimes you could succeed with that, when you had failed with everything else. So you resolved to make another effort. You tried your bob; and the first thing you knew, the old trout struck at it, and you pulled him out. He was a very large one. How you rejoiced. It was more than enough for your family, and you sent some of it to a neighbor.

Brother preacher, were you ever fishing spiritually? Had you been endeavoring for weeks and for years, with the help of the Lord, to persuade some person to yield to be saved—to embrace the offer of the gospel, but all in vain; till you almost despaired of ever seeing him embrace religion? But at last you thought of some subject which you had never used when he was present. You made another effort; the Lord was with you, and the desire of your heart was granted. You had the pleasure of seeing him come forward and join the church. So it has often been, through the help of the blessed Spirit, with the Wandering Arab, when calling sinners to repentance.

Many years ago, between the Savannah and Santee rivers,

there was a man, who was very wicked and profane—a leader of others in the ways of transgression. He was also very fond of his glass, and at times got very drunk. But this man, as far gone in sin as he was, had a mother who I hoped was in heaven, a brother for whom I had a high regard—a class-leader—and a pious wife, who often asked me to pray for him, and to try to get him out on the Lord's side. I became very desirous to see him embrace religion; and, with several others, preached near where he lived, for several years; but all in vain. I became discouraged, and felt like giving him up; but hope whispered, "Try again." And for the sake of his pious wife and brother, I still endeavored to reach his heart. I sometimes said to myself, in some interesting meeting, where the Spirit is poured out, he will at last yield; the time will come when his heart will be reached, and he will give up. But for years, I hoped and wished in vain; and one day I sent him word that "I had lost all expectation of ever seeing him on the Lord's side. I had fished for him for years, with all kinds of bait, but in vain; and I thought I would quit, and never try him again;—that I sometimes had silver fish on my hook, but he would not bite; then I had tried a nice little perch, but all in vain; and then again very small minnows, but still all in vain; that I even used dead bait, but all in vain: and that I was at a loss, and thought I would give it up, and never try again." I understood that when he received my message, he laughed heartily, and returned the following message—"Tell the parson not to despair, not to give up; he has never fished with his bob yet; to try that the next time, for some old trout can never be caught except with a bob." I did not at first know what he meant; but at last concluded that I knew what it was. I thought, perhaps, I had never given the subject a fair trial, at least for a long time. So I resolved to try my bob the first good chance I had.

A two days' meeting was appointed, where I expected him to be. I prayed much for the presence of the Lord to be granted us, and for that person particularly. We had a glorious revival; the Spirit of the Lord was graciously poured out. The meeting was protracted; several joined, and mourners crowded the altar. It was, I think, the best meeting we ever had there. I preached one day. I said, "the Lord helping me, I will try my bob now." I had concluded he meant, that as he was fond of his glass, I should speak of some of the effects of intemperance, and then of the happy change which takes place, when one addicted to it comes out on the Lord's side. So that day, in the course of my remarks, I enlarged upon the ruinous effects of strong drink upon soul and body—that without repentance the intemperate man was doomed to hell. I then spoke of the happy change which takes place when the heart is reached by the Holy Spirit—when one has been converted, and has become a new creature in Christ Jesus. I spoke of the first time that such a man would meet his wife after his conversion, and what a time of rejoicing they would have; and I represented them as travelling together through this troublesome world toward Immanuel's land. As I was passing through this part of the discourse, the man alluded to turned to a friend, a pious member of the Baptist church, and, with tears in his eyes, said in a whisper, "The parson is trying his bob now; I will have to give up." He joined the church that day. The crowd was so great, that those at a distance could not see who came up. Two ladies were standing together, and one asked, who that was who joined the church; and the other replied, she knew it was Mr. ——, by the way the preacher said "Farewell world!" And so it was. The joy of that happy wife, who had been praying so long for her husband, cannot be depicted, when the great wish of her heart was at last granted. He became soundly converted, and was a class-leader afterwards.

I have more than once heard him, in love-feast, speak of the message I sent him, and the answer he returned, and what he said that day to a friend sitting near—he could stand it no longer, for the parson was trying his bob. Many of his friends were much surprised; but he showed them he was truly in earnest, by the strong stand which he took. He was a warm and zealous member, ready at any time to take up his cross. I have been with him at several meetings. He believed in heart-felt religion, and often rejoiced aloud.

I have often since then, "tried my bob," sometimes, however, unsuccessfully. The old trout sometimes becomes frightened, and stands at a distance, or darts rapidly away. I was once at a meeting in Florida, when I was describing the case of a young man who began life under very favorable auspices. He was happily married, and for years everything went on smoothly. His wife loved the Lord, and was on her way to heaven; but in time he began to frequent the grog-shop, and after a while became quite dissipated, and treated his wife very cruelly—causing her, at times, to run for dear life, in the still hours of night. I represented that man as once going to church, where his heart was reached, and he became powerfully convicted, and was happily converted, and went home a changed man; and I spoke of the meeting between him and his wife. A man was present who had thus treated his wife; and she too was there, and was a member of the Baptist church. He afterwards sent me word that I had spoken the truth; and that, with the help of the Lord, he was resolved to change his course; and requested me to pray for him, and hoped to meet me in heaven; and said that he would join his wife's church. His friends were much surprised.

I was once at a meeting at Little Swamp, where we were enjoying a very gracious revival. I was trying my bob again. There was a man present who had travelled far on the road to destruction, who said to a friend at his side—"Squire, don't you think the parson is fishing for me?" The reply was, "Yes, I think he is." He said with a smile, "But he will not catch me." I went on for some time; when the same question was repeated, and the same reply given. This continued for some time; but after a while the Squire heard nothing more from his friend. He looked at him—he was weeping; and the Squire then said to himself, "I think he will catch you." And so it turned out. That evening he joined the church, and never stopped till he got the blessing. He was converted while at work. A faithful member of the church was present to rejoice with him in the great change which had taken place.

I have been thus often blessed while speaking of the great

change which takes place in the most dissipated persons.
I was once at a meeting in Florida where I enjoyed myself
much. It was a gracious season in that land of flowers. On
Saturday night the church was crowded, and the Lord was
graciously present. I made a strong effort to reach the
backslider's heart through grace. The sermon was finished,
a soul stirring hymn was being sung, and as usual I was
passing through the crowd shaking hands. I paused near a
bench on which several gentlemen were seated. They seemed
so confused I did not offer to shake hands with them. The
next day a brother told me, that the night before, while returning from church, he overheard some gentlemen in conversation, when one said to another, " Well, Colonel, I was
sorry for you to-night, when the preacher was speaking
about backsliders—your picture was well drawn." "Yes,"
said the others, "to the life, all that was lacking was the
name." "And," said the other, "I expected him to call it
out. What would you have done, Colonel, if, when he paused
where we were sitting, he had offered to shake hands?" "I
would have jumped out the open window." This gives you
some idea of the influence which prevailed.

The next day the large church was filled to overflowing.
The Judge and the member of Congress were present, and
there was a dense mass of closely packed people. Church
members seemed deeply interested, and I thought much
prayer was being offered to the throne of heavenly grace.
I felt the divine afflatus upon me. The Holy Spirit was
preaching through a very unworthy instrument. The congregation seemed much excited, and I noticed that one of
those honorable gentlemen was much affected. I sat down.
Some brother began to sing a favorite song, "The warfare is
over." Several joined him; the Strange Preacher could not
stand it; he was on his feet at once, and was passing through
the crowd to speak to the gentleman mentioned above; but
he, with others, could not stand the fire, and they left. A
preacher requested them to come back—we would not hurt
them. Sometimes the trout will not strike at the bob, but
will look at it and dart off.

## LEAF THE TWENTY-SEVENTH.

#### THE HEROES OF THE OLD WALTERBORO CIRCUIT.

In writing these scenes of the past, I have several times thought I ought to say something of my old circuit, and all the principal brethren in it, when I joined the church, and for some time after. At times when engaged thinking of by-gone years, I have almost fancied I could hear voices from the other side of the flood, saying, "Brother Bellinger, is it possible, in reviewing your past life, that you are going to say nothing about the friends you loved on the old Walterboro circuit, who have entered into rest, and who hope to welcome you and the rest of the old companions still behind, when you come?" It seemed to me that I could almost hear voices of loved ones gone speaking to me from many places—from Pine Grove, Green Pond, Ebenezer, Carmel, St. Johns, Little Swamp, Mizpah, and all around the old bounds. It has been thus with me while writing of the past, and I will put it off no longer.

O, my much loved friends of the old circuit, gone to heaven, I often think of you and of the others still left behind in this vale of tears. I hope you have not forgotten us here below, and that you will meet us on the banks of eternal deliverance, when our warfare is over, and we are called home. I know I cannot do justice to the dead or living; but I hope my friends will take the will for the deed, and if something is left out which should have been mentioned, in the opinion of some, remember that there is not room to mention all particulars.

Where shall I begin? If you will leave it to me, I will begin at Pine Grove. Much loved old place, how can I forget thee? Brother Aaron Smith was the class-leader; a blessed man of God; one of the old Methodists in dress and manners; a man of few words, but always to the point. How well I remember him and his whole-souled wife. What pleasant hours I have often spent with them. And that saint of the Lord, Brother Steadly, and others; and Brother Muse, who was taken into full connection in the church on the same day with me, by Brother Dunwody, and who still lives, and I hope is on his way to the better land. I cannot forget old Pine Grove; for I was treated with much kindness by the members of the church there. They bore with my weakness and my unworthiness. We often enjoyed ourselves much in class and prayer meetings. Sometimes there were only a few present; but Brothers Smith and Steadly, and a few others, would always be sure to be there. But several of my old Pine Grove friends have gone to the better land above. Many years ago, Brother Eason Smith went home. A good brother told me, that not long before he left us, he was with him at a prayer-meeting—that he was very happy, and left singing that old song—

"Here we go rejoicing home,
From the banquet of perfume."

Sister Smith, Brother Steadly, and others, have long since gone. Happy dead! ye have long been removed from the sorrows and troubles of this life. Your warfare is over. You rest from your labor, in the Paradise above. For many years, when the congregation worshipped elsewhere, I seldom passed the church without offering prayer to the Lord, and imploring his protection for myself and the circuit.

Old Green Pond! thou art not forgotten by me. The old church has long been replaced by a new one. Camp-meetings were often held there in the olden time—at one of which I was licensed to preach. Brother Allen Williams, father the Rev. P. A. M. Williams, was the class-leader—a man of strong faith and confidence in the Lord, who believed in a heart-felt religion. Brother Thomas Raysor—the most beloved of all my friends—had his membership there several years before I joined the church. Old Green Pond! what immortal memories dost thou recall to my mind! what gracious seasons we often had there! I remember a time when I went out in the crowd, to a gentleman of respectable standing, Mr. Spell, and spoke to him of religion. He joined the church at that meeting, and some years after was called to the joys of heaven. A few hours before his death, he told a friend to say to me, for him, that he was going to glory, and hoped I would meet him there; that he thanked me for going to him that day, for it was the means of bringing him to the Lord. The most of the old members of Green Pond are gone to the sweet fields of Eden, on the other side of the flood. I remember a good camp-meeting there many years ago, when a Mr. Johnson and Colonel John Raysor joined the church. I recollect the text the Strange Preacher took, "He that goeth forth weeping, bearing precious seed, shall doubtless return again rejoicing, bringing his sheaves with him." Mr. Johnson had fallen out with Brother Williams, years before. Brother W. had often tried to make it up with him, but never could succeed; but after he had been to the altar, he went to Brother W., and made it up with him, and requested him to pray for him. He was soon after converted. Sister Spell, unless I am mistaken, is the only one of the old Green Pond members left, who were in the church when I joined.

Ebenezer. There are still a few names left here of the old members. Brothers Alfred Raysor—the old class-leader, Benjamin Risher, Sley, and Martin Jaques—I have long known, long respected them. The devil has tried hard to win them back to the world; but, by the help of the Lord, they have so far held out faithful, and fought the good fight of faith; and I hope will in the end win eternal life. Brother Risher and his family have ever been very kind and true friends of mine throughout my Christian life; and I have always felt very glad to meet, and sorry to leave, them. May our blessed Lord save them all in his heavenly kingdom, for Jesus' sake. Amen.

Rehoboth. I have often enjoyed myself at the old church, for which I thank the Lord. Brothers Philip Jaques, Akerman, and Dandridge were here. They were whole-souled, thorough-going, pious men of Israel, and enjoyed much of religion. It was a great pleasure for me to see them in the congregation, in the olden times; for I know that they prayed for me when I was trying to preach.

Sheridan's Chapel. Here there was a very small membership when I first preached to them. There were two brothers, named Johnson, who were good and true old-time Methodists, in dress and manners. They are both gone to the good world, I hope. Here, too, was that good man, Brother Abram Willis, who is respected by all who know him; his house has been a home for preachers for more than thirty years. He is a modest man, of quiet, gentle manners, but full of the Holy Ghost and of faith. He was still alive, when last heard from—with his back to the world, and his face to the Jerusalem above. I have often enjoyed myself much with Brother Willis; and I hope to meet all the family in heaven.

Dear old Island Creek! Louis O'Brien—"clarum et venerabile nomen." Departed brother, all hail! Thou art gone to thy reward, and thy sainted wife with thee. What a home for the preacher was thy house in the olden times! I loved much to hear him tell of the old ministers who travelled in those parts, when he was a young man first settled in life—that they went from house to house with their saddle-bags; and how, when they preached, at times the power of the Holy Spirit would come down on the congregation, and sinners would fall right and left, like men shot through the heart, and remain motionless for a long time, and then rise and praise the Lord aloud for his pardoning grace. But Uncle Louis, many years ago, went safe to the realms above; and there went his eldest son—a blessed man of faith and prayer. The last time I ever saw him was at Island Creek, and there was only one other present; but we had a happy time together; and I preached to the two persons. The subject was—"The ways of Zion mourn, because none come to her solemn feasts." I remember another day at Island Creek, in the olden times. The service was over. I said I would like to have night-meeting there, if the friends wished it. Brother Robinson got up, and said, that was not a good place for night-meeting; but if I would come to Jones's Swamp, they would give me a congregation—but that there was no house to preach in. I gave out the meeting; a great revival broke out, and I went back there from Green Pond on Monday. I was on the circuit then in Brother Moore's place. A society was formed and a church built, which was called Mount Carmel. A camp-ground was afterwards established at the same place; and I do not remember ever having been there once in near thirty years, but that the Lord met with us, and we rejoiced in heavenly places in Christ Jesus, and felt that we were sitting under the droppings of the sanctuary. Brothers Blox, Robinson, and Blocker were yet alive when last heard from—and were whole-souled men, full of the Holy Ghost and of power. I always was glad to see them in the congregation. They yet stand as they did in the olden times, as witnesses for Jesus, who were loved of him, and were bound for heaven.

O, my soul! praise the Lord that my poor labors have been so often blessed at Mount Carmel. There was my much-respected friend, Brother Linder, who still lives to meet me when I go there, and to treat me with much kindness. There, too, was Brother Beach, at whose house I always felt at home. And those holy women of the Lord at Mount Carmel—Sisters Robinson, Beach, Blocker, and others, how I loved to shake hands with them, and hear them sing the old songs of Zion!

In by-gone years, I sometimes dreamed of Island Creek and Mount Carmel. I remember many years ago, there was a two days' meeting held at the two churches; and I stopped all night at St. John's, and dreamed that I had a good meeting where I was going, and twelve persons joined the church—but I did not mention it till the meeting was over. We divided the time between the two churches; and on Sunday, at Island Creek, the Holy Spirit was graciously present, and five persons joined. We had night-meeting at Carmel. A large congregation was present, and it was a time of much rejoicing; and seven persons joined—five in the morning, and seven at night—the number was made up. I have had many a weary ride to old Carmel—nearly forty miles from my home, and a part of the way a very bad road to travel—but I never went there without feeling glad that I had gone.

St. John's. The worthy class-leader was still alive when last heard from—Brother Joseph Risher, "an Israelite in whom there is no guile." I have never met him once in thirty years, but that I was greeted with a smile and a friendly shake of the hand, that went to my heart. If he was not one of the heroes of the Walterboro circuit, then there were none. Whenever I went there, if my faith was strong, it became stronger; if my spirits were good, they became better; if my head was aching, the pain would soon soon leave me; if I was cast down and sad of heart, and felt that I was very low down in the valley, when I had been welcomed with kind words and smiles of love by himself and his interesting family, I would soon find that a change for the better was coming over my whole nature; and then, when they sung some of my much-loved songs, my sad feelings would leave me, and the Strange Preacher would clap his hands, and cry out, " Farewell world! I'm bound for the kingdom." What a sweet oasis in this desert world, to the Wandering Arab, is Brother Joseph Risher's home. He is truly the hero of St. John's.

There was another veteran there—a holy man, good and true, who has long since gone to the realms above; he was a man of few words, silent, grave, serious, thoughtful; who had been with Jesus, and was loved of him; a man that the holy angels revered, and whom the devil was obliged to respect—Brother Duncan Stewart, another of the heroes of the old circuit. He has left a family behind him, much respected. The blood of the time-honored veteran flowing in the veins of his descendants, was freely, like water, poured out—but, alas! all in vain—for our lost cause. I have some dear friends at St. John's, for whom I often pray.

Buckhead—much-loved old Buckhead! Thy glory has departed; the voice of rejoicing is no longer heard in thy tabernacles; the voice of the preacher no longer resounds through thy old woods; the church no longer stands; the camp-ground is deserted—the place where it once stood, like the Mount Zion of the exiled Israelites, has become at last a ploughed field; and the corn or cotton now grows on the holy place over which angels loved to hover on their golden wings, and with joy carried the glad tidings to heaven, that the dead was alive, and the lost found. Dear old Buckhead!

though there is no poet or historian to immortalize thee in undying words, the Strange Preacher, with tears in his eyes, will say something of thy former glory, and thy present desolation, before he goes hence, where he hopes to meet the holy men of old, whose voices were heard in thy sacred precincts. I remember the camp-meetings which I attended there in the days of "auld lang syne." 'Twas there, too where I preached some of my first sermons, more than thirty years ago; and Brothers Talley, Bass, S. W. Capers, English, and McPhail, stand before me as large as life, when I think of Buckhead camp-ground, and Brothers McCall, Durant, and Picket, and other immortal names, whose record is on high. I remember how the heroes, from the length and breadth of the Walterboro circuit, with many others, would meet there, and, uniting their strength, bear down on the enemy—winning victories over the powers of hell, and exulting aloud in the God of their salvation.

I remember one Sunday, at the 11 o'clock service (I suppose I had sat up too late the night before), that a minister, whose preaching I admired very much, was in the pulpit, yet, in spite of myself, I became very sleepy. After preaching a while, he requested some one to wake me up, as he was going to say something which he wished very much for me to hear. I was at once completely aroused. And at the 3 o'clock service, the whole congregation seemed inclined to drowsiness, when Brother Picket got up, and at once roused up the entire crowd, by giving out the whole of a very singular chapter for his text—about the wheels within the wheels, and the eyes in the wheels—and we had a very good meeting. I recollect one night, particularly—a gracious season it was—the whole congregation seemed much impressed, and the shouts of the redeemed rang through the woods; many mourners were at the altar, and there were many happy conversions—among them a young man who afterwards became a preacher. Those old deserted camp-grounds of our Conference—Swallow Savannah, Black Swamp, Green Pond, Buckhead, Cane Creek, Goshen Hill, and many others—how sad the Wandering Arab feels at times, while thinking of their former glory, and their present ruinous condition! I wonder if the holy spirits fly over them still, as they did in the olden time; but I suspect not—there is nothing to interest them there now. I wonder if the spirits of perdition flap their dark wings over those old places as they once did; I suspect not. I wonder if our much-loved friends, departed and gone to rest, look down from those heavenly battlements now, as they did in those days when the friends left behind worshipped there; I suspect not—for what do immortal spirits care for those old grounds, so changed, and, alas! for the worse.

Much-loved old Buckhead! there was a time when good men and true worshipped in thy holy church. With several others, there was my friend and brother Charles Stewart—one of the heroes of the old circuit, who has long since gone to the green fields of Eden—a friend of the preachers and the church. The more you saw of him, the more you respected him; the more intimate you became, the more you loved him. He might be called the Gaius of the Walterboro circuit. "Vale, longe vale," to old Buckhead!

Bethel. What name comes first among her departed heroes? Brother Ulmer, the old preacher, of course. I respected and revered him much—plain, simple, childlike, full of meekness and humility, always sitting on a lower seat than that to which he was entitled. From his long life, he might have been called the Nestor of the old circuit: a man of faith, and hope, and love. It was a great pleasure, which I often enjoyed, to pass a night under his family roof. He had many interesting tales of old times to tell the young preachers. I can fancy I see him now, as he used to sit in his old chair in the warm corner of the chimney, on some cold evening in winter, smoking his pipe, telling of the old preachers—many of whom he had seen and heard; and as he talked, I listened much pleased; but after a while, his pipe would go out, and the tears would begin to fall, and he would weep like a boy whose mother is dead. I have been at many happy meetings with the old hero of Bethel. But there was another name—a man of holy longings for immortality and eternal life—Brother Edward Bryan, the exhorter, the just, the upright Christian—a man lowly and humble, who enjoyed much heart-felt religion; who got happy at home, at meetings, and everywhere. I have often been with him when the Lord revived his work. The two old heroes of Bethel have long since met in the paradise above, to part no more.

Shiloh, of which I have written a number, was in the bounds of the old circuit; but I do not know if it was always on the plan. Brother Snider was there—a good man, much thought of, much respected. He had a pleasant family; and his house was a good home for the preachers—and I have often enjoyed myself there. His wife, son, and self, I hope, are now in the happy land, far, far away. Brothers Ulmer and Bryan were with me several times at old Shiloh. Those two departed friends labored faithfully on that part of the circuit, and had many friends, both in the church and the world, who respected them much, and often attended their meetings.

Antioch. This was a small church, near Cruise's Ford, on the Great Saltketcher, which has since been replaced by another, near by the same place. I hope I will never forget the meetings in that old church, with Brothers Ulmer, Varn, and Bryan. The Lord was often present. Brother William Varn was the old class-leader—a pure, humble, heavenly-minded man—who loved the place of prayer, and who has been for years in the paradise above. And there was another who succeeded him in that holy office—Brother Godly, whom I thought much of, and who lived near the throne of grace. I do not remember ever having met him, but that he seemed cheerful and happy—ready and waiting for his Master's call to come up higher. I was very sorry when I heard of his death many years ago; but my loss was his eternal gain.

Salem. That name stands first in bold relief. Dr. Henderson—the polished gentleman, the whole-souled friend, the kind host, and the Christian soldier. Departed brother, how well do I remember thee! and, Oh! how I mourned over thy violent death! What glorious times I have seen at the Salem church! Before the Doctor joined, Brother Varn and myself had a two days' meeting there. We were at the breakfast table on Monday, and we were soon to leave for our homes. Dr. H. had not been on speaking terms with a certain member of our church for years. He was pressing us to have another meeting at Salem. Having always been very impulsive, I sometimes risk much by speaking hastily, without the least reflection, hoping and trusting in the Lord, that it will turn out for the best; but I know I have sometimes said what I much regretted afterwards, at other times, though, it seemed to have been owned and blessed of the Lord. Under an impulse, I said to Dr. H., that we would give him a two days' meeting, provided he would make friends with that brother, and forgive and forget. He paused a moment, with a flushed face—oh, what a pause! and then remarked that he would do so. We then promised him the meeting, and departed. O! how I implored the Lord to meet with and bless us at that place. The set time came, and we went, some fifty miles from home. When we got there, the Doctor told us, he preferred making friends at the altar. They met, and shook hands; and the brother told me the next morning, he still felt the pressure of Dr. Henderson's hand. We had a meeting of precious remembrance—the best time I ever saw at old Salem. Some forty persons joined one day; and it was said by some to have been the best they ever had there. On one occasion, every one present came to the altar to unite in prayer. The last one had made up his mind, as he told a friend, that nothing should induce him to come; and I was very glad to see him there.

Peniel. This church, at the place where it then stood, had declined much when I first went there; but there was still one blessed man of Israel left, who was faithful and true —Brother Lowry. He is of precious memory, full of faith and good works.

Walterboro. If there was a hero there, I am sorry I have forgotten him. But, my friends, there were some heroines there, whom I think should be mentioned. Sisters Campbell, Pye, and Henderson—pure, holy, heavenly-minded women, who enjoyed much heartfelt religion, and whose names were like precious ointment poured forth. Their whole lives were spent in deeds of Christian charity. Two of them have long been in heaven, the other yet remains to bless the church and the world.

Sandy Dam. Brother Joel Larasy—a man among men, a Methodist whom the church loves, and the devil hates—still lives to greet his friends with a smile. He has suffered much in these troublesome times; but he loves the Lord, and still holds on to his religion, and has a happy home above awaiting his coming.

Tabernacle. What minister has ever travelled the circuit —what preacher ever lived in it—who does not know who are the heroes of that church? Brother Elsey Kinsey—what recollections of strong, prevailing prayer does that name call to mind—how well he and Brother James Kinsey stood side by side in the good work, eternity will tell. How they ever welcomed the preacher; generally the first to greet him, and help him with his horse; and to request him to go with them, where they would do all they could to make him comfortable. There, too, was that good man and true, Brother Padget—a happy soul, bound for the better world. At Tabernacle, I have seen many glorious meetings. What old-time, Methodist singing I have heard ring through the church and the woods around. That good man of Israel, Brother Padget, has long since gone to the rest which remains for the people of God. The other two are still left to bless the church.

I remember an amusing thing which happened to me, nearly thirty years ago—amusing to think of afterwards, but very unpleasant at the time. I was at a two days' meeting, with other brothers; the house could not hold the congregation, and many remained out. Two of the brothers were sitting behind me, and I was trying to preach. I had not been preaching long, as I thought, when I heard those behind me talking in a low voice. At first, I did not pay much attention to it, though it bothered me. After a little, I thought I could make out a word now and then, though only spoken in a whisper; and I thought I heard, "it is most time for him to finish." I have always been easily thrown out and confused; and being a young preacher then, this disturbed me very much. At first, I felt like stopping, and not saying another word; however, I made a great effort, and went stumbling on for some time. I had almost recovered, and began to hope that I would get through without further interruption; when the talking again began in low whispers. Presently, I was sure I heard these words—"Brother B., you had better stop; you have been long enough." The distressed preacher then took his seat, feeling very much cast down. I did not raise my head for several moments. I was afraid I had been at it more than an hour; but when I looked at my watch, I found out, to my great surprise, I had not been preaching thirty minutes. I was told afterwards, that the friends had been speaking about something very different, and that they were sorry I had been so disturbed. The Lord bless Tabernacle, and the two heroes left.

Little Swamp. O! how well I remember the old church! what times of rejoicing I have seen there, and what happy seasons I have witnessed there! I have often felt that the Lord was with his poor servant while preaching his gospel in that small church so close the road, and so near the little pond—generally so full of water in the winter and spring, and so dry in the summer and fall. I remember an interesting night-meeting there in the olden time. After the services commenced, a young man stretched himself at full length on a bench, staring the preacher in the face, with a vacant smile, which interrupted him very much, for every time he turned that way he met that gaze. He requested the lounger to sit up; but he still remained stretched out. After a while, I stopped, and said to him, I thought I could preach a better sermon, with the help of the Lord, if he would sit up, and entreated him to do so; when he arose at once. The Holy Spirit helped, the church prayed, and we had a very fine meeting; and among the mourners who came up, was that same young man. How often have I rejoiced with the brethren at Little Swamp. The first to be mentioned here is Brother Paul Johnson; but I do not know as much of him as of many others—for not long after I joined the church, he moved to Georgia. He was an exhorter with us, but became a preacher afterwards. While with us, he was much respected, and was very useful and successful in his efforts to save souls. There were also at this church, Brothers Gooden, Padget, and Thomas Smith—men of hope and faith. The two last have gone to the land of the pious departed. Brother S. long since left us. I respected and esteemed him much, and he was worthy. One evening, while resting on the bed (I had been sick), my spirits were quite depressed. I thought I was forgotten by my friends—that they seldom prayed for me, when the following impression came on me very strongly—one of your friends is now on his knees praying for you, this very moment, when you think you have been forgotten by all. I at once became lifted up—I was very happy—I got on my knees and thanked the Lord. I noticed the hour of the day. Several weeks after this, I was at Little Swamp, when Brother Smith asked me to walk with him, as he wished to see me alone. He then inquired, if on such an evening, at a certain hour, I had been cast down, and thought I had been forgotten by my friends. I told him I had been. He told me that at that hour he became impressed that I was so situated, and that he must pray for me. He was then hard at work, and thought he would wait till the regular time we had agreed upon years before, which was after sunset; but the impression became stronger, and he stopped, and turned aside, and prayed for me. How good the Lord is to us!

Wesley Chapel. A place of note in the olden time—a place of renown on the old Walterboro circuit. Before I joined the church, camp-meetings were held there; and many of the old preachers, long since gone to heaven, unfurled the blood-besprinkled flag of Calvary there, in years that are past. Men, whose names will never die in the history of the South Carolina Conference, preached there, long before I realized the salvation of my soul. I have attended many interesting meetings at that place. The old class-leader, Brother Raysor, moved to Georgia years ago, and I hope is now in a better world. Brother Fulk, another of the old-time men of God, has left us. His eldest son still lives, and is bound for the better world.

Providence. A dear old church. What times of immortal remembrance I have seen there—long before the new church was built, which was burned during the late war. Most of the old friends are gone. Brother Daniel Beigler—one of the heroes of the old circuit—has long since left us for the better land, where the friends of Jesus never part, and where the weary are at rest. Brother Carson—the good, the true, the humble, and the heavenly-minded man—is still left; and the veteran still has his war-harness on, enduring hardships like a good soldier of Jesus Christ. All hail! to the old hero of Providence.

Mizpah. A chief place on the old circuit; and the first place in many respects on the Bamberg circuit. The old church has long since been replaced by a new one. Dear old Mizpah, of holy remembrance! how I loved that house of prayer and praise! How often, in the olden time, I felt the presence of the Lord in my poor soul, in that time-honored sanctuary! There were — Brother George Kirkland, the whole-souled leader; Dr. Ayer, who started with me at Binnakers for the better world. Brother Kirkland left us many years ago for the fair fields of Eden—where father and son have long since embraced in heaven to part no more. Two of the heroes of old Mizpah still worship the Lord in the new church. Brother Reuben Kirkland—the quiet, the meek Christian, the kind-hearted friend—still lives, to ask the preacher of the gospel to his house, and to make him feel at once at home in his friendly presence. Dr. Ayer was still alive when last heard from; and though in another State, that war-worn veteran of the cross has not forgotten his friends on the old circuit. James Brabham—the preacher's best friend on the Bamberg circuit—a Christian gentleman, worthy of being mentioned in the same breath with Mizpah's sainted class-leader and his preacher-son—W. C. Kirkland—still lives to bless the church and the world in these degenerate days. May their names never be forgotten on earth!

Cross Swamp. Immortal name! The dear old church, with its living and departed heroes, how much I love the time-honored place, with its heavenly surroundings! The friends here have always treated me kindly. In my young days as a preacher, they stood near me to strengthen my hands; and now that I have grown grey on the walls of Zion, they are more kind than ever. How can I forget them! I hope the Lord will enable me to pray for them while I live, and to remember them in heaven. Brother Aaron Varn, one of the old heroes, has kept the faith, has fought the good fight, has finished his course, and has gone to the paradise above, having left, among many others, the Wandering Arab to mourn his loss, and miss him much. But the good man left loved ones behind, who are faithfully walking in his steps. But, bless the Lord, some of the heroes still remain. Brother Broxton, the good and true man; Brother Murdock, the Christian veteran; Brother James Varn, one of my best friends—ever kind, ever true, ever loving; Brother L. B. Varn, my long-tried and much-loved friend—as Achates was to Eneas, as Damon was to Pythias, as Jonathan was to David, so has he ever been to me. We have stood side by side, on a hundred stricken fields, fighting with locked shields; and have won many a hard fought battle—giving all the glory to our blessed Saviour. Brother Reuben Stephens—the last on the immortal list of Cross Swamp heroes—worthy of standing by the side of the greatest of the Walterboro heroes. In olden times he belonged to Buckhead; but as he is at Cross Swamp now, I speak of him here. Before I embraced religion, Brother Stephens was one of the chief pillars of the church; and all through my Christian life, has been one of my best friends. His smile, his greeting—which always comes from his heart, and his shake of the hand, have always been to me as water to a thirsty traveller. The South Carolina Conference has few such men in its bounds, as far as I know, as Reuben Stephens—the Christian gentleman, and the veteran who has ever met the powers of darkness in the face. He reminds me much of the gallant Caleb, who after surviving all the terrors of the wilderness, stood before Joshua, and told him that he was just as strong to bear arms then as when he first left Egypt. One reason, I have thought, why he has been spared to us so long, is that the young men of the church might know that there were giants in the Walterboro circuit, thirty years ago. I hope my friends will allow me to call Brother Thomas Raysor, the Agamemnon—Brother Ulmer, the Nestor—Brother Reuben Stephens, the Ajax Telemon—Brother L. B. Varn, the Diomed—old Brother Aaron Varn, the Philemon—Brother Charles Stewart, the Gaius—and Brother James Brabham, the Jonathan of the old Walterboro circuit.

I was born in this world, in the town of Walterboro, over sixty years ago; and I joined the church in the bounds of the old circuit; and I have ever felt desirous, by the help of the Lord, to save my soul, and reach heaven at last, when my course is ended.

"Come, let us join our friends above,
That have obtained the prize;
And on the eagle wings of love,
To joys celestial rise:
Let all the saints terrestrial sing,
With those to glory gone;
For all the servants of our King
In earth and heaven are one.

"One family we dwell in him—
One church above, beneath;
Though now divided by the stream,
The narrow stream of death.
One army of the living God,
To his command we bow;
Part of the host have crossed the flood,
And part are crossing now."

## LEAF THE TWENTY-EIGHTH.

A MEMENTO OF MY MOST BELOVED FRIEND, BROTHER THOMAS RAYSOR, THE MODEL STEWARD, OR THE MAN WHOSE MANTLE NO ONE HAS YET BEEN FOUND WORTHY TO WEAR.

I have often thought, that, notwithstanding my very singular and strange turn of mind, and my many oddities, I have been truly blessed of the Lord with a great number of friends—I expect they might be counted by the hundreds—who have showed me much kindness. I know I have sometimes been treated by some of them better than I deserved. Of all these dear friends of mine, I have always regarded Brother Thomas Raysor as my first and my best-beloved; and when he left this vale of tears to enter the rest that remains for the people of God, I lost my dearest friend. I have often been requested by some of my friends—both preachers and others—to write down some of the events of my past life; and for many years I have been thinking of doing so; but did not begin the work until a few months ago. I have already spoken of several of my friends who have gone to heaven; and I would feel ashamed of myself, and feel that I had almost committed a sin, if I said nothing in these Stray Leaves of Thomas Raysor.

I was in the church for some time before I became intimately acquainted with him. He was then one of the chief stewards of the circuit, and had been for years before; and he always had the interests of the preachers and of the church at large, near his heart. His house, his heart, and his noble soul were always open, to welcome, to encourage, and befriend the preacher of the gospel. But Thomas Raysor has gone, and I am left still to feel and mourn his absence; but he is often thought of, often remembered. While he was here, if I was in trouble, I would go to him for comfort; if I was happy, I wished to share my pleasure with him; if I wanted advice, I went to him for it: and now that he is no more with me, I feel that the earthly arm on which

I loved to lean is removed. I sometimes fancy he is near me, very near; and I can almost imagine I still hear him speaking to me.

I have often felt, that if all the circuits in the South Carolina Conference, however bad the prospect, were only blessed with one man like Thomas Raysor, the preachers would be much better provided for than they are.

Near thirty years ago, one of the preachers on our circuit, through affliction in his family, had to leave his work; and I think it was by Brother Raysor's advice, the quarterly conference requested me to take his place for the time; and from that time I became warmly attached to him. Let me show what influence he had over me. I have always preferred my roving life as a preacher, to regular circuit work. Three times he advised me to go on a circuit, and I yielded each time, as he thought it was for the best. I remember a rather amusing circumstance, connected with one of those times.

Our presiding elder, Brother Walker, met me some distance from home, and requested me to take the place of a preacher, whose ill-health compelled him to leave his work. Brother Raysor was there, and I told Brother W. I would be governed by Brother Raysor's advice. He asked me if I would not first consult my wife. I told him, she would send me to Brother R. I then went to Brother R., who was near by, and he told me to fill the vacancy, which I did. After I got through the six months on the circuit, I met Brother R. at a meeting, and took him aside, and told him I had a request to make of him, and that he must grant it before knowing what it was—that he could do so very well if he would. He paused some time; but at last said he would do so. I told him, that three times in my life I had gone on a circuit by his advice; that I did not like it as well as my roving life; and entreated him never to advise me to do it again. He said that he would not, and left me for a little while, but returned again, and said that he and a brother present had a request to make of me, and that I must grant it before knowing what it was. I could not refuse. He said, I must accept of a suit of clothes from them.

He not only gave liberally himself, but influenced others to do the same. More than once in the olden time, have I gone to the class-steward to pay my subscription for the preacher, when I would be told that a brother had been there and settled it for me. I knew full well who the brother was. I once spoke to him about it; but he said, his feelings would be hurt unless I would let him have his own way; and so I had to give up more than once. I have been present when collections were being taken up for Missions, when he would say, "I give so much for myself, and so much for a brother," nodding to me. I knew him so well, that I said nothing.

When with him, I felt more at home than with any other man. He enjoyed religion, both in public and private life; and he believed in a whole-souled, heart-felt Christian life. He had a wife, who was worthy of him in every respect; and they lived very happily together for years; but death separated them at last—and she was called to the happy land, far, far away. I remember well the last night I stayed with them, before she was taken from us. Brother R. and myself sat up some time after the family had retired; and we were sitting near together—the fire having nearly died out. We were speaking of persons leaving the church; and, as if suddenly moved by a strong impulse, he said, "Well, brother, I would rather see you dead, and unburied before my gate, and the birds plucking out your eyes—as much as I love you—than to see you quit the church, and go back to the world." He always spoke out what was in his heart.

Not many weeks after this, his wife was called to her reward on high, so that I never saw her again; but she left this world fully prepared for heaven. Only a few hours before her death, she told her husband, she was ready and willing to go; and sent her last message to me—that I must never quit the church, and must meet her in heaven; that I must pray for her husband and children every night, before retiring to rest. In after years, Brother R. married again, a very worthy and respectable lady.

I have been at many very interesting meetings with Brother R., and his heart was always engaged in the work of the Lord. I remember well, a meeting many years ago, at Swallow Savannah. It was a time of refreshing from the presence of the Lord; and he seemed to enjoy himself very much. One day, we were alone, and he told me he wished to speak to me on a particular subject. He said, that he knew some of his friends thought he might be prevailed on to quit our church, and join another; but that he was resolved, by God's help, to live and die where he was. And then he said to me, that some thought, by family influence, I, too, might join another church; but he said he did not believe it. He then told me, he wished to make a bargain with me before the Lord, in whose presence we then were—that we must solemnly pledge ourselves to it. It was this: if either of us ever felt like leaving our church, he must send for the other—who must come, and remain with him until he prevailed on him to remain where he was. I agreed with him, and we shook hands on it. "Now," said he, "if any one should tell me, and offer to swear to it on the Bible, that you were going to leave our church, I would not believe one word of it, unless you first sent me word to come." I feel the impression of that pledge as strong now as if he was still with me.

Many years ago, I was taken very sick, and was brought very near the grave. Several physicians were with me, and all expected me to die. My brother, Dr. Bellinger, was with me several days; and he said, at one time he did not think I had more than two hours to live. While in my right mind, I felt much of the presence of the Lord, and the comforts of religion; and my dear Brother Raysor was with me day and night, to pray for me, and to wait on me to the last. He never gave me up; he said he had been praying much for me, and that he had faith to believe I would recover. He told my wife several times, that the Lord would spare me to her; that I would recover my health; and that he would often hear me preach again. I think his prayers, with those of many others, had much to do with my recovery. He never came to see me, while I was sick, without stopping to entreat the Lord in private for me. The Lord spared me; I was raised up again; the prayers of my many friends were heard; and, O! how much nearer to my heart was Brother Raysor afterwards than before.

But the much-loved brother of my soul has left me. He departed this life several years ago, full of peace and holy joy, to the realms of endless day. By his death, a great vacuum was made, both in the church and the world—one that never has been, and perhaps never will be, filled. He left his mantle behind; but no one has yet been found worthy to wear it.

Brother Raysor was so generous, so merciful, that while I think of him, he recalls the words of the poet—

> "The quality of mercy is not strained;
> It droppeth as the gentle dew from heaven
> Upon the place beneath. It blesseth him
> That gives, and him that takes."

I think of him, perhaps every time I pass his old home—where his eldest son now lives; and I generally uncover my head. O! how much I miss my departed brother, in these days of privation and trouble!

Farewell! Brother Thomas Raysor! I hope your happy spirit will be near when my hour comes. Thy departed children, I trust, are now with thee in glory; and those left behind, I hope, will meet thee there.

> "Thy life was gentle; and the elements
> So mixed in thee, that Nature might stand up,
> And say to all the world—Thou wast a man."

## LEAF THE TWENTY-NINTH.

CAMDEN; MEETINGS AT SALEM CAMP-GROUND, AND LANCASTER COURT-HOUSE.

In the early part of 1840, I attended an annual conference at Camden, held by Bishop Andrew, where I was ordained local deacon—which was a very serious, solemn service to me, and one which I hope I will never forget; for, O! what searching of heart I had on that holy Sabbath. The Bishop's sermon made quite a strong impression on my mind. I had never seen him but once before—which was at a camp-meeting near Bethel church, on the Blackville circuit, some years before. I remember very little of the service, however, for at that time I was a very wicked young man, and paid little respect to the services. It did not then seem probable that in a few years I would be ordained deacon by him.

Several years after my first visit, I attended a quarterly meeting in Camden; Brother Talley was the presiding elder, and my much-respected friend, Brother S. M. Green, was in charge of the church. Brother Murchison was also present. One day, while I was preaching, a powerful impression rested on the congregation, and several of the brethren became very happy, and exulted in the Lord their Redeemer.

Some days after, I left for Salem camp-ground, in Lancaster District, which was a famous place in the olden time. It was situated on the direct stage route from Camden to Lancaster. This was the first of several fine meetings which I attended at that place. Let me mention the names of several friends whom I met there for the first time. Brother Simon Fraser, a local preacher, was there—a good, whole-souled, thorough-going man, with whom I was quite pleased; but he has long since gone to the realms above. I also met the Rev. Dr. Langley and his family, and have always been happy to number them with my friends. He is a gentleman of intelligence and refinement, very courteous in his manners. His wife and daughters are also very pleasant and kind to their friends. I there became acquainted with two brothers, by the name of Cauthen—one of whom was a worthy member of our Conference; and the other was a man of weight, both in the church and in the State. There, too, was the class-leader—an Israelite without blemish or reproach; and I regard it as a fortunate moment for me when I became acquained with Brother Beckham. I once went from Camden to the camp-ground in the stage, in which I found some very unpleasant passengers, who knew I was a preacher, and behaved very badly, thereby disturbing me very much; but I concluded it was best not to reprove them, as I thought it would be casting pearls before swine. O, how I longed for deliverance from my distressing position! But at last I reached the ground; and how thankful I felt, when the friends gathered around me with their friendly greeting! At times, the Holy Spirit came down powerfully upon the congregation; and we had very sweet singing at the stand, in the tents, and in the woods. What great crowds were there on Saturday and Sunday; and the preached word found its way to the heart of many a hardened sinner who had been so long indifferent as to cause their friends to lose all hope.

I was once present at a protracted meeting, held in the church, at the same place. It was a time of much interest; the Eternal Spirit was abroad; and my faith was strong and lively. The work of the Lord was reviving in my soul. Sinners trembled, mourners wept, Christians rejoiced, and the angels were waiting to bear the glad news to heaven, that souls were converted, and prodigals were returning home. A lady was present, a member of the Baptist church, who had a very wicked son in the crowd, and it seemed that nothing could move him—neither the joys of heaven, nor the horrors of hell, appeared to make any impression. He seemed almost beyond the reach of Divine influence. His mother entreated me to persuade him, if possible, to come to the altar; and I made several efforts, but all in vain. I became very sorry for her; for she was still very urgent in her request that I should try him again. The meeting was still going on; and I went to him once more, and knelt down before him, and implored him to yield to be saved—but all in vain. He smiled in my face. "I suspect," says one, "that the Wandering Arab then left him to his fate." I became more determined to win him, if possible, for his mother, and for the church; but I changed my programme. The meeting went on with blessed results, the Strange Preacher taking no more notice of the young man than if he was not present; but in secret praying much for him. The time had not yet come for me to make my last effort. Many weeping souls were happily converted; others were still seeking the Saviour, sorrowing; and the gospel was still winning its way to the hearts of the people. Hard-hearted sinners were deeply wounded by the arrows of the Spirit, and were fleeing the wrath to come. But still that young man stayed away, and I still continued to treat him with indifference. His mother had lost all hope of ever seeing her dear son seeking the salvation of his soul. But the Saviour had tasted death for him, and the Holy Spirit had not finally departed.

The Strange Preacher was ready to make his last effort. There appeared to be a more general impression on the congregation than at any time previous. The camp of Israel was moving, at the command of the Lord, to glorious victory. Mourners were called up. Three young men were sitting near the centre of the middle aisle; the young man already alluded to occupied the middle seat. I offered one silent, brief prayer to the Heavenly Father, and walked up to the group, and spoke to the one on the right, and then turned to the one on the left—but said not a word to him. I told them, there was mercy for them if they would yield; and shook hands with them, hoping to meet them in heaven —but I took not the slightest notice of the middle one, while his mother wept and prayed. I returned to the altar, and faced the congregation. O, my soul! what did I then see? That young man rushed up to the altar, crying out aloud— "Mr. Bellinger, you said nothing to me; you took no notice of me; and I know you have no hope of me. But, O! sir, you must pray for me, whether you want to or not." That happy mother rejoiced over her returning son; and the holy angels joined with her in her thanksgiving.

Let me now tell you of the meeting at Lancaster court-house, in the unfinished church. There was a gentleman of high standing there, who, with his wife, was quite impressed by the preached word. The class-leader told me, that he had never before seen him so much interested; and that, having taken quite a fancy to me, he wished to be introduced. Strange to say, I, too, was drawn towards him from the very first. I have often been thus impressed with strangers who were not in the church, and felt a strong desire for their salvation. I have often thought, there was a preacher for every sinner; that is, that the Holy Spirit will by some means or other, reach every heart; and that, if one minister does not, by the grace of God, another will; that one sinner will be convicted by a sermon, which will have no effect on others; that a man must be awakened before he can be lost. The class-leader told me, that quite to his surprise, this gentleman was carried away with the Strange Preacher; and told me, if invited, to go home with him; for there never had been a Methodist preacher invited to his house. One night, the said person came to me, and requested me to spend the next day with him; and to bring my friend with me. So Brother McC. and myself went to his house, on the last day of my stay—for I was then to leave for a camp-meeting which I had promised to attend. I found out that the Lord was powerfully at work with him. One night at church, he rose up involuntarily, and stood during a portion of the sermon. While at his house, he selected religious subjects for conversation. The gentleman himself said to me, that he had never been so deeply interested—that he had heard of me often, and always felt a desire to see me—that he felt more drawn towards me than to any other preacher—and was convinced, if he could hear me preach a few more sermons, he would be converted, and afterwards join our church; as he considered it wrong to unite with the church before conversion. I told him, I united with the church before I got religion; and others had done the same, and realized the blessing soon after; and that if such a course was sinful, the Lord would never have forgiven them. We were treated with much kindness both by him and his wife; and they pressed me to remain, and attend the Salem camp-meeting, which was to take place in a few days—as they believed if I would go there, they would receive the blessing, and be ready to join the church. I told them there was danger in thus putting too much trust in a weak arm of flesh; for the minister was nothing without the help of the Lord, but was only the mouth through which he spoke; and unless the Spirit was in the word all would be vain. He called me, *his* preacher; and said I was sent to him; and if I went to the camp-meeting, he would be converted. My feelings were much wrought upon, and I wished much to stay, for I thought there was work for me. He had great searchings of heart on the salvation of his soul; and I was the humble instrument in his conviction; but my word was out, and I was expected elsewhere. A few moments before we started for church, they both abruptly left, and retired to their room—and I at once thought they had gone to pray. After a while, they returned, holding each other's hand, and walked up to me with tears in their eyes, and once more entreated me to stay to the camp-meeting. He said, they had retired to pray for themselves; and said he thought he knew a plan by which I could be persuaded to remain; that he told his wife in the room, if they would join the church that night, he thought I would stay, but he did not wish to do so until he had obtained religion. He asked me if that would induce me to remain. I told him, I would be very glad to see it; but I had to fulfill my promise. We had a gracious, solemn time, and the Lord was with his servant while preaching his last sermon. They knelt at their seats for prayer, but did not join the church; and the meeting was closed. They again implored me to stay; but we parted, and I never saw them again. I was quite cast down in spirit; but how much more so would I have been had I then known what was to happen in a few days.

After I got home, I received a letter from a friend, informing me of the camp-meeting at Salem—what a good time they had, and how much the friends enjoyed themselves; and that this gentleman and lady were much disappointed that I was not there. They still continued to hope I would come. There had been much good done; but the poor Major went over the ground like a lost man in a crowd, saying, *his* preacher was not there—if he could only hear him once more, he would get religion, and then join the church. They felt sorry for him. He would sometimes leave the stand before the sermon was over, and roam all over the ground; and sometimes would come to him (the writer), and say—"O! Mr. Beckham, I am sorry my preacher has not come." He left the camp-ground, and went home in the same state of mind. In a few days after, he was taken suddenly ill, and died in a few moments, without speaking a word.

It was the saddest news I ever heard—the death of one whom I had only seen for the first time just a few days before. I cannot describe my feelings. How much I wished I had remained! But I hoped for the best, knowing how merciful the Lord is; slow to anger, and plenteous in redemption.

I learned a lesson from that sad event, which I hope I will never forget. I think preachers do wrong in leaving meetings of much interest, where there is evidently work for them to do, and where they are much impressed by their own feelings to remain, and yet leave merely to fulfill a promise. It really seems to me that there are preachers to suit every sinner; so that every one will be left without an excuse. I often hear of persons, who have listened to the same minister for years, manifesting very little interest about religion; and when another came, they become more deeply interested than ever before, and, finally, are happily converted, while others still remain unmoved.

Of all the meetings I ever left with the greatest reluctance, were those of Cane Creek and Lancaster camp-grounds, and I have always regretted doing so; but what is past cannot be recalled. O! no; the past will never be seen again, till at the judgment bar we meet; and, O! that it may not condemn us there. O! blessed Father, condemn us not for the past, the present, or the future, for the sake of thy Son, Jesus Christ.

## LEAF THE THIRTIETH.

THE STRANGE PREACHER COUNTING CHICKENS BEFORE THEY WERE HATCHED; OR, EXPECTING GREAT THINGS, WAS QUITE DISAPPOINTED.

My friends, I have been telling you of very many good meetings; but now, suppose you look at the other side of the picture, for variety's sake. Let me tell you of my counting chickens before they were hatched—where things passed off very differently to what I expected. I tell you these things to show you the whole man. I have already spoken of the best meeting I ever attended—not even excepting old Binnakers, where I was converted—which was my first visit to Cane Creek. Now, let me mention one which was the poorest I ever attended, as far as my feelings were concerned. Would you think it possible, that it was the next one I was at, after I left Cane Creek? You say, that is very strange. Still it is true; but I have never been able to account for it, unless it was—which I am rather afraid was the case—that I did wrong in leaving, and the Lord intended it as a punishment and lesson for me. Let us moralize a little here. What a picture of human life! look at it. To-day, we are as happy and contented as we well can be, in this troublesome world, every thing is bright around us; the flowers are inviting us to admire them; birds are singing so sweetly, that we wonder where they learned their songs; the winds are blowing so gently, that we scarcely feel them as they kiss our cheeks. But the morrow cometh; and, O, what a change it brings! You cannot tell how or why it is so, that you are cast down, and ill at ease; and you expect every moment to see or hear something to distress you. The woods are silent and gloomy; the birds are gone; you see no sweet flowers; and the persons whom you meet do not look kindly at you; and you, more than once, feel if you still have your purse; the winds are now raging through the forest, and there is no friendly shelter near. Such is man's life in this vale of tears. O! who that has a home in heaven, would live always here? Yes, so it was; the coldest and most uninteresting meeting I ever was at, followed the very best I ever enjoyed.

Let us go back to the evening I left Cane Creek, in spite of all opposition. I have told you how sorry I was to leave; and how I turned back more than once, and went so near as to see the people on the ground; but at last turned round again, and went off. I felt all the time that I was doing wrong, but still I would go; for I had had but little experience in such things, and was expecting the meeting to which I was going to be a good one—not thinking it could be otherwise—and though sorry that I had to leave, I was comforted with the thought that I would realise the same thing again, and was full of the love of the Lord. I went on, rejoicing in the hope of immortality beyond this vale of sorrows—at times clapping my hands, and shouting aloud; and then again, a slight change would come over me—something seeming to say, " You did wrong in leaving, when your old schoolmate entreated you to stay; and when the young man came up with his sisters, you should have given up." This troubled me much; but then I would say, " It will never do to break my promise; and after all, I am going to a meeting where I expect to enjoy myself as well as I did at the one left behind—I count on there being a great revival there; and the word will be preached with the same power, and the same effect—mourners will crowd the altar, and many of them be happily converted; and the holy angels will carry the glad news to heaven as often as they did at Cane Creek." I have thought, if I had only known what was to be the true state of things, I would have gone back to old Cane Creek, and seen the end of the best camp-meeting I ever attended.

That night I stayed at a place not far from Broad river. It was late when I got there; and I had to sleep in an upper room, that was quite high from the lower floor—the stairs having no railing round them. The next morning, I got up before it was light enough to see; I said my prayers, and was hastening down, and only saved myself by a great effort. I have never forgotten my danger, and the deliverance granted to me. If that had happened to an old Roman, he would have gone no further, but would have regarded it as a bad omen. I wish I had turned back; but I still kept up my feelings by praying often. I counted on a great revival—I thought it could not be otherwise.

I had never before been to the place; and did not expect to know but two persons on the ground, and they were preachers. I stopped—as I always do on reaching a camp-ground—and prayed to Israel's God, and asked that the first person I met might be one of the two preachers, so that I might be presented to others by him. When I reached the ground, I found the congregation at the stand, and I went to the preachers' tent. The door was closed; I opened it, and found one person within, who proved to be one of my acquaintances.

Before I reached the place, I thought I felt a slight change coming over my feelings—I became depressed; and I have thought it was a foreshadowing of what was to be—some small hint that the meeting would not be as good as I expected. I have sometimes suspected that one reason why the prayer was answered about meeting the preacher, was because it was to be the last time my soul would be blessed at that meeting. I soon found out that the meeting was dragging heavily. This affected my spirits somewhat. In spite of all I could do, my good feelings were gradually leaving me. That camp-meeting was a great failure. Both preachers and people seemed to be but little interested. There was very little singing during the services; and I became still more discouraged, and at last grew quite as indifferent as others. The preaching was good—some of it excellent; but there seemed to be no Holy Ghost in it—that was the trouble. I thought the meeting got worse after my arrival, and I was very sorry I had come; for I felt I had done wrong in leaving Cane Creek. My harp was on the willows; and I never can forget how cold I became as the time passed on. Everybody decided that the meeting was a great failure. It was quite a disappointment to me; and my high expectations all fell to the ground. The Strange

Preacher certainly counted his chickens that time before they were hatched; and I have always regarded it as the coldest meeting I ever attended.

The next great failure—at least, so far as my feelings were concerned—was the one I was at after, I left Lancaster court-house, and declined going to the Salem camp-meeting, though so pressed to do so. My refusing to go there, has ever been a life-time regret. Often, in these days, after the lapse of twenty years, I still imagine I hear the Major imploring me to stay, and telling me, he thought by my remaining he would soon be converted. Do you know what I am thinking of now? It is this: if that man is not among the saved— but, O, my soul! I hope he is—I should dread to meet him on that great day. If I did wrong in not going to Salem, O, my Saviour! forgive me. The meeting I went to from Lancaster was a great failure, and I was very much disappointed.

Many years ago, I sometimes preached at a certain court-house in our State, where our church had done very little, and where the prospect promised no better. As I have already said, I think there are places at which one branch of the church does more good than another; while at other places the same church can accomplish nothing. I think it is all right; and I have often thought that if there were no other church in these States but the Methodist Church, many persons would risk the loss of their souls rather than unite with it; and so with any other denomination. After preaching at that court-house for some time, I was told by a lady, whose sister had married a gentleman of high standing, that her sister had made up her mind to join our church, and wanted to see me before going to the church at my next appointment, as she intended to join at that time, and she thought her husband would go with her. She said, I must let nothing prevent me from coming at that time. Now, this was sufficient encouragement for the Strange Preacher to begin the building of an air castle; so my imagination broke loose from all restraint, and my plan was at once arranged. I first thought of sending word to some of the preachers whom I thought would suit the place, to come prepared to stay at least a fortnight, and to fix up several of their best sermons—thinking, by the help of the Lord, to storm the village. I said to myself, "If that lady joins, and she will be sure to do so, then her husband will do as she does; and then will follow the Major, and the Captain, and many others; and we will have a glorious old-time meeting. And with the Strength of Israel on our side, we will build up the Methodist Church." My thoughts continued to rise still higher; but as I had not lost all control of myself, upon second thought, I resolved that I would not send word to the preachers, as they might have their appointments out. I knew they did not live very far, and I could send word to them afterwards. And thus I settled down on my programme, and went to work to fix up different sermons, which I thought would best suit the place. For example, what would do very well for Shiloh or Tabernacle, would not begin to suit that place. So I thought and thought, and at last had everything arranged for the meeting, and awaited anxiously for the time to come. I grasped my lance, to see if I could hold it as firmly in the rest as ever; and I examined my Damascus blade, to see if there was any rust on its keen edge; and I noticed my gallant steed, to see if all was right—the war harness, and the trappings as they should be. And my war-horse began to champ his bit, and tramp the ground—he was eager for the charge.

The time came, and I bade farewell to my family—for I expected to be absent a long time, for I intended to continue the meeting as long as the prospect was good, as I knew it was best to strike while the iron was hot. My hopes were high, and my flag unfurled. "My banner was on the outer wall, for the cry was still, they come." I was counting on a tremendous time; and thought that, through grace, the Methodist Church would at last take firm hold, where it had failed so long; and then would follow a lengthy notice in the "Advocate," that several preachers had at last stormed the stronghold of sin, at such a place. I had all my plans arranged, and my hopes had not been so high for years. I reviewed my fine sermons over again and again; when, lo! I met some one who told me, that the lady and gentleman alluded to, had a few days ago, joined another branch of the church. O, my soul! what a fall was that! The splendid castles which had been built, vanished, leaving but a wreck behind; and I was overwhelmed with disappointed hopes. After a while, I drew a long breath, and said to myself, "I am so glad I did not send word to the preachers to meet me there." I could not be persuaded to preach from one of my favorite texts; I would draw no pictures; but give them a ten cents' sermon; and leave no appointment. Do you remember those lines in "Henry VIII.," where Wolsey is lamenting his fall?

> "This is the state of man: to-day he puts forth
> The tender leaves of hope; to-morrow blossoms,
> And bears his blushing honors thick upon him.
> The third day, comes a frost, a killing frost—
> And when he thinks, good easy man, full surely
> His greatness is a-ripening—nips his root,
> And then he falls, as I do."

It was many years before I preached at that place again. Among several sermons which I had fixed up, there was one with which I had taken great pains, and the Strange Preacher was quite pleased with it, and read it over and over. He thought it was much better than Moses to Hobab, or the famous passage of the Jordan by Joshua and the children of Israel. But his trouble was to select a suitable place and time for a protracted meeting; for he thought, with the help of the Holy Spirit, whenever that sermon was preached, a great revival would break out; and he would have the pleasure of sending for Brothers L. and H.; and there would be no telling when it would close.

He went to more than one meeting, where he expected to try his favorite, but everything did not suit—something was wanting, and so he would not hold forth from the expected text. But it made no difference; he would bide his time—it would come at last. And so the parson waited for years for the set time to come. He continued to read it over again and again; and concluded he knew it much better than many a lesson he had said to Mr. Stafford, at Platt Springs, in his youthful days. He was sure that whenever that sermon was preached, a great impression would be made, by God's help; that at all meetings he should attend, the presiding elder and others would say, "Come, Brother B., give us what you preached from at such a place; the friends say it was by far your best effort." And he said to himself, "I expect when Brothers M., and S., and R., hear that discourse, they will say, 'The parson fired off one of his big guns to-day;' and as for my much-loved friends, K., and B., and H., they will be carried away with it, and will do some loud shouting before it is finished."

But the suitable place and time, and all other surroundings, had not yet come; and the Strange Preacher began to be afraid he would have to cross the flood, and go to the green fields of Eden, before he delivered his favorite sermon—and what a loss would it be to his many friends. So at last, he resolved to do as Mahomet did when he found that the mountain would not come to him—he went to it. He said to himself, "I have a two days' meeting at Green Pond, and will preach it there, whether things suit or not. I will astonish the natives there, once in their lives, if never again. And then when I take my trip up the country, I will try it at all the camp-meetings I attend;" and so it was arranged. I started for Green Pond, fully convinced that, through grace, a blessed revival would break out. It would take almost an hour to deliver my sermon; my hopes were high, and I felt that all would be right. I anticipated the pleasure of seeing the old class-leader and many others weeping, and a tremendous move through the entire crowd. I expected my voice would be drowned by the loud shouting of the Lord's people, and I would have to stop before I got quite through. I was sure that Brother H.—who generally put me ahead—would be present, and would say to himself, "The best thing to be done, is for me not to add another word, lest I spoil the great impression; but I will call up mourners at once; for this meeting will of course be protracted, and I will have enough to do."

The parson got there on Saturday, full of expectation. There were not many out; and Brother H. said, "Brother B., I wish you would preach to-day, as you are much *newer* here than I am, and there are so few out." Something impressed the parson with this thought—"You had better try the new text to-day, as the turn-out is so small; and should you make a failure, you would not mind it so much as you would to-morrow, when a crowded house will be out." But he thought there was no danger of a failure; and so he would not fire off his right-hand barrel, which was loaded with pelters, but tried something else.

A tremendous crowd was out the next day; several had to remain outside. The services commenced, and the Strange Preacher gave out his text. He hoped, through grace, to sweep every thing before him. For a while, he went on as well as heart could wish—all was bright—the congregation silent and attentive; but, O, my soul! he suddenly forgot what was to come next. He was dreadfully bothered, for he had no recollection of what had been prepared, and could think of nothing to say in its place. The perspiration streamed down his face, and he knew not what to do; but he talked on at random for a few moments, and then sat down. He wished he was anywhere else but at Green Pond; his head was bowed down, for he was in the depth of the valley. After a while, he said to himself, "Since I was determined to preach that sermon, I wish I had tried it yesterday, when there were so few out." If ever the parson counted chickens before they were hatched, that was a time.

More than twenty years ago, I had a two days' meeting at Ebenezer, on the Walterboro circuit. I thought, that if I met with encouragement, I would protract a day or two; and was in hope that it would be kept up even longer. So I went prepared for a big meeting. My friend, Brother Green was then on the circuit, and I left word for him to hurry down as soon as he could. I had some good friends there, and hoped to enjoy myself much with them. There were a few hardened sinners in the neighborhood, whose hearts I thought might be reached, which would create such an impression that it would be wrong to discontinue the meeting. These arrangements were made—such a subject was selected for Saturday, such a one for Sunday, and so on to the end. Now for the meeting, where Brother Alfred

Raysor was the class-leader—a pious, holy man, one of the salt of the earth. I knew Brother Box Robinson would be there, and would sing his old song, beginning—

" The richest man I ever saw,
Was one that begged the most.
And a-begging I will go."

There was a small turn-out on Saturday, and nothing very promising in the services; but on Sunday there was a large congregation—almost a camp-meeting in miniature. I wondered where they all came from; for there were even more than I expected. But, alas! for the preacher! the Holy Spirit was not present, as he had hoped. I became much discouraged, and my feelings were at the opposite extreme of buoyant hope. I was willing to quit, but had promised to wait till Brother G. came; and I began to wish I had not left word for him to hasten down with his flag unfurled. I gave out a meeting for the next day; but had lost all hope of doing anything. On Monday morning there was a little handful, and a very cold time. I could stand it no longer; but sounded a retreat, and called off my forces. I started for home, hoping Brother G. had not got my message; for as much as I respected him, I did not wish to meet him that day. But who was that I saw coming down the road? It was Brother G., with his "banner on the outer wall." I stopped, for I knew what to expect; he pulled off his hat, and bowed very low, expressing much surprise at meeting me, as he had been told I did not expect to return for a fortnight, and wished him to hasten to my help. He said, he expected to find me sweeping everything before me, and to hear that Captain S. and several others had joined the church. O, my soul! what a different tale I had to tell; and I remember his hearty laugh to this day.

There was a neighborhood on the Savannah river, where our church had been doing nothing for several years, and where I was once requested to hold a two days' meeting, with the preacher on the circuit. He told me, I had not been there for a long time, and the friends were anxious for me to go once more; and that as it would be a suitable time we would protract the meeting—so I must go prepared to remain two weeks. I promised him to do so, and made every arrangement; and left home expecting to be absent a fortnight. I thought of it constantly, and concluded what sermons would suit the occasion. I had some beautiful pieces of poetry, which I thought to bring in during the meeting. These I repeated to myself as I went along; I did not miss a word—all was right. After much reflection, I had resolved to use this text on Saturday—"Our feet shall stand within thy gates, O, Jerusalem!" for this would prepare the church, through grace, and they would be ready to come to the help of the Lord against the mighty. On Sunday, the house would not accommodate the large crowd; and I would preach from John xi. 48; and the meeting would be protracted; and on Monday I would take David's charge to Solomon.

When near the church, I stopped for private prayer. The Lord blessed his servant, and I was in fine spirits; and felt almost like clapping my hands, and saying, "Farewell world!" There was only one more house to pass, where I would get some fresh water, and then be ready for the meeting. I drove up to the gate, not expecting to see anybody but the servants, as I expected the family to be at church; but I was quite surprised to see the lady of the house come out. I said to myself, "She is looking for so much company, she could not go out to-day." The water was handed to me; before I drank it, she told me that she did not expect to see me. "What!" said I, "is there not a two days' meeting at the church?" She answered, that they were expecting me four weeks before—that there was a great disappointment when I did not come—the house could not hold the congregation on Sunday; and Brother C. had said he was afraid I was sick, for I was noted for filling my appointments. I never was so cast down, so disappointed, in my life—after riding so far, and not to be expected. I stood for a while without drinking the water, though I was very thirsty. O, my soul! what a fall to all my high hopes was that! I counted on my chickens there; but none of them were hatched.

## LEAF THE THIRTY-FIRST.

A MEMENTO TO MY DEPARTED FRIENDS, THE THREE GREAT HEROES OF THE OLD BARNWELL CIRCUIT, AND BINNAKERS CAMP-GROUND—BROTHERS HENRY HOLMAN, DAVID FELDER, AND GEORGE RILEY.

Henry Holman, all hail! departed friend. I never can forget thee, though thou hast long been removed from my sight. Brother H. joined the church long before I did; and was a whole-souled, devoted Christian—a man of much faith, and hope, and love—a Methodist of the old school, one who possessed a heart-felt religion. He often became very happy, when he would praise God aloud, regardless of the opinions of others; and his house was one of the most pleasant homes for the preachers of the gospel that I ever visited in all my roving life. And his children were worthy of such a father; of gentle, kind, winning manners—loving the church and the blessed Saviour. His wife was a woman among a thousand. I have spent many happy hours with Brother Holman's family. He always met me with a smile, and a shake of the hand, which went to my heart. He filled a high place in my affections, and I loved him much. He was one of the chief supporters of the Barnwell circuit, during the whole of his Christian life; was a class-leader of the primitive order of Methodism; and was famous for his constant observance of all the means of grace—attending church both on the Sabbath and week-day. He was the leader of that same church, by the door of which I rode on the holy Sabbath, with my gun across my saddle; and he told me afterwards, that at the time he had no idea of ever hearing me preach in that house.

I have had the great pleasure of numbering Brother H. among my friends, from the time I first knew him well, till the day of his death; and during the whole time, I think I never saw him, and we met often, but that he was happy and contented. He was fond of attending protracted and camp-meetings; and Binnakers camp-ground was a much-loved place to him—the earth, the trees, were all very dear to him; and I suspect he thought more of the Edisto than of all the other rivers of his native land, because it flowed so near his dear old camp-ground. I know that many of our preachers have not yet forgotten the hero of Binnakers—who generally occupied the same seat, and always appeared to like the preaching so much, no matter who was in the pulpit. He, and all his family, sung well; and it was a great pleasure for me to listen to them. I have attended many glorious meetings with Brother H.; for wherever he went he was a host within himself. I have known several persons, whose presence was a great advantage to me while preaching, and he was one of the men; for I think, with the help of the Lord, I never made a total failure, when the hero of Binnakers was in the congregation, to strengthen me with his inspiring presence. Since his death, I have missed him much; but at no time so much as when trying to preach.

I am thinking now of a time of wonderful power at Binnakers. The vast crowd seemed to be under the influence of the Spirit. The meeting was good from the first, for Dr. Capers was there; and it was a season of rejoicing for the people of the Lord. But the time of which I speak was the 3 o'clock service of the holy Sabbath, and my respected friend, Brother R. Felder, was to preach. He was at a loss what subject to take, and advised with me about it. Preachers are sometimes so situated, and it is a rather unpleasant position to be in. Let me paint the scene for you.

The horn had blown, and a large congregation was waiting. I walked to the stand with Brother F., whose mind was not yet made up. The prayer was over, and he gave out, "Come, let us join our friends above;" which was sung to a new tune. The Holy Spirit descended upon the congregation, bearing every thing before it. Perhaps such a sight was never seen before, at that time-honored place. The interest manifested was deep and wide, for the Eternal Jehovah himself was preaching; and, of course, Brother F. said nothing but "Glory!" and I think Brother H. was as happy as any one else present. Several of the preachers were prostrated in the altar. There was no sermon preached by Brother Felder that evening; for when he finished the hymn, some one requested it to be sung again, which was done. A crowd of mourners came up, and there were many conversions. It was a time never to be forgotten by those who witnessed it.

More than twenty years ago, I had returned from a camp-meeting in North Carolina, and was soon after taken very sick. I was at the gates of death; several physicians were with me, and my life was despaired of. There were two camp-meetings going on at the same time—one at Carmel, and the other at Binnakers; and it was known at both places how ill I was, and earnest prayer was offered in my behalf—and I suspect that had more to do with my recovery than all the doctors put together. One night, there was little hope of my living till morning. At Binnakers, that blessed man of God, Brother Pierce, addressed the church at some length, requesting them to exercise faith while praying for me, and he thought I would be spared to them. Brother Kirkland then invited those who wished to pray for me to come around the altar; and many who were not members of the church came forward. The next morning, Brother H. was sent to see how I was, and found me a little better. He was allowed to see me for a few moments; but was told, that unless he controlled himself, they would send him out. O, how well I remember that morning! Many days after, when I was much better, he came to see me : the doctors were not there, and we had an old-time shout together.

Farewell! dear brother of my soul; I prized thy love much more than the gold of this world. Thy warfare is over, thy pilgrimage is ended, and thou art saved in heaven; and I hope, when the time comes for me to cross the flood, that Brother Holman's sainted spirit, with many other loved ones, will be there, and my blessed Saviour, with his rod and staff, will be with me, to comfort and support me as I cross over the valley.

Father David Felder was one of the best of Christian men that I ever had the pleasure of numbering among my friends. He was worth his weight in gold, more than twice told. He had drunk of the water which the Saviour offered to the woman of Samaria, and thirsted no more for the vanities and pleasures of this world. He was a primitive Methodist in life, dress, and every thing. Whoever travelled the Barnwell circuit in the olden days, will always remember the old class-leader and steward, who always enjoyed the comforts of religion. I do not recollect ever having seen him cast down or depressed; but he appeared to be on the mountain-top at all times—ready and waiting for his summons to the better world. It seemed to me, that through grace, he was one of those sanctified men, who would be found prepared at any time for the Master's coming; and he looked to me, as if you might read these words in his face—"Come, my blessed Saviour; and come quickly." He was one of the chief pillars of the church long before I embraced religion; and he had many tales to tell of the old preachers, and of the days when the few Methodists who were in the District were shunned by others. I respected and revered father Felder much; and I often wished I was as well prepared fer judgment as I thought he was. I have spent many never-to-be-forgotten hours under his friendly roof. He was respected by all who knew him well; though I have heard that in his younger days he was wild and wicked—living without Christ in the world; and that he was convicted in a very remarkable manner. He was at a log-rolling with some friends, where they were enjoying themselves by working and drinking. The work was over, and the spirits had given out before the end of the day; and the party, at Brother F.'s suggestion, concluded to amuse themselves by listening to a sermon which he was to preach. So they gathered around where he was standing on the top of a barrel. He gave out his text, which was simply "Gin;" and spoke at some length on the ruinous effects of strong drink upon the character, health, and fortunes of men who lived such a life; and then spoke of the spiritual ruin which often followed—the eternal loss of the soul amid the flames of hell. Suddenly, he looked down to note the effect of his preaching on the drinking party, and found them all serious, some in tears. He leaped down from his pulpit, and hastened home, deeply convicted, dreading the wrath to come and a sin-avenging God. He did not rest until he found the Saviour in the forgiveness of his sins; and then he joined the church, and became a valiant soldier of the cross—the war-worn veteran of a thousand battles fought in the service of his Master.

I have had the pleasure of being at some interesting meetings with the now sainted patriarch of the Barnwell circuit; and he reminded me of some of those great heroes, who, having followed the fortunes of the son of Jesse, during all his roving life, until he was made king of Israel, became the strong supporters of his throne, some of whom had singlehanded slain hundreds of his foes. Such a warrior was David Felder—one of those immortal men whose names will live for ever. I never met him without feeling that I was in the presence of one of the princes of our Israel. My much-loved father respected him highly, and often said to me, "I wish all members of the church were such Christians as Mr. David Felder." He was a man full of the Holy Ghost, of hope, and of love. But the patriarch of Barnwell circuit and Binnakers camp-ground has long since gone to his great reward. Farewell! father Felder; you, too, have fought the good fight, you have kept the faith, and you have finished your course, and have won the crown.

While speaking of such men as Brothers Holman and Felder, I thought I would be doing wrong to say nothing of my much-respected friend George Riley—the just, the upright, and the Christian hero—the man "without blemish and reproach." As far as I know, he led a blameless life before heaven and earth. He was devoted and thorough-going, fully bound for heaven. And he was a true friend to the preachers on the Barnwell circuit. When I stood up to preach, I was glad to see him in the congregation; for then I knew there was one present who would pray for me, and who was a host within himself. He was a man of few words, but well spoken, and always in the right place. He was serious and grave, but seldom cast down; a man among men, and a hero among heroes; a true knight of the cross, whom heaven loved, and hell respected. I have often enjoyed myself much in his company. It was a pleasure to him and his pious wife for the preachers to go to see them; and they were treated so kindly, that no doubt the heralds of the cross loved to go to that home of the preachers—Brother Riley's house.

But the good man has gone to the rest which remains for the people of God. Farewell! to the three old heroes of Barnwell circuit and Binnakers camp-ground. No wonder that the holy place has seen its best days—that its glory has departed; for the three strongest members have passed away, and there are none to take their places. O, ye departed friends of my soul, I bid you all hail! and I hope you think of me sometimes, while walking the golden streets of the Jerusalem above. I can never forget you. I have seen much of sorrow and trouble since you left met; but my Saviour has often comforted and strengthened me while toiling on through this unfriendly world. Amazing grace has saved me thus far, and I hope will save me to the end of life's pilgrimage, when I hope to meet all the departed loved ones on the banks of eternal deliverance, to part no more; and, O! what a time of rejoicing it will be, when the friends who have loved on earth shall meet in glory, to be separated no more. Happy, thrice happy, dead! you are now for ever freed from the cares and troubles of life, which often press so heavily upon your friends left behind. You were taken home to rest. You were removed from the evil to come. You were spared the sad sight of your ruined country, and its departed glory. You are now saved in heaven, and are rejoicing for evermore. When done with the sorrows of earth, I hope to praise the Lord with you in endless day.

" Our old companions in distress,
  We haste again to see;
And eager long for our release,
  And full felicity.
E'en now by faith we join our hands
  With those that went before;
And greet the blood-besprinkled bands,
  On the eternal shore."

## LEAF THE THIRTY-SECOND.

MEETINGS AT OLD ZION; AND THE LAST FRESHET IN THE EDISTO.

After old Pine Grove was discontinued as a place of worship, old Zion took its place, and was one of the chief places on the old Walterboro circuit. It is on the road leading from Bamberg to Walterboro, near one of the oldest and most famous mills in Barnwell District; but I am sorry to say, I am afraid both have seen their best days. There they stand—but, O, what a falling off! Who, that remembers their former glory, does not now feel sad at their decline?

Old Zion was famous for large congregations, and lively meetings; and the old mill for the great business which was carried on there. But now a very small band meets at Zion, unless an extra occasion brings them from a distance; and, comparatively speaking, but little business is now done at the mill. But look at them in another light. At the mill, cotton was ginned, lumber sawed, and corn and wheat ground, and a great deal of money made—and the physical man was clothed and sustained. At old Zion, the gospel was, and is still, preached—and the spiritual man supported. I see that some persons have recently commenced to repair the mill, which seems to me like dressing up in bridal robes an old maid of three score years; but I hope they will succeed in restoring it to its former prosperity. How would it do for the church, sometimes, to take a lesson from the world? Suppose the friends of old Zion, try to restore, by more prayer, faith, and fasting, the old church to her former glory, and high estate. I wish so much they would endeavor, by the help of the Lord, to bring back the days of "auld lang syne." When I pass by the time-honored house, and think of the crowds which used to assemble there, and the change that has taken place, I feel like saying, "How the ways of Zion mourn, for none come to her solemn feasts." But, O! what blessed seasons I have seen there!—days of immortal remembrance! What a tale that sacred house, and those venerable trees, might tell, could they speak—but how silent they are! O! ye happy dead, who worshipped there, I hope you sometimes think of the old church, and the few friends still left behind; and while praising the Lord in the heavenly Zion, I trust you have not entirely forgotten your old Zion on the Walterboro circuit. I am sad when I pass by there now, and think of the olden times; and that is one reason why I do not have many appointments there now. I hope the friends will excuse me when I say, that I can but weep while contrasting the Zion of '37 with the Zion of '67. O! how sadly have the times changed! Did you ever see a small band of Indians, perhaps only one family, still lingering, still roving over the old hunting grounds where their fathers had been counted by thousands? So it is with the little group of friends still left at old Zion. The old class-leader still lingers near the dear old sanctuary, and I hope he is still enjoying as much of the Lord's presence as he did thirty years ago. The good brother reminds me of Cooper's "Last of the Mohicans." The ancient chieftain sits almost alone, amid the graves of his warriors long since gone to the hunting grounds of the Great Spirit—the last of the Mohicans yet worships the Great Spirit on the earth, and still sings the much-loved songs of his tribe, near the junction of the Lemon Swamp and the Saltketcher. To see the old soldier of the cross, as I expect he is sometimes seen, sitting with his head bowed down, in the old church, waiting for the little band, some one might say, "there is Marius weeping amid the ruins of Carthage." I have heard more than one of the friends of that old hero of the Walterboro circuit, remark, that they did not think he was as happy in his Saviour's love now, as in the days of "auld lang syne." Perhaps not, for I do truly believe from my heart, that I could not have held out as Brother Muse has, had I been similarly situated, for the last twenty years—worshipping at the Zion church, when her glory had departed. Without more grace and help from God than I generally have had, I know it would have been almost, if not quite, the spiritual death of the Strange Preacher. Some persons require a change of scenery and other things, to do well, and I am one of those. When I first joined the church, and after 1 had begun to preach, my loved father, who saw in me a disposition to rove, told me he wished I would confine myself all the time to two churches—Zion and Clark's chapel, preaching at the two alternately, as long as I continued to preach. Now, take twenty of my friends, who know me well, and put it to vote; and I suspect eighteen of the number would say, it would have been the spiritual death of the War Preacher.

During my long rides—for I usually go alone—I have often turned aside, and gone into the old church, and read in the blessed Book of God, and bowed before the heavenly throne, and felt my heart strengthened by my Redeemer. What times of rejoicing I have then had, when alone in the holy place! Many years ago, I was thus alone in old Zion, when some friends, who knew my horse, passed by; they stopped, and came in, and we prayed together, and the Lord of Hosts was with us. I hope the class-leader of Tabernacle remembers that morning, I have, on going there, often found the door locked, but I had been told where to find the key always.

While writing these lines, I have been wondering if the holy angels still hover over the much-loved place, as they did in the olden days; but I am afraid not; and O, my soul! what a pity! We read in the Bible about the angels of the churches; I hope if Zion has a guardian angel, he will never desert the old church. And I trust he will soon begin to come twice, where has been coming once—at least, as long as the "last of the Mohicans" lives, and continues to sing the much-loved songs of his tribe.

Near thirty years ago, I was once going there to an appointment. It was an awful day for travelling—the icy king had thrown his mantle over the ground, and icicles were hanging all around the houses. The young trees were saying their prayers with bowed heads; but the old pines and oaks, like hard-hearted sinners, stood erect. As Brother Durant would say, the storm king was rousing himself from his slumber; and it was a day as dreadful as that night, on which, Thomson says, no man ought to turn his enemy's dog from his door. My dear wife entreated me not to go—that it was wrong to do so, as I might thereby catch my death; also alleging that no one would be there. I told her, I knew three friends would be there; and I did not wish to disappoint them. So I started, but had to dismount occasionally, and walk a little, to keep from freezing. I had some ten miles to go. A young friend of mine, one of the sisters of Zion, although knowing I was noted for filling my appointments, thought I would fail that day, and then she would mark it down with red ink, and show it to me on my next visit to her home; but her husband told her, he expected me to come. She said, "no," she was sure Brother B. would be missing that day. So she sat down near a window, in a warm room (as she told me afterwards), to look out for me, and in case I did not pass, to mark me down as missing. All but five minutes of the allotted time had passed, and she was ready with pen in hand; when her husband said, "there he goes now." I was almost frozen in my stirrups, while the young trees were saying their prayers, with bowed heads, and the old pines, like hardened sinners, stood erect.

When I got to the church, I found no one there, and I walked about for some time to restore my blood to proper circulation; and soon the three expected friends came. We had faith in each other, and sung and prayed together. I remember that holy Sabbath well, and I hope Brother Muse has not forgotten the time. Old Zion, thou dear old house of the Lord! I love thee still! I will love thee always! But I go there seldom now; for it makes me so sad when I contrast the present with the olden time—when Brother Eason Smith and his pious wife, with several others, would greet me so kindly; and when sister Copeland, the sweet singer of the church, would sing my much-loved songs for me; and Brother Muse would pray as if he had a strong hold on the horns of the altar.

I have attended so many glorious meetings there, that I hardly know which to speak of; but must speak of some of the best of them. When Brother Howell—one of our local preachers, who lived in a fine house near the old mill, and who kept one of the best tables on the circuit, and always treated his friends kindly—was with us, laboring with much zeal and earnestness, we had a most glorious meeting. The house was often filled to overflowing. Brother Linda, from Little Swamp, was with us, too, with his flag waving fearlessly. He was fond of singing with his Zion friends in the olden times. . The meeting lasted almost a fortnight, and the blessed Spirit was with us. Brother H. kept an open house for saint and sinner, and made his friends feel quite at home. The altar was often crowded with mourners; and Brothers Muse, and Steadly, and Smith, and Rentz, and many others, seemed to me, if it was the Lord's will, to be ready to bid adieu to this unfriendly world, and go to the green fields of Eden. O, my soul! what immortal times we had at that holy place of prayer! and what shouts of joy went up from the holy sanctuary, as the mourning souls were happily converted, and the angels carried the glad tidings to heaven, that the broken-hearted had been healed, and the sinners pardoned! The few friends who are still alive, will remember the time. I know Brother H. preached and prayed as if he was fully sprung, and swung clear in those happy days of "auld lang syne." Every now and then, the Strange Preacher would clap his hands, and cry out "Farewell world!"

I recollect one night well. It was rather cold for the season, and a fire was burning outside. There was a large turn-out, and we had a season of rejoicing. There was in the neighborhood a gentleman of talent and position, who seldom attended church. For many years, his face had not been seen at that place of prayer and praise. But having heard so much about the great meeting at the mill, I suppose, he made up his mind to attend in a disguise, so that he would not be recognized, except by those to whom he told his secret. He remained outside at the fire, so that he could hear the preaching without going into the house. I have forgotten who preached; but if it was Brother H., the disguised gentleman might have stood farther off, and heard every word. There was a tremendous move in the congregation, and many mourners came up, and the walls rang with the rejoicings of the Lord's people. The persons outside became somewhat interested, and came nearer, that they might see better what was going on inside. One of that gentleman's party stood in the door, so as to be nearer still, and the good Spirit took hold of him, and he was most deeply convicted. The pains of hell were upon him, and he rushed up to the altar, where he fell prostrate, and cried aloud in the agony of his soul. The disguised gentleman became much excited, and wanted to go in to see what was being done to his friend to cause him to lament so. I was told he was kept back by force. O, how I wish he might have been allowed to come in! for then he might have been overthrown by the power of the Highest, and the prince of hell might have lost one of his standard bearers that memorable night. Many united with the church—among them, I think, two of Brother Howell's children. Several were happily converted. From beginning to end, the Lord was graciously manifested in our midst; and the camp of Israel moved on from victory to victory; while the flag of Calvary waved over the ransomed of the Lord.

I remember another meeting which took place there in the olden times, when two of my respected friends from Sumter were with us—Brothers Felder and Richardson. Having been with them so often, I persuaded them to give us a two days' meeting. Both were good preachers; yet there was the greatest difference in the manner and style. Brother F. was a true son of thunder—strong, forcible, and at times powerful—a famous singer, and sometimes overwhelming in prayer. When in strong supplication he besieged the throne of grace, by the help of the Lord, he swept every thing before him, and both saint and sinner would be completely cut loose from their moorings. Brother F. makes you think of a giant of the forest, with a mighty club, driving every thing before him. On the other hand, Brother R. was gentle and winning—stealing softly his way to the hearts of his hearers. At times, he was like a beautiful brooklet, kissing the pebbles as it rolled over them. And then again, he would remind you of a calm, broad lake, with snow-white swans sailing gracefully over its deep water, while the busy fisherman would be seen plying their trade, and while the palaces of the wealthy, and the humble cottages of the honest poor, might be seen mirrored low down in the deep water. And then, again, he would make saint and sinner fall in love with him, for he would remind them so much of some gallant crusader returning from the Holy Land, and winning the fair lady by sweet music played under her window, while the virgin moon wished she were nearer that she might hear better.

I met them at Midway, and pleasantly travelled with them to Zion. It was their first and last appointment there. We had been looking to the meeting with much interest; for I had told the friends of these brethren, and expectation was high. Brother R. had an old friend in the neighborhood—the honorable disguised gentleman; they had formerly been very intimate, but had not met for some time, and Brother R. was anticipating much pleasure from the meeting. He also hoped, through grace, to reach the heart of his old comrade; if no more, to cause him to think more seriously of religion than he had apparently done for years. On Saturday, we had a good turn-out for the day; and the friends were presented to the ministers, and arrangements were made for the different services. Brother R. preached the first sermon; his subject was, the Lord telling the woman of Samaria, that if she had asked of him, he would have given her "the living water." This was, in some respects, the most interesting sermon that had been delivered there for a long time. His introduction was most beautiful; he spoke of the surrounding scenery, and the holy memories connected therewith. The third great patriarch, and his family, and his many flocks browsing on the rich pastures, rose before us as large as life. He also spoke of some of the great events that occurred in that neighborhood; and then the blessed Saviour and his apostles, dust covered and weary, were seen toiling along the highway, while the gentle winds of Palestine stirred their flowing locks. And the kind Teacher, as he passed some striking object in the beautiful landscape, stopped and drew some truthful lesson from the objects before them. And thus he passed on, until he reached Jacob's well, where he sat down weary and faint, while his disciples

14

went for something to sustain the mortal life. And then we beheld so plainly the Eastern woman, as she, with pitcher in hand, hastened to the well. And a sermon which well suited the preface followed. All I heard speak of it were much pleased. Brother H. and myself expressed a strong wish that the sermon could have been reserved for Sunday. That day we dined and spent the night at Brother Howell's. Brother R. was disappointed that his friend was not out, and hoped he would be there the next day.

Brother F. preached that night, and we had quite a crowd out. His loud voice rang through the house and surrounding woods; and Brother H. concluded that he preached even louder than he himself did. What a gracious night that was, through the mercy of God! The Lord was in his holy temple; and his stately steps were heard amid the golden candlesticks. And the servants of the Lord rejoiced in the hope of heaven, when the toils of life should be over, in blessed eternity.

The holy Sabbath was a bright, beautiful day; the interesting services of the morning were over, and the hour for preaching had come. Many persons were out—some coming from a distance. Brother R. delivered the first sermon; but he was complaining of a headache, as he had not rested well the past night. And besides all this, he had heard that his friend was not there, which cast down his spirits very much. He gave us a good discourse, but not equal to the one the day before.

Brother Felder preached the last sermon, and swung clear from first to last. His "banner was on the outer wall, for the cry was, still they come." He spoke loud, strong, powerfully—and the sound of his Master's steps was heard close behind him. The shout of a king was in the camp of Israel; and the Holy Spirit came down upon the congregation. The church roused herself, and came willingly to the help of the Lord against the mighty. Mourners crowded the altar; and a desperately wicked man rushed up, as if fleeing from the open mouth of hell. We had an old-time meeting, which would have been protracted for several days, had it been a suitable time of the year.

More than thirty-one years ago—some time before I began to preach—there was a quarterly meeting at old Zion. Often in those days (I am very sorry for it, but so it was), I would be ashamed to have family prayer before persons who were not members of the church. One night, two ladies, who expected to attend the meeting, stopped with us—one of them my wife's mother, and the other her aunt, who was a member of the church. Her mother was not, and—would you believe it?—I refused to have family prayer before them. No persuasion of my wife prevailed with me. I was at the time an exhorter, and of course did wrong; I ought to have been ashamed of myself. I was told, they expected it, and asked if I did not discharge the duty; but I could not be induced to take up that cross. They sat up late, expecting me to hold forth; but not until they retired, did I o what I had done before—pray with my wife. I felt I had done wrong, but so it was. The next morning, we went down to Zion. I was much cast down, for my wife had told me how sorry she was that I had acted as I did; that her aunt was quite surprised at it. That Sabbath was a famous day at the old church; and all the services were solemn and interesting. The preached word did not return empty; but the good pleasure of the Lord was accomplished. A good impression rested on the congregation; the Holy Spirit was strongly manifested in reproving of sin, of righteousness, and of a judgment to come. The camp of Israel marched on in glorious triumph; and the flag of redemption waved over the host of the Lord. The door of the church was opened, and, to my surprise, Mr. Carson and his wife, who had not long moved down from the up-country, joined, and he is now the leader of Providence. And, to my still greater surprise and pleasure, my dear wife's mother also united with the church. It was a gracious meeting, of happy remembrance, at time-honored Zion. I got a great blessing that day, though I deserved it not; but it was of the free, boundless mercy of the Most High. I was much encouraged—much strengthened; and I went home rejoicing in the hope of immortality, far beyond the "blue throned stars," where sickness and sorrow are known and felt no more.

And I firmly resolved, by the grace of the Lord, that I would never again refuse to conduct family prayer before the world; and thus far I have faced that fire, bless the the Lord, O! my soul.

"But," says one, "what about the last freshet in the Edisto?" I will tell you; but you must not require names. It is not a very pleasant subject to me; which is my reason for putting it off so long. You must know, then, that when the Wandering Arab is much excited, if he receives an unexpected check, or damper to his spirits, the reaction is sometimes tremendous, and the tide turns down the other way, with the force of a mountain torrent, bearing every thing with it. Or, in other words, the preacher is as suddenly depressed, as his spirits have been exalted; and if this comes from an unexpected quarter—from some one whom he considered very zealous, and enjoying much religion—he feels nearly as distressed as the great Cæsar did, when the much-loved Brutus stabbed him. But, alas! for the Strange Preacher; he cannot yield to his fate with the grace that the mighty Roman did.

Well then, my friends, you must know that once in the olden time, in the month of July, there was a very high freshet in the Edisto, a few days before a meeting at old Zion. The time came, we had a large crowd out—persons from a long distance all around. I do not remember who preached, but I know that the impression was very good. It was deep, tremendous, overwhelming, and every thing bowed before it—a time of great excitement. But the most roused up of that great crowd was the Wandering Arab. He was cut loose from all his moorings; and was rushing over the bar, at the rate of thirty miles to the hour. He sprang to his feet, he clapped his hands, and shouted at the top of his voice, "Farewell world!" And he went on shaking hands, expecting to pass through the entire crowd, perhaps even to have gone to some who were outside, and to beg them to let him pray for them. All this time, there was a brother, of whom the parson thought much, seated with his head bowed quite low. The Strange Preacher had noticed him, and expected, that though very quiet, he was enjoying the meeting as much as any one; for you know, it is said, that "still water runs deep." On went the Wandering Arab, shaking hands. Brothers H. and L. threw their arms around him; and his good friend, "the last of the Mohicans," gave him an embrace which he expects to remember on the other side of the flood. And on went the War Preacher, with every flag unfurled, and his "banner on the outer wall, for the cry was, still they come." He clapped his hands, and called out, "Farewell world!" About the eighth person with whom he offered to shake hands, was the gentleman who was sitting very still, with his head bowed down. The parson was so much excited that it was with difficulty he kept his feet. He told the brother, he knew he was enjoying himself very much, and that he was glad to see it; and he hoped they would meet at last, when the warfare was over, in the green fields of Eden, at rest for evermore. The brother slowly raised his head, and with a sigh, "*imo pectore*," from the lowest depths of his troubled heart, and the tears streaming from his eyes, he said, "O, Brother Bellinger, Brother Bellinger! the last freshet in the Edisto has drowned all my corn; and it is too late to replant."

"Tell it not in Gath, mention it not in Askelon, lest the daughters of the Philistines rejoice." O! my soul, what a fall was there! The far-famed War Preacher—the brave soldier of a hundred stricken fields, fell from his gallant steed, as if shot through the heart. We are told, that in ancient times, "the woods, the streams, the flowers, the birds, and the stars all wept," when Bion, the poet, died. And I hope all my friends who read these lines, will feel very sorry for me; for I expect never to forget that mournful fall, and the last freshet in the Edisto.

But it is time to close. All hail! to the old Zion church, and her time-honored class-leader. All hail! to the "last of the Mohicans," who sits almost alone, amid the graves of his warriors long since gone to the hunting lands of the Great Spirit; and who yet sings the much-loved songs of his tribe, near the junction of the waters of the Lemon Swamp and the Saltketcher.

## LEAF THE THIRTY-THIRD.

MY SECOND VISIT TO ROCK SPRINGS CAMP-GROUND, NORTH CAROLINA, AND THE STAR OF H. H. DURANT AGAIN IN THE ASCENDANT.

Well, friends, we were off again for another trip to the far-famed Rock Springs. I met Brother Durant at the place of appointment, and we greeted each other as friends do, who have loved, and who have been separated for a long time. Everything was ready, and after an early dinner, we drove from Lincolnton to the ground in due time. Brother D. had been drilling me since we met, that I might speak loud enough to be heard by the many thousands who would be present. He placed himself about one hundred yards off, and I was to give out a hymn loud enough for him to hear. After trying very often, I succeeded in making him hear. After sixteen years' absence, I was at the renowned camp-ground once more; and the friends who remembered me gathered around, and gave me a warm welcome. The immense multitude did not impress me as at first, for I had become accustomed to crowds; and, although there may have been more persons out than at my first visit, I did not gaze at them with so much wonder. The several hundred tents were still there, thronged to overflowing; but, O, my soul! how many who were there before had passed into the spirit world.

I found many ministers on the ground—both local and travelling—all armed with the panoply of heaven, prepared for battle against the king of darkness. All classes of people, from the highest to the lowest, could be seen there—many from over a hundred miles away, who cared very little for the preaching at the stand, for they seldom went there. Some never went at all; but spent their time in eating, drinking, and talking politics, and everything else but religion. Some met there as on a kind of middle ground, and exchanged visits, and drank wine, and enjoyed themselves as they pleased. Members of Congress met there, to settle national affairs. And there were some present, who dressed so differently from the majority around them, that you wondered what brought them there. They moved about, and talked, and looked, as if they wished it understood that they were not made from the same clay as the crowd around; and they kept to themselves as much as possible. Their motto seemed to be, "I hate the profane vulgar." What cared they about religion or preaching, particularly that of the loud-shouting Methodists? And if, by mere chance, they happened to be at the stand, when there was any noise or excitement, they left at once. Others went there regularly; you never missed them, their places being always filled; but they had no wish to be spiritually benefitted, and if you expected it you would be disappointed—for they were there only to find fault with the services. In their opinion, those preachers were the poorest they had ever heard—they could do better themselves; and as for the singing, that might have done, had it not been quite so loud! They believed in a silent, decent sort of religion—so silent, that no one knew whether you had it or not, and which would not prevent you from attending the theatre, race-ground, or ball-room. And then when they felt like sleeping under a long sermon, they had only to drop their heads. And after a while, when mourners were called up, some preacher would come, who thought they were under conviction, and ask them to let him pray for them—which would be a fine joke to tell their friends when they went home, how the poor man was so cast down when they looked up and smiled in his face, and asked him to excuse them. And they could also tell their friends of a very Strange Preacher who was there, who told them about the old-time heroes and men—about Brutus, and Cæsar, and others—who sometimes made them laugh a good deal, and then again they would cry in spite of all they could do.

Go with me to the good spring not far off—how cool and delightful the water is! But let us turn aside, and sit down on this old log, and notice the different groups as they pass to and fro. Look at that aged couple, how slowly they climb up the hill, with buckets of water, so heavy for them to carry. The most of their children and grandchidren are dead, or gone to the rich lands of the West, or to California to dig for gold—and they are all alone. Are you not sorry for them? Their youngest son is a preacher, and has been travelling for years, from the mountains to the sea-board; and their youngest daughter stayed at home to take care of them, but was taken from them by death, a few months ago. But let me tell you some good news about them—they love the Lord, and are bound for heaven. They joined the church fifty years ago, when Methodism first came into the country; and they have been coming here to camp-meeting ever since the first one was held. They are happy and contented, and expect to cross the flood before long. They have some interesting tales to tell of old times. They have a snug little house in a corner of the yard, which they call the prophet's room. And when the preacher stops there at night, you ought to be there to see how much they make of him; and when he leaves in the morning, the old lady will be sure to have something to send to the parsonage. And they always have a little to throw into the hat when it is passed round. The preachers would be well supported, if all the members were like that old man and his wife, who are carrying water up the hill. They expect a minister to dine with them to-day, and are glad; perhaps it was that they were speaking of as they passed us. Come now, tell me the truth; if you had known all this, would you not have offered to help them?

Look to your right, at that group of young women, who are coming down the hill with pails and pitchers. Notice those two behind the rest, with their arms around each other, with sweet flowers in their hair. The one nearest you has black, the other blue, eyes. Which is the prettiest? It is hard to tell. Do you know what I think of them? It is this—I doubt very much if the Assyrian maiden who won Jacob's heart at the well was more lovely than those two daughters of the old North State.

Now, turn to your left. Did you hear that loud laugh? See those young men with their coats off, and each with a large bucket in his hands. They are coming to the spring for water, and they hope to be in time to help those young ladies. And perhaps they were laughing about which of them should wait on those girls with the flowers in their hair. Let us see who it will be. Now they have all passed. Was it not a fine picture?

But here comes another party of loud-talking men. How rough and savage they look! I suspect they are party of "blacklegs" of the lowest grade; for there are a number of such on the ground, and they were up last night playing cards. They are coming to the spring now, I guess, to take at least two drinks of rum, and then they will retire to the woods, to play until near sunset. Those men are up to any thing that is bad; and I would be afraid to meet those two desperate looking fellows in front, in some lonely place by myself.

But the crowd is constantly passing and re-passing. Who comes next? How silent are those who are now passing! Let us watch them. See, they have passed the spring without stopping. Let us stand up, and notice them as long as we can, and try to find out what they are going to do. Now they stop, and uncover their heads. I know now who they are. They are a company of young men who have been up for prayer, and they have a class-leader among them, and they are going to spend some time in humble supplication before the throne of grace. They will remain out there, even if they miss the next service at the stand; for some of them are expecting to be happily converted before they return. And I suspect this is not the first time they have been out there. Perhaps that class-leader got religion there years ago, and he has a strong faith that some of them will be blessed there this time—for he is full of the Holy Ghost and of power.

Now let us sit down again, and view the groups still coming. There are some six or seven grave, serious-looking men coming down the hill; and I hear one or two of them singing in a low voice. The one who walks behind seems to be in deep study. I suspect they are a party of preachers, coming down to the famous spring, to drink the water fresh and cool—and I rather think the one behind will preach next, which is the reason why he is so wrapped in thought. I do not think he will return with them, but go off to pray for the blessing of the Lord, and to read over carefully the sketch he has with him. I hope we will be in time to hear his sermon, for I suspect it has been well arranged; for report says he is very pious, and much beloved by the church, and that the Lord has blessed him with some fine revivals, and that all are wishing he will be sent back the next year. The preachers have passed back, but I do not see him; I suppose he is now looking to the hills, from whence his strength cometh.

How many different classes of persons have passed! This is a curious world in which we live, is it not?

But who are those coming now? There seems to be something wrong. Hear how loud they talk. And see, they strike together their clenched fists. What can it mean? I suspect one of two things—they must either belong to that party of rowdies, who came to the stand last night after most of the people had left, and only a few remained with the mourners, and behaved very badly, creating quite a disturbance, and doing much to break up the meeting, some of whom the stewards had arrested, and I suppose they are bent on having satisfaction; or, perhaps they are some of those rough customers who will attend camp-meetings, and who have had a quarrel, and are going to the woods to settle the difficulty by a rough and tumble fight. They have passed the spring, so I suppose the last guess was right.

See, that young preacher is returning by himself. And now there are two young persons coming together. Both seem much excited. I suspect they are two happy lovers, and all is again right between them. Some time back, there was a breach between them; for you know it has been said, " true love never runs smooth." They had each sent back the other's letters, and other mementoes, and were quite wretched for months. But while going to the stand last night, it was all made up again. And they are quite alone now, to converse together, and perhaps appoint the wedding day, and also to settle who is to have the pleasure of uniting them for life—

whether the young preacher on the circuit, or the old minister who has charge. Is that not a lovely picture, when 'tis finished by saying, that both are in the same church, and enjoy heartfelt religion? And that was the reason why the lovers' quarrel was made up so easily. I trust they did not see us as they passed, for they were thinking only of each other. Did you notice what a sweet kiss the happy youth gave his betrothed while at the spring? I do not think they saw us.

I wonder who that large party of men are, who are coming yonder. They must be conversing on some very interesting topic. One takes out a piece of money, and hands it to another. They have been for some time trying to swap horses, and that money paid closed the bargain.

See that other party approaching now—one talking while the others are listening. He is the same young man you saw in the preachers' tent yesterday, who was so very polite. He is a candidate for Congress, and is trying to make those men believe, that unless he is elected, the government will fall to pieces. On their return, he seems as much interested as ever.

But who are those now going by? A party of women, with bold, wicked front, and painted faces, and gay dress. Those fallen ones are they of whom the wise man said, "Let not thy heart incline to her ways. She has cast down many wounded; her house is in the way to hell, going down to the chambers of death."

Do, my friends, excuse me for having kept you waiting so long; but I wished to show you some of the many sights that were to be seen at that famous camp-ground.

The horn had sounded, and the time for preaching had come, and the young minister was in the pulpit. What immense multitudes of immortal souls bound for eternity were before us, who were sailing on the river of life which empties into the ocean of eternity! As they lived here, so will it be in the world to come; for "he that soweth to the flesh, shall of the flesh reap corruption; but he that soweth to the spirit, shall of the spirit reap life everlasting." How far, do you think, those thousands could have been heard, as they sung with strong, clear, up-country voices? As far as Beatty's Ford, on the Catawba river, which was a few miles off? If the wind was blowing that way, perhaps they might have been heard most of the distance. What strong voices they had! Do you think a preacher with such lungs could ever break down? The prayer was over, and the young preacher gave out his text—but I have forgotten what it was. He appeared to be deeply in earnest, and to weigh well what he was saying. His words came from the heart, and went to the hearts of his hearers. And how much of hope and truth was in that glance which he occasionally raised to the heaven above. His subject was well arranged; and as he went on, he became still more deeply interesting. I was sorry to hear the loud crying of that baby far back in the crowd, and was glad when the mother quieted it so soon. And then those dogs barked so loud; how much better had it been, if they had been left at home. But at last every thing became quiet, and nothing was heard but the voice of the preacher—who was telling us of the green fields of Eden. How he wept when he told the sinners of the joys of the better world—where so many of their loved ones had gone, and where they would never go, unless they repented of their sins. His feelings became too strong for him, and he sat down. Then some one got up, and at once invited mourners to the altar. They went up, weeping and begging for mercy. And there was a loud shout heard: some good man—whose son had strayed very far from the right path, and seemed bent on destruction, and who was at last convicted, and made to dread the wrath to come—was rejoicing over his returning son.

"But," says one, "what about H. H. Durant, the great revivalist?" He was moving and directing the form and order of the great battle; and was overlooking the entire battle-field. He was the great champion of Prince Immanuel's forces—that is, as to the troops on earth. He was the presiding elder, and controlled every thing—planning the different attacks on the powers of darkness, and his presence alone was a host, whether he spoke or not.

Saturday night had come, and it would soon be the hour

for service. Brother Durant and myself had been talking of how many persons we thought could be seated under the arbor, independent of the multitudes who would surround the stand, accommodating themselves as best they could. We made a calculation, and concluded that near six thousand could be seated. We had a great season of grace from the presence of the Lord that night. Did you ever hear Brother D. preach when the Holy Spirit was with him—when he soared high, and took the crowd with him, far above the "blue throned stars?" Did you ever hear the shout of a great crowd, while he was speaking of the glories of the better land—loud enough to be almost heard by the sleeping dead? That was the way he preached at Rock Springs. And it seemed to me that he took such lofty flights, you might almost have heard the harps of the redeemed, as they walked the golden streets of the Jerusalem above. It appeared to me, during the meeting, that the battle seemed so evenly balanced—the tide of victory changing from one side to the other, as if each would gain the day—that a stranger looking on could not tell which side would eventually triumph, "for each adverse host was gored with equal wounds." But if H. H. Durant would show himself, the Lord being his great help, the victory would be won by the host of Israel. I know I am not the best judge, but I thought Brother D. must have suited the people of Rock Springs as well as they had ever been suited. But he did not preach as often at those meetings as he might have done, in my opinion. He was glad to see all the preachers at work; and I suspect the prince of hell was more or less alarmed when Brother Durant was present, and in full force—for he could not tell when he would suffer most, whether when his enemy was preaching, exhorting, or praying, for he was tremendously powerful at each engagement.

I have been three times to Rock Springs, and I think Brother Durant was the man for that place, if there was one in the Conference.

We had a glorious time; and Brothers Hill, Asbury, and others, came up gallantly to the help of the Lord, and bore themselves bravely in the thickest of the fight, driving the powers of darkness from the strongholds which they had held so long. And I rejoiced when I saw those good men and true passing through the crowd, singing, exhorting, and praying, while the shouts of happy converts climbed the hills of glory.

While thinking of H. H. Durant, I am reminded of one of the scenes which took place before the classic walls of Troy. It was doubtful for a long time which party would gain the victory, but it was at last decided in favor of Troy by a mighty chieftain, whom Homer calls Sarpedon, and of whom he thus speaks—

> " Nor Troy could conquer, nor would the Greeks yield,
> Till the great Sarpedon towered amid the field—
> A chief who led to Troy's beleaguered wall
> A host of heroes, and outshone them all."

My friends, did you ever read Sir Walter Scott's "Ivanhoe," where he is describing the great passage of arms at Ashby? I hope you have not forgotten that field of honor. Do you remember the knight who was called the Black Sluggard? Brother Durant might be compared to him, at more than one of the meetings at which I have been with him. Do you remember how that knight stood aloof from the general battle, taking no part in it, until he saw that the time had come when his party would be routed without speedy help; then how he would shout his battle cry, and bear down on the foe with the strength of a falling avalanche? So, while the Strength of Israel was with him, have I seen Durant do, on more than one battle-field; and that was how he did at Rock Springs. Do you remember, again, the fight at the castle, when the friend of the knight was sick and imprisoned; and when the battle was described to the wounded man, by a spectator, so much to the life, that he said he would give all that his heart loved most upon earth, for the pleasure of fighting for one hour, in such a well-contested field, under such a chief? I regard it as a great honor, which I ought never to forget, that the War Preacher, once in his life, at Rock Springs, did battle for glory and for heaven, while H. H. Durant led the charge.

It was Sunday; and the great hour of the meeting had come, and an immense crowd was present—I presume, from eight to ten thousand persons were in and around the stand. I was requested to go with others around the tents, and try to form some idea of the number of persons who would not come to the stand; and, after looking about, we concluded that from two to three thousand were still absent from the stand. But we returned in time to hear the sermon; and I think it was Brother D. who preached, and that he gave us one of his happiest sermons. It seemed to me, on several occasions, that while he only stood up in the altar or pulpit, and leaned over the book-board, and shouted aloud, or only sung one of his much-loved songs, the Spirit being with him, that a victory was gained, as if some strong sermon had been preached. Do you remember, friends, when the Trogans had set fire to the vessels of the Greeks, and their final ruin seemed as if then come, that Achilles came out unarmed, and standing on the top of the wall, shouted out aloud three times; and that at the sound of his voice, all Troy fled back affrighted, and the vessels were saved? Thus it was with Durant at Rock Springs. It appeared to me, if he only shouted, sung, or prayed, it was a battle fought and won for the hosts of the Lord.

## LEAF THE THIRTY-FOURTH.

MY FIRST VISIT TO SPARTANBURG, WHERE I HAD TO PREACH MORE THAN THE TWO PROMISED SERMONS.

While on my second visit to Rock Springs, with Brother Durant, I became so desirous of returning home, that all his efforts failed to persuade me to remain longer. So he agreed to let me off, if I would promise to preach two sermons in Spartanburg, as I passed through. I was sent there by Dr. Miller—a gentleman of much worth and respectability, a member of the church, and a friend of the preachers, and one of the leading men of the old North State. Brother D. gave me a letter of introduction to Brother Moore, in which he told him I was to preach two sermons—the first to be on the night of my arrival. I reached Spartanburg late in the evening, and went to Brother M.'s, and delivered my letter; and requested him to have the bell rung, as I wished to preach my first sermon that night, and I intended to preach my second the next evening, and then leave. He told me, it was so late that but few persons would be out; and urged me to wait until the next evening, when he thought I would have a better turn-out—and I at last consented to do so.

It was rumoured the next day that I was in town; and I had an opportunity of looking about, and of becoming acquainted with Brother Bobo, and several other friends, who treated me with much respect. I also had the pleasure of seeing sister Wright—a lady of much faith and love, who was one of the old-time Methodists, and was well known and respected by all; few such are seen among us these days. Brother Mouzon was on the circuit—a man much beloved and esteemed by the church, wherever he has travelled. And he was, perhaps, the most popular preacher that ever was sent on the Walterboro circuit, and one of the best in the South Carolina Conference. I was warmly greeted by him and his family, and felt at once quite at home; and he made me do the most of the preaching.

At my first appointment there was a good turn-out. There was only one more sermon, and then my promise would have been fulfilled, and I could leave for home. But the Holy Spirit had work for me to do that I knew not of, and I found Brother M. to be of much help to me. His advice, his strong faith, and his prayers were a host on the Lord's side against the powers of darkness. On the second night, the presence of the Lord was so manifested, that the friends earnestly requested me to remain; and I thought myself I ought to stay longer, for there was evidently a good work going on. Many of the mourners were much affected, and appeared deeply in earnest. The brethren, too, were becoming more zealous; and in the congregation there appeared to be more attention than usual; and now and then a shout would be heard in the camp of Israel, and the Spirit of the Lord was abroad in the crowd doing his holy work. And thus things passed on for some time.

One night, as is often the case, I became cast down; and having been very desirous before leaving Brother D. of returning home, I said publicly, that I thought I would leave the next day—but Brother Mouzon and others so entreated me, that I resolved to remain. A lady of position and much intelligence sent me word by a friend to be sure to remain, for there was a much greater impression on the people than I thought, and that I would be doing wrong to leave. She was the same lady who gave me the name of Wandering Arab. So I decided to remain a few days longer; and Brother M., who is a very pleasant man, and fond of a harmless joke, said the next thing to be done was to apprize the friends of my determination to stay, and that I must be paraded on the streets, so that all might see I had not left. And so I had to walk about with him through the business part of the town, as he said, that all might know that the War Preacher was still at his post. I was glad when the marching about was over. And from that time the meeting continued to increase in interest—the whole place was under religious influence, and members from other churches came forward and took part in the services; and some of the children of the chief families were among the mourners and converts of the meeting. The congregation generally remained after preaching, singing and praying together. And some of the brethren were very useful in pushing on the work of the Lord, which was widely extending, embracing all classes of the people. By this time I had been to see several families of our church, and as usual, I tried to be engaged in the service of my Master—advising and praying with them all the time; for I think almost as much good is done in that way as by the preaching of the word. Moreover, many persons from the country, who had heard of the meeting, were present with us, thus adding to the pleasures of the occasion. But of course, there were some there, as at all such places, who did not seem much pleased with what was going on—only as it served to pass away time, or to spend what is termed an idle hour. And doubtless there were some present to find fault with and make sport at what they saw.

One night in particular, there was a great outpouring of the blessed Spirit, and I have seldom seen a more general interest than was then manifested. Some of the members were, perhaps, more influenced than they had ever been before; and some were at length prostrated by the Holy Ghost, which rested upon them. Brother M. himself, was much more affected than any of us had seen or heard of before. He seemed to be completely transported with holy, happy thoughts, as if he was exalted to the third heaven, far beyond the "blue throned stars;" as if he heard the hallelujahs of heaven; as if he was hearing the sweet harps of glory. I have been to hundreds of places where the Lord's work was much revived, but to very few where there was more of the demonstration of the Holy Spirit. By this time, there were several bright and happy conversions among those seeking the forgiveness of their sins; and the voice of rejoicing was heard among the children of the Lord; and some desperate spirits on the way to destruction, rushing like the horse into battle, were arrested, in their mad career, and were ready to close in with the offers of salvation. Several said there had not been such a religious feeling in their midst for many years. I rejoiced very much, and praised the Lord for his gracious displays of power, and for the hope of eternal life when free from the trouble of earth.

Brother Mouzon surprised me one night, by saying to me, that I had disappointed several persons very much, who had been looking for some manifestation on the part of the War Preacher, which they had been led to expect; and that he was afraid, if they were not soon gratified there would be a falling off in the interest of the meeting; and he said that was why the crowd remained so late at the last service, and they said that if the display did not take place the next night, they would not come again, as they had so often been dissappointed. I asked him what it was. He said, he had told them that at times I had been known to wave the flag for the friends, which always resulted in a happy effect, and that he told them he thought I would do it there, and that there was a strong wish in the congregation to see the waving of the War Preacher's banner. He also told me, that his wife and sister took it by turns to stay at home with the children; and whenever it was his wife's turn to remain with them, she almost cried at the thought of its being done in her absence; and he requested me to do so the next night. I told him I would, if the Lord would grant us a good meeting. I suppose it is generally understood that I am a very singular person and preacher; for which reason I am allowed to do what for other persons would be considered quite out of order; for strange persons are expected to say and do strange things. So the next night, there was the largest turn-out that we had yet had; and one could see that there was something unusual on foot. I had been praying for the divine strength of Israel to be granted to us on that occasion; and I remember well what a gracious season of rejoicing we had. The stately steps of Prince Immanuel were felt and heard among the golden candlesticks; and the right hand of the Lord did valiantly in the great crowd present. The sermon was over, and the excitement was very high; and I thought that the time had come. So I told them I was sorry to learn that several persons had been much disappointed at not seeing the War Preacher wave his flag for the congregation; and that I understood, among the ladies particularly, there had been a great expectation, and that I did not have the heart to keep them longer in suspense. I then gave the proper order, and the entire crowd —men, women, and children, saints and sinner—faced the music splendidly. They rose to their feet as if moved by one impulse; and the banner was waved in the name of the Lord of Hosts. Such a glorious time I have seldom witnessed in all my roving life of more than thirty years from Montgomery to Fayetteville. O, my soul! praise the Lord for that immortal night in Spartanburg. The meeting was kept up till near twelve o'clock; and I spent nearly a fortnight, embracing two Sundays, in the place.

So I had to preach more than the two sermons which I had promised Brother Durant; and he told me afterwards that he expected it to turn out just as it did; and that from the day I left him, till he heard from me, he prayed much oftener for me than he had ever done in the same length of time before. When I left, the meeting was still going on. It is fifteen years since the time of which I have been telling you; but I was there again recently, of which visit I expect to tell you in another number.

## LEAF THE THIRTY-FIFTH.

HOW THE PROTRACTED MEETING AT G—— WAS BROKEN UP, WHEN THE GHOST SHOOK HIS GORY LOCKS.

Many years ago, I was at a camp-meeting on the Cooper River circuit, with Brother C. B., the presiding elder of the District, and Brothers M. and S., and several others. I remember but very little about the meeting; but I will say that I was treated with the same kindness and respect by Brother B. that I have always enjoyed ever since I have had the pleasure of knowing him. I have also known Brothers M. and S. for many years, and I respect and love them much. When absent from them, if I should be asked which of the two I would rather see, I would say, Brother M.; but if I was going to leave them both at the same time, I would rather shake hands with Brother S. last, for I expect I could feel his grasp the longest. If I was sick and in trouble, and both the true friends were present, I would wish Brother M. to pray for me first, and then Brother S. If I wanted a sermon to be preached particularly for the church, Brother M. should do it, of course; but if I desired a great effort to be made to reach the hardened sinner's heart, and if there was a score of preachers present, I would choose Brother S., and request him to preach the same sermon that he did at Centre camp-ground, North Carolina, when I was present.

Well, friends, we all met at the stand on Monday morning for the last public service. A chapter was read, a hymn sung, a prayer offered, a benediction pronounced, and we were dismissed. Brethren M. and S., and, I think, another, whose name is forgotten, and myself, left together; and how pleasantly the hours passed by, with those dear brothers in Christ, while I could not tell which I liked best—Brother M.'s hearty laugh, or Brother S.'s grave smile. The houses and trees seemed to fly by us, as we hastened onward to the village of G——, where a kind welcome awaited us. I have often thought, if I had known what was before me for the evening, I never could have enjoyed myself as I did. But so it was—the Strange Preacher, so famous for the wild wanderings of his fancy, never once thought of what awaited him. I have often thought, what a blessing it is, that we do not know what awaits us in the swiftly coming future; for if we did, how many of us would drink the cup of sorrow twice, when once is more than we can bear aright, without the help of Heaven. So it was a good thing for the Strange Preacher, that he did not know what was in store for him; or he never could have enjoyed himself so much that evening. Not even M.'s laugh, or S.'s grave smile, could have made him forget the coming trouble.

But, as I have said, we got to the village at last, and sister S. met me with the same calm smile with which she had years before welcomed me with in the village of B——, and I soon felt at home in her friendly presence.

After we had rested and refreshed ourselves a little, and when I was anticipating a very pleasant time, a note was presented to Brother M., from a preacher of another denomination, who had been for several days carrying on a protracted meeting in the place. The writer said, he understood that there were several Methodist ministers in the village, and he requested one of them to preach for him that night; that he would take no excuse, for out of so many, he hoped there was one who would grant his request. Brother M. sent word back that one of us would do so.

Now, you must know, that during the meeting then going on, it had been declared boldly from the pulpit, "that once a man had been converted—that once he had become a child of the Lord—never mind how great a sin he might commit, he was still in the favor of the Lord, and that if even he should die without repenting of it, he would nevertheless be sure to go to heaven—that he could not be lost." The preacher made mention of David's great sin; and said he was sure of heaven, if he had died without repentance—for having been once a child of the Lord, he could not have been lost. Some one who heard it, told us there was no mistake about this having been said; upon which Brothers M. and S. made up their minds that no one present should preach the requested sermon, happen what might, but the Wandering Arab; and that he should not even be permitted to choose his own subject. I saw at once what was before me, and determined to escape if possible—to leave no stone unturned to save myself from what I saw staring me full in the face. So I begged very hard for some one else to fill the appointment. I told my two brethren it would do so much better for one of them to preach; for I had several relatives and friends who were members of that church, and for their sake, if no other, I would rather not do so. But it was all in vain. I took them aside, one at a time, and entreated them, for the sake of the pleasant memories of "auld lang syne," to let me off; but it would not do—they remained immovable. So I said, if I must preach, I thought several other subjects would suit much better—either "Moses to Hobab," or "I would not live alway," or "My feet shall stand within thy gates, O, Jerusalem!" But they said, nothing would suit so well as, "Solomon, my son;" that the ghost must shake his gory locks. I told them I had never been so situated before, and had no heart to face the music; and that the War Preacher never would return from that field, with his flag waving fearlessly, and his lance held strongly in the rest, as I knew they wished him to do. But they would not yield. They said none but the Strange Preacher should fill the appointment, and his subject should be chosen for him, and that he should reserve his whole strength for the "casting away for ever." Alas for me! I could not prevail with my friends. So I said that I had always found sister S. kind to me, and I would go and ask her to save me. I told her of my trouble, and entreated her to help me. I told her, I thought "the passage of the Jordan by the children of Israel," much more suitable—that I remembered how she enjoyed it that night at B——; and that I knew, as Brother S. thought so much of her, he would give up if she asked him. But she said, that in her opinion, there was nothing, from Genesis to Revelation, that would do so well as "Solomon, my son." I felt that I was doomed—that it was all over with me. But I resolved to make another effort; so I went back to my brethren, and urged and entreated them; but all in vain. I promised to come to any of their meetings, and to stay as long as they wished, and to let them choose all the subjects for me; but they would not yield. S. no longer smiled gravely, but seemed more firm than ever. He recalled to my mind that scene in the "Lady of the Lake," where the brave knight, surrounded by his foes, placed his back against a rock, and then, drawing his sword, said, "This rock shall fly as soon as I." I was told by both of my friends, that they would never think as much of me as they did before, if I did not preach from "Solomon, my son," and make the ghost shake awfully his gory locks, and reserve my strength for the "casting off forever." Before yielding finally to his fate, the Strange Preacher went to sister S. once more; and the gentle lady would have come to his rescue this time, but M. and S. had been there already before him. He told her, he never felt so little like preaching as he did then; that the fame, small as it was, that he had won in many a desperate battle, would all be lost that night; for that he had no heart, no strength, to break a lance in such a field as was before him. She replied, that she was very sorry for him, but he must face the fire; that she would pray for him more than ever; and that M. and S. had set their hearts upon it, and would remember him before the throne of grace—that the ghost must walk the stage and shake his gory locks.

And so we started to the place of appointment. The sweet Swan of Avon tells us that "Time travels with different degrees of speed with different persons; that he walks with some, and trots with others; that he ambles with some, and gallops with others; and that with some he even stands still." But I think he must have moved as fast as "the weaver's shuttle," with the Wandering Arab to the place of trial. If he walked by the side of M. and S., he was told to remember "Solomon, my son;" and the Strange Preacher wished himself far on the other side of the Savannah river, or anywhere else but in the village of G——. And if he passed to the side of sister S., he was told not to forget the "casting away forever," and she would not be so hard to move the next time he wished to get off from preaching.

We arrived at the place of worship, which was at a private house. It would have been a small turn-out for a church, but was a very good one for the place. The preacher who wrote the note met us very friendly; but I suspect, if he had only known what was to come, that invitation would not have been sent. But the other minister, who had made the declaration we had been told of, seemed a little distant; and I guess, if he had foreseen what was to come, he would have been found missing. I had to stand very near him, and could almost have touched him with my hand. I gave one last glance at my friends—there was no hope left. And feeling like the man who had all the bridges burned behind him, and knowing there was no way of retreat, I resolved at last to go the whole figure, hoping I might never see the village of G—— again in this unfriendly world, if I had to be so unpleasantly situated.

Song and prayer were over, and the text was read out—it was, " Solomon, my son." The Strange Preacher then looked at M., and the glance which was returned said plainly, "that's right, face the music;" and S.'s serious face said plainly, "do not forget the gory locks;" while the expressive countenance of sister S. said, "I am praying for you, but remember the 'casting off forever.'" Many of you, my friends, have often heard me on that subject. But on that occasion, I felt very differently from what I have done, as often as I have tried to preach from it. Once, for a moment, when excited by what I was speaking about, I almost forgot my surroundings. But on I went, drawing still nearer to the much dreaded passage; and sometimes, during the short pauses I made, I almost made up my mind to take "French leave" of those most dreaded points; but I knew if I did, my friends would be done with me forever.

Still I went on, putting off the great trouble as long as possible; but. at last the much-feared Rubicon rose before me, overflowing both banks. I paused—I felt more than tongue could tell—I turned once more to my friends, to see if there was any pity for me in their eyes. Alas! there was none. And I at once made up my mind to do or die. I looked to Heaven for help, and unfurled my broad banner to the breeze; and I felt like saying, "Once more, my friends, to the breach, once more." I drew my Damascus blade, and threw away the scabbard; I spurred my gallant charger on, and swam the Rubicon which was overflowing both banks. And when I stood once more upon the firm earth, I said to myself, "Farewell world! for with the help of the Lord, I will go the whole figure once in my life, if never before. I will raise the ghost, and he shall shake his gory locks; and I will spread myself on the 'casting away forever,' so that all this congregation, both saints and sinners, will remember the Strange Preacher in the village of G—— to their last hour." And I paused a moment, to gather all my strength for what was to come.

I painted the king of Israel on his death bed, with the great men of his kingdom around him, and as, perhaps, he thus slowly and seriously expressed himself: "My dear son, you will soon fill my throne; remember what I now say to you. That sad day of which I am going to speak, was before you were born, my son. I loved the Lord, I was fully bound for heaven; for I was a man after the Lord's own heart. One day, in early morn, I offered prayer to the Holy One of Israel, with as much faith and earnestness as ever; and if I had died then, I would have gone safe home to glory. But before the sun had gone down, I had sinned—I was guilty of a great crime, and deserved death by the law. If I had died that night, without repentance, I would have gone to hell. O! my son, what a fall was that! But that was not all. I sinned still more, in the sight of earth and heaven. I caused the death of a brave man—the noble Uriah. If it had not been for me, my son, that man might have been now standing with those heroes who are present, and whose names will never die. If I had died then, my son, without repentance, if there is a hell for the wicked, I would have found it. O! Solomon, never forget what I now tell you. If you forsake the Lord, and do not return to him, he will cast you off for ever. Those persons who have never professed to love the Lord, cannot forsake him; for they have never belonged to him. When I had thus so greatly sinned, if I had then died without repentance, I would have been eternally lost, and I never would have reached the blessed Canaan above—where the pious Jews of all ages have gone—where the sainted Samuel and my much-loved Jonathan are now happy for ever. One day, the prophet Nathan came to me with a message from the Lord; he told me there was a poor man, who had only one lamb, that lay in his bosom, and ate at his table, and was to him as a child; and that there was a rich man, who had large flocks;'and a traveller stopped all night with him, and he took the only lamb from the poor man, and dressed it up for the wayfaring man. And I at once said, he should die. Nathan said, I was the man, and charged me with this great sin. An awful conviction at once possessed my soul; and when the morning came, I expected to be in hell before night; and when the night came, I was afraid to go to sleep, lest I should awake in the pit. And I felt sometimes almost tempted to take my own life; but I knew if I did, I would only the sooner be cast off forever. And then, when worn out with watching I dropped to sleep, it was to dream of the noble Uriah, and cruel murder. And often, when I was awake in the still hour of midnight, the ghost of Uriah would stand before me in his bloody robe, with his death-wound in his breast, and his dark hair all clotted with blood, and he would shake his gory locks at me, and say, 'You murdered me, and you will, without repentance, burn forever in hell.' And feeling more than tongue can ever tell, I would at times reply to the spirit, as he stalked to and fro, with his noiseless steps, before my couch—' How can you say I did it? You fell in battle, by the hands of the children of Ammon!' But he said, 'You told Joab to place me there, and when the fight began, to leave me alone. I will shake my gory locks at you, for you did it; and without repentance, you will burn in hell forever.' The spirit would at times come very close to me— within arm's length,'and say, 'You remember the time when you sent to our camp, to our Captain Joab, to send me to you; and you gave me to eat from your own table; and when the next morning, you found out I had not gone to my house, you asked me why I did not go?' And then, my son, the ghost seemed to come so near, that his bloody robe almost touched me. And he asked me if I had forgotten his reply—that he knew I never would forget it. And the spirit said, 'I told you that the host of the Lord, and my lord Joab were in the open field; and you sent me back to the camp with my death-warrant in my pocket. I was told where to stand. The enemy rushed out, and I was left alone. I will shake my gory locks at you, for you caused my death; and without repentance, you will burn in hell forever.'"

Much more was said; but I must hasten to the close. The ghost played well his part: he walked the stage, shaking awfully his gory locks. The preacher did his best on the "casting away forever." And before he sat down, he spoke as he always does while preaching from that text: he dwelt upon King David's repentance, and his restoration to the favor of the Lord; and that perhaps he said to Solomon, with a smile of heaven upon his dying face, "My son, whenever you read that Psalm which has these words in it—'As far as the east is from the west, so far has the Lord removed my sins and my transgressions from me,' remember that I then had repented, and the Lord had forgiven my sins, and restored me to his favor once more." And the king of Israel was represented as taking his departure from earth, escorted by holy angels, to Abraham's bosom.

The parson, before sitting down, turned once more, and looked at his friends. The expressive glance which M. and S. gave him, seemed to say, "Your banner hung on the outer wall to-night; and we will let you choose your own subject the next time." He then turned to sister S. The same smile was on her face that he had seen there years before, at Bennettsville, when herself and husband, by their very kind greeting, made him so soon forget his long, weary ride from Fayetteville. The last hymn was sung, and the last prayer offered to the throne of grace; the benediction was pronounced, and the protracted meeting at G—— was closed.

# LEAF THE THIRTY-SIXTH.

### TWO VISITS TO GEORGETOWN BY THE STRANGE PREACHER.

Some fifteen years ago, I went on my first visit to Georgetown, to attend our Conference, with my dear friend, Brother L. B. Varn, who was ordained there. It was my first trip on a steamboat, and for a while I enjoyed it very much. The ocean scenery was novel and interesting to me, until I became sea-sick, when all pleasant feelings at once left me, and I was cast down and discouraged, and wished myself at home.

I had read so much of Georgetown during the days of Marion and Horry, that I had often wished to see the time-honored place. When we got there, we were met by a crowd on the wharf, among them many of the preachers; and I was introduced to a number of persons. My sea-sickness had not entirely left me. Brother Varn and myself had our places allotted to us, where we were pleasantly situated, and treated kindly; but it was rather far to walk to Conference. The next morning we were in the assembly of preachers. There were over a hundred present, and Bishop Andrew presided. He was the right man in the right place. I saw many familiar faces—some of whom smiled at me, some nodded, and others came over and shook hands. The Conference at times seemed to be attending very closely to the business before it; and at times something rather serious would be brought up, and then all but the members were excluded—which was rather unpleasant to me at first, but after a while I became accustomed to it. I saw several of the chief men of the Conference—men who had made their mark in the world, and whose names were known to fame. I saw some venerable men, whom the church loved much, and whom the world respected. They were known and read of all men, and their record was on high. I noticed some one speaking to the presiding elder of the District, Brother W., who rose up and said, he understood that Brother B., of the Walterboro circuit, was in the room, and he hoped he would preach in such a brother's place, who would not be able to fill his appointment. But I had not yet gotten over my sea-sickness, and was in the act of rising to ask to be excused, when Bishop Andrew remarked, that he understood Brother B. was always ready; and I felt that there was no escape for me. I was in a bad state for preaching; but I took something to relieve me, and tried to do as well as I could; and trust there was some good done. Brother Varn concluded the services for me. I think I learned something in that Conference, for those preachers dealt very plainly with each other; and if a brother needed reproof, he got it well put on, you may depend on it. I witnessed all the services of the holy Sabbath; and I hope the Lord owned and blessed that Conference Sunday in Georgetown. Bishop Andrew gave us a very strong, forcible, and impressive sermon, which was after the fashion of sermons to which I love to listen. The ordination service was quite solemn to me, and I trust was so to all present.

The last night came, and we were in the church to hear the appointments read—which I enjoyed very much. The house was crowded, every place seemed filled; but the crowd was quiet; and the venerable Bishop rose, and gave his last advice to that body of ministers before reading out the appointments. There was a short pause before the names were called out. Let us look around a little. What a picture! How eager, how wistful some of those preachers looked! Several of them were on very pleasant circuits the past year, and were hoping to be sent back to the same place. Perhaps the last thing some wife said to her husband before he left was, "Tell the Bishop, I say, 'please send you back, and I will pray for him more than ever.'" There was another one who expected to be sent back; and how sorry he would feel if he knew that his presiding elder had been told by the stewards, that they did not wish that brother to be sent back; so he was not returned. There was another preacher who had been two years on the same circuit, in the up-country, and he was wishing to be sent to another one near by; and I suspect he was quite surprised when he found he would have to go to the sea-shore. And there was a presiding elder, who had been two years at work on one district, and was well pleased; but the general wish was that he might be changed; and I guess he was somewhat surprised when he heard that he was to go to some rough circuit in the up-country. Several ladies were present, with their husbands, fathers, and brothers, who were also interested in the reading of the appointments. You could see some of the preachers change countenance: their faces were first pale, and then flushed; and then there were others who seemed perfectly indifferent. They had become accustomed to change, and did not mind it much. But some were feeling more than they were willing to confess, and that indifference was only assumed. Did you notice that brother who was looking so earnestly at the Bishop? He had an interview with him the day before, praying to be returned to the same circuit. He, however, dropped his head after a while, and I saw him wiping his eyes; for he saw in the speaking glance of the venerable man that his request could not be granted. Were you not sorry for him? The Strange Preacher was.

This is always the most interesting part of the Conference to me. The appointments were read out slowly and distinctly, beginning with Charleston; and as they were read out, several persons were busily employed in recording them. Did you notice those pieces of paper which were passed about so quickly? Those were the "plans" of the different circuits; but you could see more than one man holding on to the plan he had before. These were sent back to the same work. And did you notice how reluctantly one man gave up his paper? His whole heart was fixed on going back to the same place, but how sadly did he return home; for he dreaded to break the news to the mother of his little boy; and he imagined he could already see the tears in her eyes, when she was told they had to move, and go to a place where the preacher, after working last year very hard, got a poor support—hardly enough to keep soul and body together. And I would not be surprised if he took more than a day longer to get home, than he did to come down to Conference; and I suspect, when he got nearly home, that he called on the Lord for strength and grace to take up the cross like a Christian hero. If I had been in his place, I think I would have stopped at that good class-leader's house, who lived near the village, and have begged him to break the news to my wife, while I was putting up my horse, and providing for him after his long drive.

The Strange Preacher felt the tears falling fast from his eyes, as he bowed his head, and said to himself, "that is one reason why I like my roving life the best; for I can go where I please." Did you notice that young minister, with a very expressive face, and black eyes, and hair as dark as the raven's wing—how he suddenly drew back, and hid himself behind some one who was standing near him? He had been for some time engaged to the lady of his heart; but the understanding between him and her parents was, that if he was sent back to the same work, they might be married soon after his return; but if he had to go to a distant part of the Conference field, he would have to wait another year. And he was sent to a distant part of the State. Were you not sorry for him? And did you not notice how the good Bishop's voice trembled, when he read out that appointment? He was well acquainted with those young people, and sympathized with them.

And did you hear that audible sigh which came from those ladies who were sitting near the pulpit? It came from the troubled heart of an aged mother—a widow, whose only child, a young minister of much promise, but feeble health, was sent to a sickly part of the Conference. He was her only support this side of heaven; and she feared he would be in his grave before the end of the year. I hope more than one prayed to God to spare that mother's only stay on earth.

The appointments had all been read, and the benediction pronounced, and Conference closed; and I returned safely home.

A few months afterwards, at the request of Brother James Stacy, I returned to Georgetown. I took the train at Bamberg, and soon reached Charleston, where I took the boat, and by the mercy of the Lord, arrived safely at the place, where Brother S. met me with a kindly greeting, and we began the meeting. We toiled on, praying and looking for the salvation of Israel; we pleaded the promises of the holy Book; and implored the Lord to visit his earthly Zion in that town. We preached and labored on, trying "to look to the hills from whence cometh our help."

I spent many happy, heaven-blessed hours with Brother S., Dr. W., and other dear friends in that place. I saw much more of Dr. W. during my second visit than I did at my first, and I was quite pleased with him—he was so courteous and kind, and a Christian man in every respect, and his family too, was very interesting. I wish the whole world was filled with such families; for then the Saviour's reign would be universal. But our much respected brother has been for years past at rest in the green fields of Eden— "where friends shall meet again who have loved."

The meeting grew more interesting; the Lord was on the giving hand, and the church was rousing herself up. Zion was dressed in her beautiful garments. We had good congregations; and serious impressions were made on the hearts of several present. The preached word had not been in vain; for the Lord's will was accomplished, and his work revived.

I must now tell you of something which occurred during the meeting, which was not very pleasant to the Strange Preacher; and between ourselves, I think that is the reason why I have been so pressed [not to leave Georgetown out, while writing these "Stray Leaves."

One memorable night of the meeting, some of the sisters were singing a song, which the Strange Preacher enjoyed very much, and he requested that it might be sung over again. He was much strengthened; his hopes were high, and his banner was on the outer wall. The Holy Spirit blessed the word, and a good impression seemed to prevail. Some of the members were very happy, and the mourners were seeking the salvation of their souls. Some one began one of the parson's much-loved songs, and he was mounted on his gallant steed, with his flag waving bravely. He passed through the throng, and cried out, "Farewell world!" He passed on, exulting that the Lord was in his holy temple, and the flag of Calvary waving over the hosts of Israel. The Strange Preacher felt more and still more the excitement of the hour. He saw a gentleman with his head bent slightly forward, who looked as if seriously impressed. He went up to him, and said he hoped he was enjoying the meeting. The man was hard of hearing, and held his hand to his ear. The preacher spoke a little louder, but still without being understood; and the Wandering Arab wished he had passed on, without saying any thing to him. But with a still greater effort, he said, "Friend, do you wish to get to heaven?" "Yes," said the stranger, "but not in the steamboat fashion you Methodists have of getting there." O! my soul, how the tide of feeling suddenly turned the other way. The parson cooled down very suddenly, wishing himself on the other side of the Alabama river, or anywhere else in this troublesome world, at that moment.

But on the whole, the meeting was a good one. I remember one day particularly, I told my dream of meeting my mother in heaven, which, with the blessing of God, made a serious impression on the congregation. It was to me the happiest hour of the meeting; for the "voice of rejoicing was heard in the tabernacle of the Most High." Brother Stacy was so much pleased with it, that he had it written down and published in the *Advocate* the second time.

## LEAF THE THIRTY-SEVENTH.

ENGLISH CHAPEL; OR THE WANDERING ARAB, TAKING THE WATER WITH FEAR AND TREMBLING, COMES OUT BETTER THAN HE EXPECTED, WITH THE EXCEPTION OF PULLING HIS BOOTS OFF.

English Chapel was one of those wayside churches of the olden time, like Shiloh of sanctified remembrance. It stood not far from the public road; plain, modest, and unassuming in its appearance, as if it wished to shun observation, and preferred a small band of faithful worshippers to a large congregation. And it really seemed to me, that a small turn-out suited it better than any place I ever saw—I mean a handful of whites; for the negroes turned out in crowds. And I have seldom heard better old-time Methodist singing than we had there. But the much-loved old church has gone the way of all the living. It was burned down several years ago, and its glory has departed; but it still lives enshrined in the hearts of many who worshipped there in by-gone days. I have not forgotten the modest, humble, little sanctuary, with the friendly trees which encircled it so lovingly; for I have often enjoyed myself much there with the kind friends of the neighborhood. But what a sad change has cruel war, with its train of woes, brought upon that portion of our Lord's vineyard! O! the times, how mournfully have they changed, since first I raised my voice in the sacred place, calling sinners to repentance.

Before I say any more about the meetings at the chapel, let me tell you of its remarkable class-leader. I have seen and heard of a great many class-leaders, but I have never met, or heard of such another one as the leader of that little church. Since I began these "Stray Leaves," while I have been writing of many persons and things, I have scarcely yet felt my utter inability to do justice to my theme, so much as now, when I undertake to describe the leader at English Chapel. I have never yet seen just such a man, and I never expect to. I know I am perhaps the most singular person that the reader has ever seen or heard of. One of our Bishops told me once, that since the days of his early youth, he had never seen but one preacher who reminded him of me. But the leader of the English Chapel is alone in his glory. He was a man fond of a good joke, never mind at whose expense; and he seemed to prefer having an amusing story to tell of a preacher, or a pious member of the church, than of any one else; and he enjoyed a good laugh better than almost any one I ever saw. He also enjoyed a joke on the Wandering Arab very much—it was quite a treat to him. But he was also a warm friend of the preachers, when they needed help, and was very generous in supporting the ministry. His house and his heart were always open to them; and he enjoyed a good meeting very much. He never neglected his private or family duties; and few persons listened with more pleasure to a good sermon. He lived in a splendid mansion, in fine style, with every comfort around him—was fond of hunting—kept fine horses and hounds, and was a capital shot. Such is a very imperfect picture of the leader at this chapel—a man of a kind heart, and a free purse. I always respected him much, and regarded him as a true friend—though often dreading him, he was so fond of a joke. Long live the leader of English Chapel! I have attended several good meetings there, at all of which my much-respected brother took an active part. The Rev. L. B. Varn was with me several times, laboring as he always does, very faithfully.

We had a very interesting time there many years ago. There was a gracious season of rejoicing from the Holy One of Israel; and several hardened sinners closed in with the offers of mercy. Some, who were so far gone in the ways of transgression that they seldom attended preaching, were so powerfully wrought upon one night, that they had to leave the house, being afraid to remain longer. And there was a man, whose wife was a member of our church, who was very wicked, and much opposed to the Methodists. His wife was afraid for the preachers to come to their house. But at last, he was powerfully awakened; and was converted, and became a zealous member of the church.

"But," says one, "how about the Wandering Arab taking the water?" I will tell you. You know, whenever persons join our church, they are baptized in whatever manner they prefer—either by immersion, pouring, or sprinkling. But I was preaching many years before I was requested to baptize by immersion. I always knew I was awkward and absent-minded, and I was afraid I would make some great mistake, and thereby cause much sport to the sinners who are at such places; so that, to tell you the truth, I always dreaded to undertake to baptize persons in that manner, and felt grateful that I had never been requested to do so. Besides, I was afraid that I might make a false step, either in going into or coming out of the water, and fall down; or perhaps I might keep the subjects under too long. So I hope my friends will excuse me for making a full confession, and saying that I dreaded very much when I should have to face that fire. I felt like thanking my stars that I had so long escaped this trouble; but it came at last very unexpectedly. I had always thought I would have a long notice beforehand, and thereby have an opportunity for preparation. I had been indirectly spoken to on the subject; but had always persuaded applicants that some other preacher would be more suitable for performing the solemn service. I may judge my good friend, the famous leader of the chapel, wrongfully, but I suspected him of having an agency in bringing this great trouble upon me, as he was well acquainted with my views on the matter, and I think he moved the wires on this occasion.

Brother Varn and myself had a two days' meeting at the chapel. I had been praying for and expecting a gracious season. I had, some time before, taken in several persons at that place, and was hoping that others would unite with us on this occasion, and that the old members would become strengthened, and take a fresh start for the better world.

I got there safely. Were you ever, friends, on some pleasant day, when all was bright above and around you, surprised by a storm suddenly coming upon you, for which you had made no preparation? So it was with the Strange

Preacher on that memorable day. Almost the first person to meet him was our good brother the leader, who told him, without preface, that there were several persons to be baptized, who wished to be immersed, and preferred him to any other preacher. The ceremony was to take place on the following day, a little while before the public service began. Do please feel sorry for me, my friends. I at once began with my excuses—first one and then another; but nothing would do—and he evidently enjoyed my confusion. The friends had fixed on me, he said, and would take no denial, and there would be a great disappointment if I refused—I must not think of such a thing. I told him, I wished he had sent me word, so that I might have had some time to think about it, and have come prepared; that it would have to be put off. But he said, it must be done by me the next day. But I had no change of clothes with me. He had arranged that, too; and I was to go to a house near, where I would find every thing ready for me. But, the parson said, the creek was some distance off, and it would not suit so well. My friend had obviated that difficulty also—a spring branch near by had been dammed up, and would be ready by morning, and he carried the Strange Preacher to look at it. I told him I did not think it would be deep enough by morning. "O!" said he, "you and Brother Varn can pray for the rain; and though there is no sign now, I would not be surprised if there is plenty by morning." I was in for it; and so the service was appointed accordingly. I confess freely, that I doubt if five minutes elapsed, except while I was asleep, in which I did not think of and dread the coming trouble. I cannot tell whether the meeting was good or indifferent—whether the preachers swung clear or got in the brush—I know nothing about it, for my mind was taken up with other thoughts. The class-leader looked all the time as if he were enjoying my confusion vastly. I had been in that neighborhood often, and always found the brethren kind and respectful; but on this occasion, I admit that I spent a very unpleasant time, until the great trial was over.

Some of my friends, the class-leader in particular, drilled me again and again—showing me how to stand, and place my hands. I remember he said, with a smile, "Brother B., if you are still uneasy, I will go with you to the creek, and you can practice with me to your heart's content—an hour if you want to." Do not laugh at me too much, when I acknowledge, that had I known what was a-head of me, I would not have had the meeting at that time. I could scarcely for a moment think of anything else; even while in conversation my thoughts were on that all-important subject. We spent the evening at a good sister's house, which was truly a home for the preachers. I had spent many pleasant hours there in other days; but on that never-to-be-forgotten evening, the first and only subject with me was the confusion and embarrassment of the coming baptism. My true friend, Brother V., was a great help to me. I have often felt glad to have him with me, but perhaps never more so than on that occasion. I am truly sorry to say that I was so confused, but so it was; and in writing these "Leaves," I wish to give you a correct picture of myself, as well as of others. Brother V. thought with me, that unless we had rain, the pool would not be deep enough; and so we did not forget to pray for it, as we had been advised. There was a great fall of water that night; but I suspect, if the truth must be told, the Strange Preacher would have been very willing for the rain to prevent the people from going to church next day. The clothes I was to use were given to me; I tried them on; they answered very well, so I could not make that an excuse for declining. Every hour brought me nearer the dreaded Rubicon, soon to be crossed; and I suspect the good friends noticed my absent manner.

The holy Sabbath had come, and the rain had stopped. The blessed day had calmed my mind somewhat, but still there was much anxious thought lurking within. And the Strange Preacher thought he would be sure to make some blunder, when some would laugh aloud, while others felt for him. When we arrived at the church, we found several persons there—among them the fun-loving class-leader, with a suppressed smile on his face. Even his gentle, heavenly-minded wife, had a marked expression on her countenance, which seemed to say, "Brother B., I am sorry for you; I wish you understood it as well as our preachers do—there would be no mistake then." We went to look at the water; all said it was deep enough. The crowd increased; there were only a few moments left, and I knew there was no way of escape. We were at last prepared for immersing the subjects—some fifteen in number, among them several young ladies. We had to descend a little hill, which had been made slippery by the recent showers; and some one whispered to me, to be very careful in going down the hill, lest I should fall. I had been thinking of it myself. The leader, who was the master of the ceremonies, came up to me, and said every thing was ready, and I had better not wait longer. He told me to begin with the young ladies, and take one on each arm down into the water; and charged me to be cautious how I walked, for, said he, "you know, Brother B., it would be dreadful to fall with a lady on each arm." I said nothing, but thought to myself, if that does happen, the Wandering Arab will never have another appointment at English Chapel.

The service begun by the singing of an appropriate hymn, the class-leader doing his full part. The usual questions were asked and answered, and prayer was offered. During all this time, I thought it best not to look around, lest I should see a smile or something that might confuse me. The procession began; we marched down the slippery hill—the Wandering Arab, with a young lady holding on to each arm, walking very carefully, dreading a fall, with the words still ringing in his ear, "Brother B., that will be awful, with a lady on each arm." But, through the mercy of God, I reached the water with my fair charge safely, and silently asked help from on high. I had heard persons say, that they did not think the subjects were always sunk deep enough; and I said to myself, "I will try to make all sure; there shall be no mistake this time." I began with the two young ladies who came down with me, and performed the service as solemnly as I could, bearing the subjects as deep under the water as possible. I was by this time well drenched; but I continued to baptize the others, assisting them to and from the temporary pool, dreading each time a slip and a fall, and with my mind firmly made up, that if that happened, I would be seen no more at the chapel. One by one they were baptized, and then the procession marched up the hill—the preacher, with a lady on each arm, walking very carefully, with his clothes very wet, and his boots clasping his feet very closely. I suspect, if the great enemy of mankind ever wished to trip up the feet of the Wandering Arab, literally, he wanted to do so at that famous immersion scene at the chapel. But, through help from the Lord, I marched down and up the hill safely, which cannot be said of all the heroes of this world. When the service was over, I was congratulated by some friends on the performance; and the general impression was, that the subjects had been buried fully deep enough.

It was now almost time for preaching to begin; and I retired to the woods to change my garments, and the fun-loving, but still good and true brother, offered to assist me. I expressed myself as thankful at having got through safely and my friend observed, that he trembled for me as I walked down the hill, adding, "for you know, Brother B., it would have been dreadful, had you fallen with a lady on each arm." "Yes;" I said, "and if it had happened, it would have been my last visit to this place." "But," he replied, "you got through very well; and there is no mistake as to your burying them deep enough." But the Wandering Arab seemed to be bothered in pulling off his boots; and I do not know if he could have got through in time, if his friend had not helped him. So he sat on the ground, and the class-leader pulled away as for life, dragging him about for some time, all in vain. Was he not in a fix? At last, the parson took hold of two little trees to steady himself; and once more the class-leader pulled for dear life. The boots were off at last, and the parson was fixed up in time for the meeting. On his way to the church, some one who should have been there before, came up to him to be baptized; but the Wandering Arab requested to be excused that time.

## LEAF THE THIRTY-EIGHTH.

THE PROTRACTED MEETING AT D—— CLOSED AND RENEWED AGAIN; OR, THE BEST OF THE WINE AT THE LAST OF THE FEAST.

Very many years ago, when our land could have been truly called the "Sunny South," I started on the cars for the town of D——, but missed the connection at Florence, whence I had to go on in a small hand car. I found a kind welcome at the house of a brother, whose wife was the daughter of a much-loved friend of mine—the Rev. H. S., and I soon felt at home. Now, brother preacher, if you have ever been in D——, I suspect you have been in few places where you found the friends so kind, and the congregations upon the whole so well-behaved and attentive. O, how can I ever forget my first visit to the place. Dr. S.—whole-souled, noble-hearted Dr. S.—one of the princes of our Israel, how glad I am that I knew and loved thee, before thou wast called to the Jerusalem above! I met him first at the famous Gully camp-meeting, and had heard much of him even before that. But as much as fame had said in his favor, I found she had not done justice to him; and I think I would have borne the sorrows and trials of life better than I have done, if I could have had the pleasure of meeting him oftener—for I have known but few persons whose presence encouraged me more than that of Dr. S.

I also became acquainted with those two whole-souled men and true Christians—having the blessed God for their Father, our Saviour for their elder Brother, and the holy angels for their kindred—those preachers of the cross—knights of Zion—Brothers H. and B. I think I met them there for the first time; and there was something very captivating about them, which made you feel that they had been with Jesus, and were loved of him. I have since then often met Brother H., and the more I saw of him the better I loved him. I am sorry I have never seen Brother B. since, for I know he would have won still more of my good opinion; but I hope to see more of him in heaven than I have upon earth. One was a Methodist, and the other a Baptist, preacher; and both the church and the world would be much better off than they are, if there were more of such men among us.

I remember well how Brothers G. and M. met me; and I was much strengthened in their friendly presence.

I never can forget my first text. It was our Saviour's question to the apostles—"Will ye also go away?" A serious, attentive congregation was present; and I think there was more than one person praying for me in that crowd. Minister of the Gospel, hast thou not often been convinced whilst attempting to preach, that there were present those who were remembering thee before the throne of grace? It was so with me that day. I have often preached from those words; but perhaps was never so aided by the Holy Spirit; and I had faith to believe that the Lord would bless my poor labors among the people of D——.

There was a gentleman present, who had once loved the Lord, and who had once fought the good fight of faith, and endured hardness like a good soldier; but, alas! he had fallen from his high estate, and gone back to the world. He invited me home with him, and showed me much respect. He told me of his sad condition; and said, that after leaving the church that day, he fancied he still heard the words of the text—"Will ye also go away?" and also those other words, which I repeated more than once, "You may go away, if you wish"—that I was standing at his side repeating them—"You may go away, if you wish." Poor man! perhaps it was the Spirit of the Lord making a last effort for his restoration.

We had a gracious season at almost every service; members of other churches were present, and seemed to enjoy themselves very much. Other preachers besides those of our church favored us with their presence and help; and that Baptist brother I was telling you of, seemed much interested; and I was very glad to see him among us.

Mourners came up, and in the congregation there were

signs that the good work was going on; but it was not so manifest, so general, as I had hoped to see it; and the mourners were not so deeply affected as I thought they ought to be. They did not linger at the altar as long as they often do; and the congregation, though serious and attentive, did not seem so deeply impressed. This discouraged me; for unfortunately, I am of sudden impulses—sometimes very high up, and then again, in the depths of the valley—as Brother Durant would say: to-day exalted, almost above the "blue throned stars;" and to-morrow very low down in some gloomy vale—to-day thinking that the meeting ought to be protracted for a long time; and to-morrow believing it should be closed, and requesting the friends to wind up. I had felt depression creeping over me for some time during the day; and at night I was much cast down—more so than I would have been, perhaps, had I conversed with Dr. S. before service. O! how well do I recollect the time—of all the night-meetings that I have ever attended, perhaps few are so well remembered by me. It was raining—not so as to keep those away who wished to attend, but enough to serve as an excuse to any who felt inclined to remain at home—and we had quite a small turn-out. I resolved to close the meeting—to wind up the banner, and call a retreat. I concluded not to consult any one, lest I should be advised not to do so. I had before this, expecting what might happen, sent word to a preacher at M——, to expect me at such a time.

When the services were over, I told the congregation I would close the meeting; but suddenly I was powerfully impressed, and told them I had something to say to them before they were dismissed. I told them, I felt convinced that there was a much better feeling prevalent than I thought there had been a short time before; that there were a lady and gentleman who had never before thought so seriously of religion as they had done since the commencement of the meeting—particularly that night. I repeated the remark again, that I knew it was so; and if I never realized it in this life, I would go to the judgment seat, feeling I had spoken the truth; and if it could be proven otherwise, any one was welcome to do so. I then dismissed the congregation; and the protracted meeting was closed, and the small congregation retired to their homes, with such thoughts as will only be known in eternity.

I went home that night with Dr. Z., with such feelings as I have seldom experienced, strongly impressed with the truth of the declaration which I had made. I retired to rest, not to sleep, but to think of the conviction still upon me—believing firmly that if I knew no more of it in this life, I would hereafter. In the morning, the same feeling was upon me, and I concluded that I would have to renew the meeting; but I thought it best not to say any thing of my determination. And, O! how I longed for the presence of some of my much-loved friends, that we might advise and pray together; but I kept my thoughts to myself. The family expected me to leave the next day, and Brother Z. said, "I will go to D—— for your trunk, and you can take the cars from this place." If I had told him what I felt, I would have informed him of my change of mind; but I said nothing, and the Lord only knows how I tried to pray while he was gone—still convinced that the meeting would be renewed.

Dr. Z.'s house was a green place in this wilderness world, where I spent many happy hours, never to be forgotten. Preacher of the cross, have you ever been there? If so, I know you enjoyed yourself. And did you not feel like saying, "sin has not blighted all on earth;" mother Eve has yet some pure and heavenly-minded daughters in this fallen world? But Dr. Z. has been called from earth, where he did so much for his Saviour, to see, adore, and praise him in the Paradise above. Farewell! thou prince in our Israel; I hope to meet thee again, to part no more.

When Dr. Z. returned, there was a marked expression on his face. He said, "Brother B., I have brought your trunk; but I do not expect you to leave." When he inquired for it, he was told a letter had been left for me, which had been sent by a very respectable person of the town; and although he did not know its contents, he was so sure that I would renew the meeting, that he came near telling Brother W. to give out an appointment for me. I opened and read the letter, and I am sorry it was burned with my house. It was from a lady, who said, I had never spoken a greater truth than last night; and she reminded me of saying, I might never know more until at the judgment; but she wished me to know before leaving the place, that there were two persons present, herself and husband, who had never felt so much of religious influence in their lives as they did that night—though they did not know each other's thoughts until they left the church; that on their way home her husband told her how much distressed he was; that she said she felt the same, that he knelt at his seat for the first time; and that one preferred the Presbyterian, and the other the Episcopal, Church; and she asked me to pray for them. Those of you who know me well, can fancy how I felt. I then told Brother Z. how I had felt ever since I had closed the meeting, and of my conviction that it must be renewed; and I told him to give out preaching for me on such a night. How thankful I felt that I was so soon to realize my prophecy; how I prayed for a manifestation of the Holy Spirit; how I longed for the presence of my absent friends! If I could have had my wish granted me, how soon would Brothers S., and M., and D., and R., and others have been with me to assist in the good work.

We were again at the church; and, O! how I felt the Strength of Israel with me. I think my faith was never more strongly fixed on the Rock of Ages; and I was sure of a blessed meeting—as sure of it, as Brother Postell was at Cattle Creek, in the days of "auld lang syne." I felt the presence of the Lord as distinctly as ever before in my life. I had only heard of two persons whom I might expect at the altar; but something told me others would come. I invited up mourners, and said there were five persons who would come—that nothing could prevent them; and up they came at once. You know it is said, "Ask, and ye shall receive; seek, and ye shall find;" and I asked the Lord to give me twenty-five or thirty more, and soon the altar was crowded. It was one of the happiest moments of my life, for there was joy on earth and in heaven; and of course, the

Strange Preacher clapped his hands, and said, "Farewell world, I am bound for the kingdom." The writer of the letter and her husband were the first at the altar; and I felt as much interest in their conversion as if I had been told they were going to join our church. I called to see them more than once; and I can never forget them. The lady told me one day, that the night before, after two o'clock, her husband woke her up, and said he felt worse than ever; and that nothing would do but that they should get up and dress. She complied, and they went into the parlor, when he read the Psalm that I had last read.

The meeting continued to increase in interest; and Brother Z. one day said to me, "Have you noticed how the children seem to be becoming more impressed at each service. I expect to see many of them at the altar at the next service." And so it was. They came up for the prayers of the church. The work of the Lord was gloriously revived; many weeping souls were happily converted; and we had "the best of the wine at the last of the feast."

I have never seen that lady and her husband since; but I hope to meet them in heaven.

One thing more, and I will be through with the meeting at D——. One day, as I was passing through the streets, in company with that good Baptist brother, a little girl, with a sweet smile, said to me, "Uncle B., mother told me to tell you that we had a good meeting last night." I said, "Yes, we did." She said, "Mother says, she has faith to believe we will have a better one to-night, and I have too." And with tears in his eyes, the Strange Preacher said, "Yes, my child, and I have too." And the good brother said, he also had faith to believe it. And so it was. Bless the Lord, O! my soul; and praise him all ye powers within me, for that never-to-be-forgotten night. I was glad that that letter was written; for we had "the best of the wine at the last of the feast."

## LEAF THE THIRTY-NINTH

MEETINGS ON THE COOPER RIVER CIRCUIT, WITH MY MUCH-LOVED FRIEND AND BROTHER, THE REV. J. W. KELLY.

I met Brother Kelly for the first time at old Cane Creek; and I suspect he thinks as much of the place and its surroundings as I do—for we both have good reasons for remembering Cane Creek. I have always loved Brother K., for he has always shown me much respect and kindness, and has always been a true friend. I will ever regard it as a happy day for me, when I first met him and his now sainted parents; for I have seen only here and there a family like Brother Kelly's. I have been with him often in private, and at many good meetings—from Rock Springs to Cooper River; and I know him to be a workman that needeth not to be ashamed, for he rightly divideth the word of the Lord, giving both saint and sinner their portion in due season. He is a whole-souled, thorough-going man, and a good, upright, devoted Christian. All hail! to J. W. Kelly—my true friend and brother.

Many years ago, I started to meet him at a quarterly meeting, thence to go with him to other places. I have forgotten many of the events of that trip; but I know that I enjoyed myself very much, and found friends who were kind and attentive to me. I had a much longer ride than I expected. I left home on Thursday, expecting to reach the place in time for preaching on Saturday. The first night, I stayed at Brother Appleby's—a local preacher, and a man much respected by his friends—a pure child of heaven, too good for this sinful world; but he has been for years in the land of the pious departed—the happy place of which he so often told us. I had the pleasure of attending many meetings with him, and always found him faithful and kind—a man you could depend on. He told me that he thought if I would stay at Brother Williams's the next night, I could arrive at my journey's end the next day. I was off by time the next morning; but remember little of that day, except that I had a long, dreary ride, with nothing to interest me. I went several miles out of my way, by taking the wrong road; but by the aid of Providence I reached Brother W.'s about sunset—where both horse and rider found rest. I had never met him before; but I found his house a pleasant, quiet place; and I felt glad to think I was so near my destination. After resting a while, I observed, that I expected to reach such a place on the Cooper River circuit early the next day. I can imagine that I see Brother W., as he looked surprised, and said, "You will do well if you reach the place in time for Sunday;" and if I ever was astonished in my life, it was at that time. Was it possible that I had a long day's ride, before even reaching the neighborhood of the place for which I was bound? I became cast down, and for a time wished I had not started; but I knew it would not do to turn back; and hope, the child of heaven, smiled upon me, and I was resolved to go on. I spent a very pleasant night at Brother W.'s, and made an early start in the morning, and got to Monk's Corner to dinner; but was still some distance from the place, and I again became much discouraged. Saturday night, after dark, I reached a house, much used up, and when I inquired how far off I was, I was told, it was only five miles to the church. Only five miles! I could hardly believe it, and I felt at once much revived; and began to have somewhat the feelings that the exile has when he has almost reached his long absent but much loved home. Only five miles! I will be there soon in the morning. I stayed near a church called Hickory Hill—a wayside house, somewhat like old Shiloh of sanctified remembrance. I thought of Brother K., and bygone days at other places— Cane Creek, Goshen Hill, and Fish Dam. How they stood before me, with other friends of "auld lang syne."

Sunday was a clear, bright, lovely day. How well do I remember the day, while writing these "Stray Leaves," amid the ruins of my much-loved Mamre! I was in hopes of being in time for love-feast; but I could not leave as soon as I wished to. The five miles seemed rather long, but I at last reached the place, when I found the love-feast was not over, but the doors were closed. I had been a long time coming; Brother A. was wrong about the distance. The doors were opened, and the crowd came forth; and I felt like forgetting my long, weary travel, when Brother K. gave me one of his unequalled shakes of the hand, and said, "How are you, Brother B.? I am very glad to see you." And Brother S. W. Capers came up with a firm, strong step, and a pleasant smile on his noble face, and gave me a greeting which would almost have made a captive prince forget for the time his palace home. I was almost tempted to clap my hands, and cry out, " Farewell world!" Bless the Lord, O, my soul! for that Cooper River welcome. May I not forget it on earth, and think of it in heaven! All hail! to my dear departed friend, S. W. Capers, in glory. All hail! to my much-loved friend, J. W. Kelly.

I would have written a whole number as a memento of the immortal S. W. Capers, but I was afraid to make the effort; not because I did not love and respect the man, but because I knew too well that only a Homer could describe an Achilles. So please let that be my excuse. Those who have more than once heard him preach on extra occasions, when the Lord was with him, I think, should never forget him; and those who were less fortunate, missed what they would have remembered long with much interest. As I have alluded to the departed hero, if you will excuse me, I will say a few words about a sermon I heard from him. Though not on an extra occasion, the Lord was with him. The subject was about growing in grace; and among other things, he told us of a man whom he once knew, who ran well for a while, and grew in grace when very poor, and when the world frowned upon him; but who made a sad decline in his after life, when he owned riches and the world's favor. He described him so much to the life, that I almost fancied I had known the man. He began with him when he had just entered upon life, and was poor and homeless, and had to work hard for his bread. He at last bought a few acres of land, and erected a small log house, and then married a poor woman. They were converted at the same time, and started together for the better world. They continued to grow in grace, and were very devoted to the church. They had to go some distance to church, across a large swamp, and sometimes she had a child to carry in her arms; but they loved the Lord, and had some little to give in support of the gospel. One day, he took an axe, and cut a foot-path through the swamp, and threw a tree across the creek—thereby shortening the distance. Sometimes, each one would have a child to carry; but they often got very happy, and shouted aloud the praise of the Lord. After a while, he began to rise in the world; and they both came to church on one horse; but they did not get happy as often as formerly. And after a while, he bought a buggy; but they were not so regular in attending church as in their days of poverty. He continued to prosper, and ere long had a fine carriage and horses; but they were fast declining in grace, and seldom went to church, except on extra occasions. He finally became a public man, and was sent to the Legislature; and then there was a fine church built near his house, but he scarcely went there once a year—for he had lost his religion, and gone back to the world. The picture was so truthful, so like poor human nature, that it made a great impression.

But let us return to Brother Kelly.

I am sorry I have forgotten so many things of interest which transpired on that trip; but I will tell you of what I remember. I preached the first sermon that day. There was a large crowd out, and my subject was, "Solomon, my son"—which is one of my old favorites. The church must have prayed that day, particularly the preacher; for the Holy Spirit came down in much power. Several persons crossed the bar, making for the deep sea, under the influence of a mighty spring-tide, which swept every thing before it; and some of the sisters were as happy as I thought they could well be this side of the river of death; and the grand old woods around Hopewell rang with the shouts of the ransomed of the Lord.

I recollect one picture well—of a backslider, who had gone back into forbidden paths. The Spirit of the Lord took hold of him, as it were, and held him over the open jaws of hell.

He was a tall man, and wore his boots on the outside. He came up with an expression that seemed to say, "all the devils of perdition are close behind me."

After an interval, Brother C. held forth; and we had a most wonderful time. The meeting was kept up till near night.

Brother K. told me of an event which took place while I was preaching, which if I had known at the time, might have unhorsed the War Preacher, or at least caused him to reel in his saddle. There was an old local minister, who was very deaf, and who was much excited, and wished to hear every word; and he would now and then say, "Talk louder, I can't hear you." Brother K. said he tried to stop him, telling him he would disturb me; but he would soon begin again.

Brother K. had a series of appointments, at which I was to be with him; but of some of them I have no recollection. I think the next place we went to was the church where our old deaf brother lived, and he was going to play the same game again; and Brother K. could only stop him by telling him to sit nearer, and that I would speak louder. I was with Brother K. at Hickory Grove, where we had a gracious season; after which we passed through a gloomy section of country—through swamps of awful names and dismal surroundings; and I felt like saying to myself, "Jordan is a hard road to travel, and so is Cooper River circuit." But my Cane Creek friend was with me, who kept me from being cast down and sad of heart. I have often wished I had the fine flow of spirits that some men have. But the Wandering Arab sometimes passes rapidly from one extreme to another. I do not remember ever having seen Brother K. with his harp on the willows. He reminds me of some bold river, which flows on in its bold channel, whether heavy rains fall or not; and I have scarcely ever seen a more suitable travelling companion than Brother John W. Kelly. If I was discouraged because of having made a failure, he would tell me of a time when the Lord was present, and the parson swung clear. If I was disappointed on account of the small turn-out, he would remind me of a time when the large church was thronged, and the word went to the hearts of the people. In my opinion, there are few such men to be found, taking him up one side and down the other. He must have entered the world in one of Nature's happiest moods; and I suspect the first sweet kiss he received was from the lips of some holy angel, who smiled kindly as he bent over the new-born infant. "May he live longer than I have time to tell his years; ever beloved and loving may his life be; and when old Time shall lead him to his end, goodness and he fill up one monument."

We had a meeting near a place called Hell-hole Swamp. What a name! But the church was called Dawn of Hope— a small house and congregation; but the Strength of Israel being with us, we had a most glorious meeting, and an old-time shout in the camp. We also had quite an interesting love-feast, with a gracious season from the Lord. There was a good German brother present, who took quite a fancy to the War Preacher; and who, I was told afterwards, often prayed for me in public—mentioning me as the Walterboro preacher. That season of refreshing at that small way-side church was, I think, hard to beat; and I told Brother K., I thought the name should be changed from Dawn of Hope to Hope Realized.

We next went to a church called the Fort's Church, which was one the chief places on the circuit; and I think we there had our best meeting. It was a time of great rejoicing and happy remembrance. The congregation seemed to be under the direct influence of the Holy Ghost. There was a Brother John Forts there, one of the princes of our Israel—a young man of strong faith and works, full of hope and love. I was much impressed in his favor, and was glad to form his acquaintance, and to meet him at other places. I remember one day particularly, at this church, there was an old lady of over eighty years of age, who was still unconverted at that late hour of life. And there was a great manifestation of the Spirit in the crowd, and the church was filled with the Divine presence; and that old lady was deeply convicted, and made a complete surrender of herself to the

Lord, and passed from death unto life; and her friends rejoiced with her.

We then had a two days' meeting at a church called Bethel, where there had been camp-meetings many years before;' but the tents were then in ruins, and the old place looked as if it knew its glory had departed. The meeting was a pleasant one, without a great manifestation of the Lord in our midst—but the church was somewhat comforted and strengthened. We stayed mostly while there with a lady who lived near the church, which was a place of quiet and repose for the preacher of the gospel, where, when tired and cast down, he might rest from the troubles and turmoils of life. I was much pleased with that quiet hermitage, and its gentle mistress, sister Layton, who lived so near old Bethel, and its forsaken camp-ground. I see the cottage now, so lovingly surrounded by its friendly trees, and Brother K. and myself seated close together. O! what a sweet place in this desert world was that to the preacher, on the Cooper River circuit!

Some years after this, I went to another part of the circuit, to be with Brother K. again. I went down on the railroad, and got off near Summerville; but there was some mistake—I was expected to come from Charleston by the morning train, and the person who was there to meet me had left before the down train arrived—so I was at the end of my rope. Those of you who have passed the L—— Turnout, know that it has not a very promising look; and it might be regarded by some as one of those jumping-off places of which you have heard. I hope I may never have to get off there again, with no one to meet me. I did not know what to do with myself; and felt the "blues" coming on rapidly. If I had been called on then for a sermon, I suppose it would have been from, "Why art thou cast down, O, my soul!" I began to think of my distant home, and that my roving life had some very unpleasant pictures connected with it—such as my present unpleasant situation. I have never tried that place since; I am afraid of it. But hope smiled on me, and whispered, "better days a-head, when you step off the cars above, at the Mount Zion depot, on the other side of the flood; many friends will be there waiting for you. Your much-loved mother will be there, among the first to greet you with a sweet kiss on the left cheek, as she did that night in the dream, and will say, ' welcome home to heaven, my Methodist son, I am glad to see you.'" And the Strange Preacher was at once on the mountain top; and should he have been called on for a sermon then, it would have been from, " I was glad when they said unto me, let us go unto the house of the Lord."

Some one told me, there was a free negro, named Lamb, living near, who was a clever person, and a member of the church, who would help me on my way. So I went there, and found every thing very comfortable around him, with plenty of money and servants; but he kept his proper place. A good dinner was served—himself and wife waiting on the Strange Preacher; after which he sent me to Monk's Corner. But I was still some twenty miles from the church. I was told there was to be night-meeting, and that I could reach it in time, by riding an old horse which had been placed at my service—which, they said, did very well with a spur. And so the Strange Preacher started off, with the tide of feeling again turning. That was in some respects the most unpleasant ride I ever had. I found the horse very slow, moving at a snail's pace; but by using the spur frequently, he would go off in a long, jolting, rough trot, which would not last more than a hundred yards, when he would again relapse into his slow gait. Did you ever see a horse that would trot all day under the shade of a tree? Did you ever see a horse that, it seemed to you, whenever you spurred him on one side, *that* would move while the other stood still? I thought I was riding such an one that evening. I only went a few miles, and stopped all night at a good Baptist brother's house. He knew the horse I was riding, for he once owned him; and he said he was sorry for me, for he was the meanest saddle horse he ever saw; and I was yet a long way from the church. I was completely used up; but the family were very kind, and did all they could to make me feel at home, and I spent some pleasant hours under that friendly roof. My slumber was profound; and Sunday morning found me much refreshed and strengthened. My kind Baptist brother was sorry for me, when he thought of my having to ride that rough horse again; and said, he had two good spurs, and would mount him himself, and see if he could not make both sides go at the same time; and he had a gentle horse that I could ride, and his wife would go too. So we started off for church that holy morning. How different was the morning ride to that of the past evening. The roads, woods, and weather were all the same; and yet the situation was very different. How was it? I was better mounted, and had friends with me who loved the Lord: and, what a difference that makes!

We arrived safely, and there was another Cooper River greeting. Brother K. had given me out, and regretted much my not having been met at the Turn-out. We had a fine old-time meeting of much interest—at least in one event, if no more. There was a Major Durant there—a relative of Brother Henry Durant, whose wife was a good member of the church, but there was little hope of his ever becoming one. Brother K. had no expectation of his ever embracing the terms of salvation. His was a fine family, and I took quite a fancy to them. I was much pleased with the gentleman; and began to pray for him, and hoped he would join before I left. We stayed with them; and although it was my first visit, it seemed to me that I had known them for years. I felt sorry that he was so indifferent, and hoped yet to see him start for heaven. My faith became still stronger, and I counted on his coming, and began to call him "brother." Brother K. told me he thought I had best not do so, as he was afraid his day of grace was gone; but he thought if he ever joined, he would become a zealous member. They got Brother K. to baptize their child; but at the last day he had not joined. Still my faith was strong. I preached; Brother K. exhorted; and we had a glorious time—but when the door of the church was opened, Major Durant did not come forward. My faith did not waver. I told Brother K., as it was his last time there, to exhort again, and then bid them farewell—that he must give him another chance. And we had a strong, forcible exhortation. Still the Major did not come forward, but knelt at his seat. Though we were dismissed, I had not given him up, and I made a last attempt: I have never made such another effort in all my life. The Strange Preacher took his last arrow, and as he drew it to the head, heaven, earth, and hell looked and listened—for the fate of an immortal soul was trembling in the balance. We were outside the church. Shall heaven or hell win? O, glory to the Lord, heaven was conqueror! And we shouted on earth, while angels rejoiced in glory. I stepped up to Major D., but did not call him brother, and told him, I was sorry he had disappointed me very much. He asked how? I told him, I had counted on his joining the church, but he had not. "Mr. Bollinger," said he, "I am sorry I did not; but it is too late now." "No," I replied, "it is not too late." "Not too late?" said he, "then, please sir, put my name down." O, my soul, what a happy time we had! Those of you who know Brother K. and the Strange Preacher well, may guess how much we enjoyed it. We had the best of the meeting after being dismissed on the last day. And I regard it as one of the most delightful moments of my life.

Brother Durant began at once to work for the Lord. After some time, he came to me and said, that an old schoolmate of his wished to join, and requested that his name might be put down. I think I enjoyed myself that never-to-be-forgotten time as much as ever in my life.

I never saw Major D. again; for a few months after, he passed to his reward. Does it not look as if that were the last offer? And was it not coming in at the eleventh hour? I know the effort was out of the usual way, but I have never regretted it.

Farewell to Brother J. W. Kelly, and to the Cooper River circuit.

## LEAF THE FORTIETH.

### PROVIDENCE CAMP-GROUND, FISH DAM, AND BELMONT, UNION DISTRICT, SOUTH CAROLINA.

I started, about the first of August, to attend the Providence camp-meeting, and after that, to fall in with Brother Fleming, of the Spartanburg District. One of my namesakes, the son of an old and valued friend, Dr. Bates, had written a pressing letter to me, requesting me to come to the camp-meeting; and although I was expected at other places, I concluded to go to old Providence once more. No one met me at Orangeburg; but through the kindness of Brothers Barton and Snell, I reached the ground the next day, in time for the three o'clock sermon. This is one of the old camp-grounds of the State—a holy place of immortal remembrance. I have attended several remarkable meetings there in the days of "auld lang syne." What a band of noble, generous, Christian men—some of them gone over the flood, but several yet left behind—stand in sublime relief, when I think of time-honored Providence! S. W. Capers, J. C. Postell, H. H. Durant, W. C. Kirkland, David Appleby, Dr. Boyd, and others, are departed. 'N. Talley, C. Betts, W. G. Connor, A. M. Chrietzburg, Rufus Felder, and many others, are now living. How plainly do I see them before me now, as when listening to their burning words, which at times almost made me fancy myself in the green fields of Eden! Bless the Lord, O, my soul! that I have so often felt my blessed Saviour comforting and encouraging me at old Providence. I have found the friends of the church there very kind in these troublous times. O! that the Lord would save them all in his heavenly kingdom. I have been at some wonderful meetings there, with Brothers S. W. Capers and N. Talley. When I went there last, I missed some of my old friends very much—Brother Mallard, the just and upright; Brother Thomas, one of the sweet singers of our Israel, and a very useful and faithful servant of the Lord, full of joy, and faith, and love, but too good for this rough world; so the Lord took him home to heaven. I fancy I see his hope-inspiring face now, as I often saw it in days gone by. And father Evans was not there to greet me as in former years; he was on the old Cypress circuit what father David Felder was on the Barnwell. And that old hero, Brother Daniel Dantzler, was not there to cheer me. What a pleasant place was the house of Brother D., for a weary preacher to stop at just at sunset, when the stars were beginning to gem the heavens!

I remember now, almost as if it had occurred yesterday, a scene that took place at old Providence many years ago. Brother C. was the presiding-elder. It was a season of great rejoicing. I preached; and the Lord, in answer to the prayers of the church, must have blessed me more than usual. There was much of the Divine presence in the congregation. I had drawn the picture of a happy death-bed—which I wish you had to hang in your room, that you might often look at it. The next morning, a young preacher was rather late getting up. Brother C. awoke him, and reproved him for his late sleeping; when he said, with a tear in his eye, "I am so sorry you woke me up, for I had a most beautiful dream. I thought I was in Charleston, and some great painter had just finished Brother B.'s picture; and several persons had just retired to a certain distance, that they might get a right view of it, when you roused me up." Brother C. told him, he was truly sorry; and advised him to go to sleep, and try to dream it over again.

I was grateful that several of my old friends were still left to greet me, and to rejoice with me last year. Brother C. received me with a smile, and Brother W. G. Connor with a kind greeting and a look from his expressive eyes that went to my heart. I saw a good man there—one of the heroes of Rock Springs memory, a strong, faithful, fervent Christian—Brother Little. We had not met for fifteen years; but how swiftly did my thoughts go back to Rock Springs, and I heard once more the songs of that tremendous congregation. He preached twice, I think—a good sermon each time, strong and forcible. At times, there seemed to be a good work going on among the people. I had the pleasure of meeting Brethren W. H., and S. G., and I., all good preachers, and famous for their good singing. The elder preached only one sermon; but it was one of those efforts which both saint and sinner might listen to with profit. All that I have heard from him for years have been of the same style. And if there is a presiding-elder of the South Carolina Conference who can preach a better sermon than the one I heard at Providence, I would be glad to hear him. He made only one remark that I wish had been left out. He represented the devil as a fisherman, and enlarged on the idea, leaving out nothing. He then paused, and looking at the Strange Preacher, he said, he knew the picture was not finished, but he thought I could do it, and he hoped I would, and rather thought the friends might expect something on that from me one of these days. You must know that I have thought several times of something to add to the picture, but my imagination could invent nothing; and I am afraid of being reminded by some persons that they are anxious to see the finished picture; and I expect to keep clear of old Providence for some time, unless the friends will promise not to insist on my putting the last touch to the picture of the prince of hell as a fisherman.

And Brother W. G. Connor gave us a finished sermon on the prodigal son. He is in some respects, in my opinion, one of the most interesting preachers I ever heard, and his effort on that occasion was one of his best, I think, not even excepting that never-to-be-forgotten time at Aiken, when we listened with so much pleasure while he told us of the time when the morning stars sang together, and the sons of God shouted for joy, when—to use a phrase so well known to some of the preachers—he turned the corner so splendidly at the rate of twenty miles an hour. There were several things of which he told us in his sermon, that, it seemed to me, ought to have reached the hearts of the most hardened sinners present. The unfortunate youth, on his return to the much-loved homestead, stood so life-like before us; the kind and sorrowing father taking his stand by the road-side before the morning sun arose—before the lark had sung his hymn of praise to Jehovah—watching and praying, still in vain, the weeping father stood; and when the sun had gone down, and the stars had come out, he was still there—weeping, hoping, looking; and at last the prodigal came, and then the fond embrace, the kiss of love. I wish all the exiles from a mother's or father's heart could have been there; for I think they would have started at once to return home.

On my way up the country, I stayed one night in Columbia, where I had the pleasure of seeing Brother William T. Capers, a son of Bishop Capers. How much he reminded me of his sainted father—the same sweet smile, the same gentle greeting. I have always enjoyed his preaching.

I started the next day for Fish Dam, and Brother Fleming's meetings; but I found out that the stage would not go to Spartanburg that day, and that I would have to stop at Alston, which was not the most inviting place one ever saw by a good deal. But a kind Providence directed otherwise. A gentleman on the train got off there, and took me home with him. He was a member of our church, but I have forgotten his name. I spent a delightful time at his house. His wife was from the old Concord neighborhood. And while there, I thought often of those old heroes, Brothers Barr, and Spann, and Smith; also of one of the sanctified of earth, still living—Brother Joseph Holmes, once of the Conference. If I ever saw a man of whom it might be truly said, "He lived each revolving day as if it was his last," Brother Holmes is the man. I spent a night where he had lived many years before; and I preached by request that evening, which I hope was not in vain.

I took the stage the next morning for Shelton's Ferry on Broad River, where we would reach the cars. But I had the misfortune to have some very unpleasant travelling companions. Did you ever, preacher of the gospel, travel many hours in close contact with a party of drinking men, who had no respect for your feelings? I have experienced it more than once; and I know it to be very trying. I hardly know which was most unpleasant—the twenty smokers, near Gunter's Bridge, or that stage ride to Broad River. If it was not for one exception—the presence of Major M. G.—I would have preferred being mounted on that old horse that travelled all day under the shade of a tree. But there is an end to all things; so I at last crossed the river, and reached the train. How thankful I was that it was past!

I arrived a day after the time appointed; therefore I was not expected. I got off at Sims' turn-out, within walking distance of Brother Kelly's. The day was very warm; and I had two carpet-bags, an overcoat, and an umbrella, to carry. I was cumbered with many things; and while passing a house, a tremendous dog rushed out upon me. Both hands were engaged. What was I to do? He seemed ready to spring at my throat; and I thought, "is this to be the end of life's pilgrimage with the Wandering Arab?" O! no; the lady of the mansion came to my rescue; and I reached Brother Kelly's safely, and was greeted as I had been on Cooper River, and soon all was right with me. I found one of his sisters and her children with him; and their dear parents, and old Cane Creek, rose before me in fond remembrance, and I felt at once at home. We talked over old times, and I found him the same true friend. He was living at the place his father left him.

Sunday morning, we were off in time for love-feast. I had been there before, but not in that church. It was one of the oldest Methodist preaching-places in the State, and some of our venerable bishops had preached there. The famous presiding-elder of the Spartanburg district, Brother Fleming, was there, with open heart and hand to welcome me, and it seems to me that I still feel the shake of his hand. I wish I could have such welcomes oftener than I do in this unfriendly world. I can never forget those happy hours.

The meeting was one of comfort to me, and to the church generally, and it was said to have been the best they had had for years. I saw once more some of the heroes of Cane Creek—Brothers G., and S., and H., and J., and others; and O! what a happy time we had; and I thanked the Lord that I had met them once more. I would not be much surprised if the news went to heaven, that the Strange Preacher was visiting again the scenes of early years, and some happy spirits were bending over the golden walls, and regarding with pleasure the meeting of old friends upon earth. I hope the departed saints—Brothers Kelly, Thomas, Jennings, Gillam, Glenn, Postell, and others—were near us, and that they were mingling in the throng unseen, rejoicing with us.

Brother Fleming fired off his right-hand barrel on Sunday, loaded with pelters. I had not heard him since he was on the Orangeburg circuit—when he wrote those verses on the Wandering Arab. I always considered him a good preacher; but found that he had improved in the course of time. The word went home to the hearts of those who heard; and the work was revived. The Strength of Israel was with us; and the banner of the Lord waved in triumph; and the meeting was protracted. Brother F. had already told me, that his entire work was in a state of revival, except at two points; and he hoped and prayed that those places would be visited from on high. He left us on Monday, and I was to remain a day longer. Brother Mood was with us one day; I had not seen him for a long time. He preached a good sermon; but I have never known him make a failure.

Dr. G. took me home with him. I had been sick during the first of the year, and had not entirely recovered—I needed rest. He was to take me to the next meeting, on Brother Ervin's circuit, where I had the pleasure of meeting Brother Joseph Holmes. It has always been a treat for me to be with that war-worn veteran of the cross—the hero of a hundred fields. In going home with Dr. G., I passed over the old Goshen Hill camp-ground; there was only one tent left. It was about dark, and silence reigned all around. I thought of the blessed times I had had there, and the dear friends gone home to glory. Brother G. reminded me of the night when I preached my snow-storm sermon, as the friends called it; and how, when I was describing an awful storm, the weather changed, or seemed to change; when some thought that the thermometer had fallen thirty degrees; and one gentleman said, if the cotton was killed in August, the Strange Preacher ought to be arrested before he left the district. I remembered the night well, and also what one of the preachers told me at the time. He said, he found himself suddenly becoming cold, although he had on a thick coat; and he turned up the collar, and buttoned it up close; and would have put on a cloak if he had had one.

We got home some time after night, and the Doctor's wife gave me an old Cane Creek welcome; and all was right with the Wandering Arab once more. What a house for the preacher! How his comfort was looked after, and every kindness shown him! But I am afraid we will never see each other this side of the flood; for Dr. G. moved to Texas not long after.

Dr. S. came to see me, and we went over the dear old times again. And we went to an old Baptist church close by, and prayed together. O! how I love those private devotions in the house of the Lord; for I have often thus found my Saviour to the joy of my heart. Brother, dost thou love to bend the knee alone, with no one near but the God of earth and heaven? Art thou regular in thus retiring from the world to seek the Son of David? O! that you may always find him.

Dr. G. and myself started to meet Brother F. at Belmont Church. We spent a little while at the house of a sister Rice, of Goshen Hill memory; and I was sorry I had to leave so soon—for the family was apparently as heavenly-minded as I have ever met with in all my roving life. And they gave much more than a cup of cool water to refresh the weary traveller.

I passed where old Mount Prospect academy stood—where I went to school more than fifty years ago. I thought of the years long gone by; and I saw the old pear-tree still standing, from which I had eaten fruit when a school-boy; but there was only one limb alive. What a tale of olden times could that old tree have told, if it only had had a tongue! I wondered if it had forgotten when we played under its shade over fifty years ago; and if it still recollected the merry laugh and hearty shout that were heard near it in olden times. I am afraid it had much oftener heard the angry word and horrid oath, than the holy song of Zion. O! thou old pear-tree, if thou art still standing, one of those boys, and I hope others, who more than fifty years ago often sported with his school-mates near thee, has long been preaching the gospel, and hopes through grace, when life's pilgrimage is over, to pluck the immortal fruit from the trees which grow on the banks of the river that maketh glad the city of the Lord.

We stopped that night at Dr. Hill's, and were well provided for. The next morning we started for the church, and reached it in time. But let me first tell you of the situation and surroundings of Belmont.

Next to old Springtown, it is the finest-looking place for a church, I have ever seen. All hail! to Springtown in Barnwell, and Belmont in Union District. For beauty and loveliness, you surpass anything I have ever seen for a place of prayer and praise. I had been wanting to see Belmont for more than twenty years; and I have often longed to attend the camp-meetings held there in former years.

After shaking hands with many of the friends, and after seeing the many noble trees that stood like guards around the holy place, and after passing through the grave-yard, I felt like saying, "O! that I could have been here many years ago." Brother Ervin was a friend that I was glad to see; for I had known him before he began to preach, and his presence recalled to mind dear places and loved friends. Old Salem, in Lancaster District, was before me as large as life. Brother Beckham and his wife, with Brother Frasier, and many others, were in fancy present; and we greeted each other as in the days of "auld lang syne."

Brother F. came, and the meeting began, and embraced two Sundays before it closed; and it was a time of rejoicing for the people of the Lord. The Holy Spirit was present, and a tide of happy feeling was rising, and there was a good prospect for an old-time meeting. In the evening, the subject was, "Let us go unto the house of the Lord." The meeting began finely, and the friends were expecting a revival. I met with a kind greeting generally—very much so from some. Brother G., with his pious wife and daughter, won the Wandering Arab's heart by their kindness. and I hope to remember them on earth, and meet them in heaven.

Sunday was the great day of the meeting, and many persons had to remain outside of the house. We had an interesting love-feast, and then Brother F. preached an impressive sermon; and it was manifest to all that the Lord was in his holy temple, walking amid the golden candlesticks. Brother F. showed me as much respect as I have ever met with from any presiding-elder in all my life; and he told me he wanted me to preach a particular sermon at every place I went with him, and he was to choose the time when it was to be delivered. I tried it there; it was the passage of Jordan by Joshua and the children of Israel; and Brother F. gave us the distinguished gentleman from Ethiopia on Monday. I learned something that day, and enjoyed the service very much; but he left us in the evening.

The meeting continued to be interesting; and I enjoyed the singing there better than at any other place during my trip of two months. Many mourners crowded the altar—among them a blind gentleman. And, O! how much I enjoyed the singing of the ladies of Belmont. I was told, that the church had not been thus visited by the Holy One of Israel for many years.

Brother Melton was with us, doing good service for the Lord; and Brother Ervin came gallantly to the help of the Lord against the mighty. He is a noble example of the Christian gentleman—so kind and winning in his manners. He is a man that all the church should love. I do not think I could remain cast down in his cheering presence.

I was six days with the friends there; and, O! what a happy time was the last evening! It was with reluctance that I left them. Dr. Cumming, from Spartanburg, took my place; and the meeting was kept up with blessed results to the end. Bless the Lord, O! my soul, for that visit to Belmont.

## LEAF THE FORTY-FIRST.

MESOPOTAMIA, UNION DISTRICT.

On Friday morning, I bade farewell to my new-found friends at Belmont. A member of our church kindly offered to take me to a place called Mesopotamia, where I was to meet Brother F. I had a very different ride on this occasion from the one in the stage—for there was a brother Christian with me. We crossed the Tiger River, and at last entered upon a famous section of country—the much-talked-of Pea Ridge neighbourhood. I was there at last. All hail! to the Pea Ridge country. I had often heard of the region before, and had been invited to attend some meetings up there, but something always prevented me. At last, however, the Strange Preacher was in that famous stronghold of the devil. But I had yet to preach my first sermon on Pea Ridge; and I thought I would not be able to unfurl my flag in that notable land. I was afraid that the prince of hell had very little trouble with his friends in that vicinity; for, with but few exceptions, all went on to suit his pleasure. On we toiled through that remarkable portion of the up-country—seeing the same sights all the time. And I felt my noble war-horse more than once bearing strongly on the bit, as if he were longing for a charge on the powers of darkness; and the Wandering Arab felt like calling out, " Once more to the charge, dear friends, once more." And he more than once grasped his Damascus blade, and longed to be in some famous passage of arms with the hosts of the Lord against the legions of Satan. But we are told, that " every cloud has a silver lining," so there must be some lovely pictures to be seen, spiritually, if not temporally, in Pea Ridge. So let us fondly hope—though we have often heard that hell's throne is set up there—that the Holy One of Israel has some followers there, who are bound for heaven; and that some who are now in the Jerusalem above, once lived in that region. For I must believe, that though the visits of the holy angels to that country are "few and far between," yet they surely come sometimes on missions of mercy and love, and sometimes carry the unexpected and, therefore, glad news to heaven, that some mourning soul has passed from death to life, whose home was in Pea Ridge. I would feel too sad, if I thought there were no glorious death-bed scenes connected with that country—that no saint of the Lord has fought the fight of faith, amid the trials and temptations of that noted region. For sweet flowers are sometimes found growing in the most desert places of this world; and they are far more lovely, and more likely to win the notice of the passing traveller, because they are so unhoped for.

As I was leaving that famous region, I took off my hat, and bade it farewell. O! that some preacher of the gospel may yet be raised within its limits, who will be valiant for the truth, and the hero of a hundred battle-fields. And, O! that the Wandering Arab may yet, through grace, save some souls for heaven from the noted Pea Ridge country.

It was now near sunset. Where shall we stay for the night? was more than once asked of my companion. And I was told, that at the house of a gentleman from the low-country, a Mr. D., was a very good place. I observed, that I knew a family of that name, whom I respected very much —though I had no idea this was the family. But I was told that the eldest brother had married up there.

It was some time after dark before we reached Mr. D.'s. I called at the gate. A voice within, said, "Brother, Mr. Bollinger has come." I was recognized by my voice. It proved to be the same family I knew, and I was greeted with another Cooper River welcome. We were glad to see each other; and it was a pleasant reunion mixed with some sad thoughts—for we had all lost some dear friends, and some still more loved relatives, since we last met. I was most kindly entertained, and was pressed to remain longer. Brother Fleming, wishing to take me by surprise, would not tell me of their being up there.

The meeting began the next morning. Brother F. was there, with his flag on the outer wall. The services began under very favorable auspices, and continued good from first to last. Nearly everybody was a stranger to me; but I met with a kind welcome from all. The signs were promising, and we expected a good time; and, bless the Lord, we were not disappointed. Brother F. opened the battle—in person charging at the head of the hosts of the Lord; and a victory was won over the powers of hell. I was introduced to a young Baptist preacher, who appeared to be very pious, and devoted to the good work. He was unfortunately blind, but took much interest in the meeting, and remained with us till the end. Brother Watson was the preacher in charge, and said he remembered seeing me, before he was grown, near Cokesbury. He made a strong impression on my mind—more so than many young preachers I have seen. I have met with but few who pleased me more, than the noble and generous-hearted Brother Watson, who fought for our lost cause, but failed to win; for the earthly flag under which he marched was struck at last. But bless the Lord, O! my soul, he has been for years fighting spiritually under the blood sprinkled banner of Calvary, which has never yet, or ever will be, lowered to mortal or immortal foes. All hail! to Brother W., who came up so gallantly to the help of the Lord against the mighty.

I became acquainted with several ladies and gentlemen, who paid me much attention. Brothers S. Walker and Littlejohn seemed to be the chief men of the church; and I felt much drawn towards them.

The first Sabbath of our meeting was one of the days of the Son of man. There was such a crowd, that not more than half could be accommodated. We had a most interesting love-feast; if I could only be in such a one once a month, I would be a far better man than I am, and would live nearer the throne of grace than I do. But such blessed feasts of love in this wicked world, are "like angels' visits, few and far between." Many told us of what the Lord had done for them; and Brother Watson sung a few lines of some suitable hymns—while the fires of love burned upon the human hearts, and the Lord was praised by mortal lips. Our young Baptist brother was much moved, and reminded me of Dr.

S. in his first love-feast. He spoke with strong emotion, and a fine impression was made. O! my soul, how the Wandering Arab exulted in the Lord, his Strength and his Redeemer.

When the congregation assembled, every place was filled; and Brother F. made one of his happiest efforts; and by the help of grace many sinners were wounded by the arrows of truth. Among other things, he told us of a wonderful revival at a wicked place in the old North State, when every one in the place, except two, became members of the church; and that one day during the meeting, a gentleman thus privately addressed a friend—both of whom had been officers in our late war for freedom—"You remember such a battle? Just before going into it, I promised the Lord, if he brought me out safe, I would try to serve him." The other replied, "General, I made the same promise." "And now," said the first, "I intend to fulfill my vow." The other replied, "And so do I." And I think both joined the church at that meeting.

I preached in the evening, at the request of Brother F., on the crossing of the Jordan by the children of Israel; and the Lord revived his work—many hardened sinners were cut to the heart, and many mourners were seeking salvation. Bless the Lord, O! my soul, for the outpouring of the Holy Spirit on that day.

His work calling him to other fields, Brother Fleming, as usual, left me to go on with the meeting; but there was a local minister with us, whose name I have forgotten. He was very zealous and devoted, and a whole-souled man of God, fully bound for heaven. He preached twice for us, and prayed at times as if he had hold on the the horns of the altar, and would not let go without the blessing. This was, in some respects, the best meeting of the trip—many were soundly converted, and the glad news was known in glory. The colored people turned out in crowds, and appeared to enjoy themselves. Our Baptist brother preached two good sermons for us, and was of much service to us in prayer-meetings. Members of other denominations seemed to enter with interest into the services, and seemed to be drinking of the wells of salvation; and I had the pleasure of spending many blessed hours of joy and comfort to my heart. How much those dear and newly-found friends reminded me of some much respected in the bounds of the old Walterboro circuit. Brother W. is a man among a thousand—a prince among princes. Some one said, if I had seen his departed brother, I would have been more pleased with him. That might have been the reason why they were separated—that one might serve in the upper temple, while the other was left to bless the church and the world in these degenerate days.

I hope long to remember that nine days' meeting; and Tuesday after the first Sunday in September, 1866, I hope was a day of rejoicing both in earth and heaven. Let it be regarded as one of the happy days of the year; let it be marked down, as an old Roman would have done, with a white stone. At least, so says the Wandering Arab—for I think it was the happiest day, spiritually, that I had seen for ten years. At that Black Swamp meeting, mentioned in a former number, I was blessed more than I thought I had ever been before; and so far as I understood it, I thought I had obtained the blessing of perfect love, and I enjoyed it for some time; but, alas for me! after a while, I declined in my spiritual life, and I know that I did not love the Lord as much, and serve him as faithfully, as I had done; and, though living in the comforts of religion, I had lost the greater blessing. Now, I do not say that my soul was sanctified on that Tuesday, but I believe it was the happiest day I had seen for many years; and I hope I have been getting on better since that day. To the Lord, Most High, be all the glory.

Day after day, the blessed revival went on. Hardened sinners were convicted, and fled to the cross for salvation. At times the crowd was not so large, as some were compelled to remain at home; but Jehovah was ever present in his temple, to bless all who drew nigh to him in spirit and in truth. There was one young man, who was regarded as almost beyond all hope, who was powerfully impressed, in spite of all his efforts to appear indifferent.

The last day of the meeting had come, and, by request, I preached twice on that holy day. Praise the Lord, O! my soul, for that closing blessing. With many tears, I bade the friends farewell. And after I left the church, a stranger came up to me, and threw his arms around my neck, weeping very much; and the Wandering Arab said to himself, "This must be one of the old-time shouting Methodists." I asked his name, and he said he was a member of the Baptist church; that he had enjoyed the meeting very much; and he asked me to pray for him, that we might meet in heaven.

Farewell to the dear friends of Mesopotamia, where I saw the best meeting of my long trip. Farewell to all the Methodists and Baptists there, who treated me so kindly. Farewell to the gentle maid, named after her own river—the "Pacolet." Farewell to the kind ladies of that place.

# LEAF THE FORTY-SECOND.

##### MEETINGS AT CANNON'S CAMP-GROUND, AND IN THE TOWN OF SPARTANBURG.

I started for Spartanburg, where I had been expected for a month, but was prevented from going at the appointed time by protracted meetings. Brother Watson and myself went up in Brother Walker's carriage. Brother Watson has a pleasant family, and no wonder he loves them so much. I spent my last night with him. We travelled on very slowly, but agreeably, for several hours. I had been from home a long time, and often felt like returning. Dr. Littlejohn was expecting us, and I was afraid we would be late in reaching the place. When we got there, he had given us out, and had dined without us; but something was soon fixed up. The good Christian gentleman had the prospect of a total failure of his crop. He was very cheerful, however; and seemed to be a well-read man, of much general information; and his wife and children were very agreeable. In the evening, we stepped over to the house of the local minister, whose name I have forgotten, and spent a pleasant time. The Doctor had several impressive incidents to relate of the days of '76, which he had heard from his father. And within a few yards of his house, was the encampment of Colonel Washington's horse, a few days before the battle of Cowpens, which was fought only a few miles from his place.

I had not been to Spartanburg for fifteen years, and my thoughts were both sad and pleasant while musing on my second visit. I was told that religion was at a low ebb there; and I wondered how the friends would receive me, after so many years' absence; and whether the Lord's work would be revived or not.

Dr. L., who went with us the next day, was well acquainted with all that region of country, having lived there many years ago; and he knew almost every man, woman, and child he saw on the road; and every place seemed familiar to him. He told the histories of some families whose houses we passed. He was an interesting talker; and we listened with more interest than to some sermons we had heard. We stopped at his mother-in-law's for dinner—a good place for the preachers to rest, as they passed on their missions of mercy. That good sister must have often entertained the servants of the Lord. We found that Brother Sharpe and his family had been spending some time there.

We arrived at Spartanburg safely, after a long day's drive. I went to Brother Fleming's, and shook hands with cousin Carrie and the family; and then spent the night with Brother Lester—a much-respected friend.

In the morning, Brother W. and Dr. L. returned to their homes. Was it possible, I was in Spartanburg once more? What was to be the result of the expected passage of arms? Which side was to win, heaven or hell? What flag was to wave in victory, that of Calvary or perdition? Who were to be convicted, and who converted? Was the church soon to be moved, or would it require heavy and hard blows to rouse up the children of Zion, so that they would willingly come up to the help of the Lord? Would the old friends give me a warm Cooper River welcome? Such thoughts as these often possessed my mind.

I had not yet seen sister Wright, Brother Bobo, and many others; but I hoped to see them soon; for I could not feel at home till I had. I had time to look about, and I met several friends who greeted me as in olden times. And that warm-hearted man—Brother K., had greeted me with a gentle smile; but I said to myself, "this is not up to Cooper River yet; but it will do very well." So I thanked the Lord, and took courage. Some of the kind ladies of the place had looked for me long, and had made ready to receive me with something nice and inviting. You know, some things will get out; so, it had been noised abroad that the parson was fond of a nice rice-pudding, and some of the ladies had prepared it for him; but he did not come, and they were discouraged. But though cousin Carrie had been disappointed more than once, she had faith to believe that the missing one would turn up some time, and resolved to try it once more; and so it was, for the absent one was at last at her house, where he met some warm friends, who greeted him with a Cooper River welcome. His faith and hope were strong; and his war-horse was bearing hard on the bit; and soon he would be ready to hang his banner on the outer wall.

At Brother F.'s, I met Dr. Smith, whom I had long known and respected—a friend of the olden times; also Professors Dupre and Carlisle. They are all well known to fame, and are faithful servants of our Saviour. And the hours passed by very agreeably. Brother Black, from the Greenville Station, was there, and appeared glad to see me, and wanted to put me to work before I had rested enough. Brother F.'s children treated me with much respect; and his dear little Agnes, with her winning ways, made a life-time impression on me. And before I left, I found out that Spartanburg had two little angel girls living there, who, I trust, will often remember me in their prayers; and I hope our Saviour will be unto them, "as the shadow of a great rock in a weary land." I was glad to see my dear friends, the Mulligans, of whom I think so much. I had met them in much happier circumstances, in the days of "auld lang syne." While writing these lines, something seems to whisper to me, "those two little angel girls prayed for you last night."

Before beginning with the meeting at Spartanburg, I will tell you of the meeting at Cannon's. Brother F. took me there on Saturday morning. It was my first visit there, though I had often wished to be there. We overtook a horseman moving slowly along, whom Brother F. appeared glad to meet; and I was introduced to Colonel Ballinger. And I said to myself, "Is it possible that this is the man whom I have been wanting to see for twenty years?" Our names were very much alike. I had been told that I looked like Colonel Ballinger, of Spartanburg District; and was asked if we were related. And so I had long been wanting to meet him. I told him of my desire to become acquainted with him; and he said that he had been as anxious to meet me. He was one of the stewards on the circuit. Our first meeting came very near being a fatal one to him, for his horse stumbled, and fell on him, hurting him seriously.

We reached the ground; but, from what I was told, the friends did not think they could support a camp-meeting; but at last they concluded to do so. I found the ground very much out of order; many of the tents were fast going to ruin, and that old battle-field was very much on the decline—hence the first appearance was very unpromising. I expected that many a struggle between light and darkness had taken place there: sometimes one party seemed about to gain the day, and then the other side would recover and finally gain the victory. I hope truth always prevailed.

Brother Sharpe, and the preacher on the circuit above, united in their labor of love; and I understood that they had been blessed with great times generally; and through grace there was no failure this time. If those two ministers are spared to the church, they will, with the help of the Lord, accomplish much good. I became acquainted with many persons, some of whom noticed me closely; but this seems to be the case wherever the Strange Preacher goes. Brother Fleming wished me to lead the way. I heard some of my favorite songs, and enjoyed them very much. Whenever I visit a place for the first time, it requires some little time for the friends to become accustomed to me; but there must have been more than usual prayer offered up now; for things went on as if I had long been known to them; and, through grace, there was a season of refreshing, and the hosts of Israel struck their tents and started for the green fields of Eden. We had the promise of a fine meeting. I would have been glad to have remained at the time-honored place; but the meeting in Spartanburg had begun, and I could not well attend both; for after having been at so many places, I did not feel able to do much work. So we left in the evening, expecting to return the next day.

Sunday came, and I started on my last visit to the camp-ground. The great crowd would be out—the upper ten, and the lower ten, and all; and there would be a general gathering there that day. I was ordered to open the battle again. We had old-time Methodist singing—how it climbed the hills of heaven; and we had a glorious time. Mourners crowded the altar; and many of the friends crossed the bar in splendid style. Brother F. preached at three o'clock, on a rather singular subject—Samson's riddle. He swung clear, and I learned a thing or two; for I found out that there were more good fishing places on that creek than I thought there were. Farewell to the old camp-ground; but I will not soon forget it. . The meeting continued for nine days, with happy results; praise the Lord!

Spartanburg had improved a great deal, in some respects, since I was there before. Two flourishing colleges, a much more suitable church, and several fine houses had been built. But what were the religious prospects of the town? For that was the thing of most importance. I had seen the pious, devoted sister Wright; and she was glad to greet me once more. I noticed many things; and was a little afraid of the result of the battle about to begin; but I looked to the hills, whence cometh my help.

The first night of the meeting came. I thought things looked a little changed; but I said to myself, "Now for some of those old songs I enjoyed so much when Brother Mouzon was on the station." But, hark! what was that I heard? There was a melodeon in the church—which was quite a change. The friends had heard that the parson did not relish such things as much as they did, and so they did not use it every time; but he became more accustomed to it, and sometimes thought it added to the interest of the service—particularly when Brother Dupre sang that simple lay that took the Strange Preacher's heart by storm, "There's a light in the window for thee, brother."

The service went on from day to day; but I had been to so many good meetings, that I was a little cast down that this did not compare favorably with them. But I hoped and prayed on. I went, one morning, to Brother F.'s, and my little Agnes came to me with a sweet smile, and said, "Uncle Bellinger, I can repeat the Psalm you preached from on the first night: 'I was glad when they said unto me, let us go into the house of the Lord. Our feet shall stand within thy gates, O Jerusalem!'" I felt strengthened and encouraged, and thought there was a better day coming for our meeting; and I said to myself, "She must be one of my little angel girls of Spartanburg; but I hope I will find another, for I would rather have two."

On Friday night, the turn-out was larger, and I began to feel a little more at home, and felt sure that Brothers B. and K., and sister W., were praying for me.

The meeting went on slowly at first; but on Saturday night there was some slight advance; still I was cast down, and concluded that it was a hard place to move. For two nights, rain prevented many of the people from attending church. Dr. S. prayed once or twice, and the Wandering Arab began to feel the heavenly influence coming upon him; and Brother Fleming said it was time to cross the Jordan, for the services had been improving. Brother Lester prayed, and the heavens seemed to be coming lower down, and the earth rising. And Brother Dupre and his choir had sung again, "There's a light in the window for thee, brother;" and the parson felt the tide gradually rising. When Brother Bobo told me good night, he smiled, and I thought to myself, "You have not forgotten the old times in 1851." My head-quarters were generally at his house.

I felt quite at home with Brother Kirby and his kind wife and interesting children; and I often thought, while with him, of my much-loved friend, Brother Durant, and of the pleasant times I had had with him at Rock Springs.

One day, while riding in the town, a dear little girl said to me, "Good morning, Uncle Bellinger." I replied, "Good morning; but I do not know you." Her large black eyes looked a little disappointed as she said, "You don't know me! Why, I am Mr. Lester's daughter; and you were at our house the other day." And I said, "O! yes, I remember you now, and am glad to see you. Did you say your prayers last night?" "O! yes," she replied, with a smile of love in her bright eyes, "and I prayed for you, too." I told her, I was so glad; and that she must come to church, and sit where I could see her. She said, "I will be glad to come, but father says I will go to sleep; but if I was to sleep in the evening, then I could keep awake." I replied, "Go home, and tell your father, that I said, he must let you come to church, and sit where I can see you." She seemed much delighted as she tripped off, and the Wandering Arab said to himself, "I have my other little angel girl, and we will have a good meeting yet." I rode on, and found a little boy with three apples. He gave me one, and said, that he too prayed for me; and I felt like clapping my hands right there, and crying out, "Farewell world." Bless the Lord for praying children.

That night the Lord was graciously present, and was walking amid the golden candlesticks. And the church came up bravely to the help of the Lord against the mighty. And my little angel girl sat where I could see her—there was no sign of sleep in her beautiful black eyes. And Brother Dupre sang again, "There's a light in the window for thee, brother;" and, bless the Lord, the holy work was at last revived, and several mourners came to the altar—some of them thereby surprising their friends very much. And I said to myself, "We will, through grace, have a revival among these friends yet."

One morning, feeling very tired, and nearly used up, and feeling a little home-sick too, I was in my room seeking repose, when one came in, with a smile of heaven on his face, and a tear of joy in his eye, and speaking to me, said, "Sir, I can say 'Farewell world' now, feeling as happy as you did last night." It was one of the young converts. I was at once on the top of the mountains, and ready for another charge. Old Spartanburg was once more on the eve of a great revival. Not unto man, but unto thy name, O! Lord, be all the glory given.

I called, one day, to see the wife of my much-loved friend, Brother W. C. Kirkland. It was a sad meeting for both of us. I do hope the Keeper of Israel will always protect that family from all evil here, and save them in his kingdom hereafter. How lonely and distressed she seemed for her sainted husband in rest above.

I spent one night with Brother Dupre, the rain keeping me there. I was not very sorry it turned out so, for I saw more of that good man's family; and I expect to remember the time always, and wish I could spend many more such evenings.

A great revival began, and was kept up for several days after I left, with much interest to the last. I was present at more than one good prayer-meeting while there; but I am sorry I did not hear Brother Lester preach. I was glad to listen to Dr. Smith, one night, from—" How long halt ye between two opinions?" And the Lord was powerfully present. I had not heard him for many years, and it reminded me of the days long gone by. And I was glad to find that his "bow still abode in its strength."

I was expected soon to unfurl my banner in Greenville—therefore I had to leave while the revival was still going on. I must take my farewell of Spartanburg. When shall we all meet again? Perhaps never again in this life. But how will we meet? Saved through grace, will it be? I hope it will be as friends who have loved, never to part again.

Farewell to all the kind friends of Spartanburg! While writing this number, I have been thinking, that if such a thing could be, when I am called to cross the river of death, I would like to have some of my Spartanburg friends, with other loved ones, present; and Brother Fleming to offer the first prayer, and then to read the 122d Psalm—"I was glad when they said unto me, let us go into the house of the Lord;" with Brothers Bobo and Kirby near by, and the two angel girls at my right side; and then to have Professor Carlisle to pray; and then to have my much-loved family to bid me farewell; and then to have Brother Dupre and his choir to sing—"There's a light in the window for thee, brother;" and, as I am passing away, to have Brother Lester to pray as he did that night in the church; and to have Dr. Smith to perform the funeral service.

Farewell to my Spartanburg friends; may we meet in heaven!

## LEAF THE FORTY-THIRD.

JACKSONVILLE, FLORIDA; OR, THE STRANGE PREACHER REQUESTED TO STAY TILL AFTER SUPPER.

Come friends, and go with me to the "Land of Flowers." I will not keep you long, as my stay there was short. I went from Bamberg to Charleston, and thence to the St. John's River, and in due time I arrived at Jacksonville. It was my first visit, and I scarcely expected to see a single person I knew. I was accustomed to such things. Before I left the vessel, a young man from my District came up and spoke to me, and seemed very glad to see me.

The next morning, I called to see the preacher of the station, Brother G., a young man of much promise; and I discovered that his wife was a daughter of a local preacher of South Carolina. I had first seen her at Abbeville court-house, when a little girl; and I met her, years after, in Jacksonville, the wife of a minister. She remembered having heard her father speak of me. Brother G. said he would like me to fill the pulpit for him at the next service; but that it had been given out that he was to preach the funeral sermon of a member of the church; so he wanted me to try it that night, which I consented to do.

I was glad to meet with an old acquaintance from our State—a Brother R.—who was a local preacher, and a gentleman of pleasing manners. We had not met for several years.

After service, I was requested to spend the evening at a brother's house, where I was treated very kindly. Brother R. and his wife were also there; and I hope the time was not wasted in vain discourse. My spirits were good, and I was in hope that we would have a good night-meeting. Remembering that I had to preach at night, I did not indulge at dinner as much as I sometimes do; and I spent some time alone, thinking of my discourse for the night. But late in the evening, I was again in their company. My spirits were high, and I requested Brother R. and his wife to sing some of my favorite songs. I suspect there are but few persons upon whom singing has such an effect as upon me. Sometimes I am carried beyond all self-control, and feel as much impressed as by the best sermons I have ever heard. And at times, when I am very much cast down—quite low down in the valley—some of my friends, who know what songs I love to hear, will sing for me; and by degrees, my feelings are raised, until I stand on the mountain-top. When thus excited, if I meet with an unexpected check, I am very suddenly depressed.

Now, that evening in Florida, one sweet song followed another, and the parson's feelings continued to rise—he was enjoying much such songs as, "Jerusalem, my happy home;" "There is a happy land, far, far away." The tide of feeling rose higher, and he was soon on the mountain-top, or, as Brother Durant would have said, he was almost above the "blue throned stars." The impression on the little party was strong; and the preacher requested that they would sing one more song—"I would not live alway; I ask not to stay." The tide of feeling was bearing every thing before it—as when Dr. S. spoke twice in his first love-feast. And the preacher was soon on his feet, feeling as he had often done, while crying 'out, "once more to the charge, dear friends, once more." He told his friends, he wanted "to live a Christian here, he wanted to die shouting." It has been said by some one, that the War Preacher is never seen in all his glory, only while passing through the congregation, shaking hands, with his flag flying. But you should have been there. He never was much more impressed than on that Sabbath evening. The lady of the house had never met the Wandering Arab before; and he doubtless appeared to her a very singular person. But on, and still on, the sweet singing went; and he shook hands with each of the little party, and told them how happy he was—that he was bound for the kingdom, and hoped to meet them there. Brother R. was much impressed, and gave the Strange Preacher a strong grasp of the hand; tears were falling fast around; and on the parson went, fully bound for the green fields of Eden, on the other church. I was requested to preach. Now, in those days, I kept no record of my texts; but I thought I would try something *new* to the friends; and I hoped they would be pleased with it. I said to Brother K., after we left the church, "I guess you never heard me from that subject before." I remember his reply, and the expression of his face, to this day. "Brother B.," he remarked, "I hope you will not mind my saying, that when you read out your text, I said to myself, 'I think this will make the *fourth* time!'" The preacher was let down somewhat. There was no denying, he felt the tide turning rapidly the other way.

We were soon overtaken by a heavy shower, and got well drenched. When we arrived at the house, I retired to put on some of Brother B.'s clothes, who was not as large a man as myself. I never was in such a fix before in all my life. In those days, very tight pants were the fashion.. The preacher had been told by his friends to hasten, as the dinner was ready. He strove to get into the pants, but it would not do. Now, a knock at the door; some one said, "Please come now, the soup is cooling." The preacher pulled and twisted; but still there was no admission. The writer of these "Stray Leaves" was evidently in a close place. Now again, a long pull, a strong pull, and a pull altogether; but still in vain. Another knock, "Do come; what can be the matter? You must be through with your prayers by this time." A low voice within answers, "Do not wait for me." The reply is, "Yes, we will; but do come— the soup is cold now; are you not through with your prayers yet?" A low voice from within replies, "I am not praying; I cannot get the pants on." Now, I stood on a chair, and held the pants as wide open and as tight as possible, and jumped into them, and twisted and strained desperately. At last, they were on; but, *such a fit*—so awful tight. Now the door opened, and out came the preacher, with such feelings as he never had before. It was a custom to stand up, in those days, to say grace. He thought all eyes were upon him. When he was standing up, he was afraid to sit down; and when seated, he dreaded very much getting up. What a relief it was for the preacher when the hour for repose came! The parson retired to bed, saying to himself, "I am afraid the friends have found out that I never got the pants on till the drawers were left behind."

But to return to my narrative. Next morning, I went to the house of Colonel J. M. Brabham—a friend long known and much respected. I was not expected, but it made no difference with them. I hope I left a blessing behind me here; for I know I found one in the very pleasant hours spent with those pilgrims to Zion's hill. Next morning, I started again, Colonel B. going with me, to see me safe over the Great Saltketcher; and, through a kind Providence, we got over safe. And now we part. O! when shall I see that lover of my Saviour again? If no more on earth, I hope we may meet at last in the green fields of Eden, at rest forever more.

Now I move along very slowly—my old horse reminding me much of that famous one I once rode near Monk's Corner, which was said to trot all day under the shade of a oak. And now I pass by the burned stores, where many thousands of dollars were once made, and by desolate homes, and I felt like saying, "*sic transit gloria mundi.*"

What is that which now attracts the attention of the writer of the "Stray Leaves?" for his imagination is now spreading her wings for a flight. It was an old oak standing near an old homestead. Friend, did you ever see an old tree or house, that seemed to you to have a melancholy tale to tell? I have noticed such more than once in my roving life. You know that the Bible represents the trees as speaking sometimes.

Let me tell you first of an old house, for which I feel very sorry. It stands within the bounds of the present Bamberg circuit, near a famous old mill that has had several names, but is now called Nimmons' Mill. I was passing there not long since, and it appeared to me that the old mansion looked more sad than ever before. I could almost fancy I could hear it sigh, and say:

"O! Roving Preacher, I know you. Do you not feel sorry for me? My glory has long departed; my happiest days are gone; I have often wished that my overthrow would come. There was a time in the days of 'auld lang syne,' when I was very happy, and enjoyed life much; but a mournful change has come over me. There was a time, when preachers stopped here, and rejoiced together, and praised the great Eternal. I remember when you seldom passed without entering my now deserted halls. But now, your visits are less frequent than the angels' to this sin-cursed earth—for they come sometimes, but you never. Once, many years ago, I think it was when that much-loved preacher, the Rev. W. P. Mouzon, travelled the Walterboro circuit, you were riding by one day, and stopped, and seemed much moved at my sad state. You dismounted, and came into my silent rooms. There was no family living here then. You at last knelt down; you were quite excited; you wrestled much in prayer; you were blessed; you rose from knees, and said, 'Farewell world! I am bound for the kingdom.' You cried out aloud, 'Bless the Lord, O! my soul; and praise him, all ye powers within me.' You then rode off, trying to sing,

'I want to live a Christian here;
I want to die a-shouting;
I want to feel my Saviour near,
When soul with body's parting.'

"I now said to myself, 'a Methodist preacher has come here at last, who very often led in family prayer here in the olden time.' You had not gone long—I know you had not reached the old Clear-pond—when I said, 'I am afraid he will never stop here again; the last preacher has come and gone of the many who used to stay here so often in the happy years long gone.' 'I then said to myself, 'I wish I could be overthrown; I wish the lightnings of heaven, or the strong winds, or the fires that so often burn the woods around, would destroy me.' For then, the next time you came by, on your way to the Zion of the Walterboro circuit, you would feel very sorry for me, and pray among the old ruins of the old homestead, and think of the immortal heroes of the old South Carolina Conference, who often worshipped their Saviour in these now lonely halls. You would remember the great Achilles — S. W. Capers, Samuel Dunwody, H. H. Durant, Colin Murchison, H. A. C. Walker, Theophilus Huggins, P. F. Kistler, and that war-worn veteran—Henry Bass. But now I am sad of heart, and tired of life."

Let us return now, my friends, to the venerable oak—standing near the burned homestead, on the south side of Rivers' Bridge, on the Great Saltketcher. That lonely tree seemed to have a sad tale to tell. I could almost fancy it thus addressing me:

"Traveller, who are you now going by? I have a melancholy history."

I hope, my friends, some of you will enjoy this picture—that of the venerable tree telling its tale of woe to the Roving Preacher. It now, after several mournful sighs, seems thus to speak:

"It was long before these present United States were formed, and in the early days of the colonies, that I was but a very small twig—only a few feet high. But many large trees were around me, with their lofty heads towering heavenwards. Something within me told me, that as they are now, so would I be, in the distant future. I believed the thought, and my heart was glad. The rains fell, and the sun shone, and the summer's heat and the winter's cold came, and I grew rapidly. All was a mighty forest around me then.

"Many years passed by, and then, one bright Spring day, the first of the frontier men came along; and he put up a little tent not far off. Still, old Time rushed by rapidly, and more of the advance men came, and the sound of the axe, and the report of the rifle, roused the silent echoes of the woods. And still the years flew by; when one day, the unexpected news of General Braddock's defeat spread through the land. I was a young tree then, with a bright future before me—large enough for the sturdy hunter to fasten his horse to one of my lower limbs, as he listened to the distant cry of the hounds, and waited much excited for the coming of the antlered monarch of the forest.

"Years still flew by swiftly; and now, when the glorious days of '76 were come, I was a young prince of the woods, glorying in my strength. The sporting squirrel had raised more than one family in his nest amid my branches; and the monarch eagle had many a time soared along in wide circles over my proud head. I was happy then; I exulted in my might. The savage panther had often startled the midnight hours with his child-like cry, as he roamed through the forest around; and he more than once, in the hot summer's day, had sprung down upon the passing deer, from his hiding-place among my thick green leaves. I grew fast in strength then, and defied the raging winds as they swept along.

"And now, the immortal days of the Revolution were come; and the land rang with the report of the Declaration of Independence; and the bloody struggle went on; and the war-cry almost reached the blue heavens; and old Time still rushed by. And now, a small bridle path went by near me, and the Whigs from above were hastening down to Savannah—for the war-loving French had come to our help, and we expected soon to take the city; and more than one straggler from his legion was hastening on to his place in the ranks, under the heroic Pulaski; and some of the passers-by reposed for a while beneath my ample shade; and the brave soldiers wept as they thought of their loved ones far away.

"One night, the moon was shining beautifully, and silence reigned all around, when I heard the sound of the coming horsemen, who slowly and sadly rode up, and they stayed near by till the coming day. And now, I heard them tell of the fight, and the defeat at Savannah of the noble Polander, who fell, fighting bravely to the last; and how the hero of Fort Moultrie, the gallant Jasper, even in death, saved the flag he loved so well. Before they left, they resolved, that after they went home, and stayed with the dear ones there a while, they would join other leaders—Sumter, Marion, or Pickens, and still fight on for the green graves of their fathers and their native land.

"The years still rolled by, and the victory was ours, at Eutaw Springs; and at last, Cornwallis had surrendered to Washington at Yorktown, and the land had rest from the strife which had lasted so long.

"I still lived on, prosperous and great. Old Time flew by still on rapid wing, and several settlers came, and fields were opened up around, and houses were built, and one erected very near me. The merry voices of children rang around, and I was pleased and glad for the change which had come.

"By this time, the bridle path had become a broad highway. One day, early in the morning, the young farmer came with his sharp axe in his hand, to cut me down. He said that I checked the growth of the green corn near by, with my ample shade. I trembled much now, for I thought my time had come. I was very fond of life then. He paused, and looked up, and said aloud, 'My father often sported here, and was happy under this tree. I will not cut it down; and I will tell my children, that when I am gone they must spare the old oak.' He then left me; and I was glad that I had escaped.

"Traveller, let me tell you of the happiest day in all my past life. It was one bright, warm evening in October. The sun was nearly down; the birds were singing in my branches, and the squirrel was eating the corn he had taken from the field near by. A young man now rode up, weeping with bowed head—his bridle lying loose on his horse's neck, his hands hanging by his side. He was repeating aloud,

'Come, humble sinner, in whose breast
A thousand thoughts revolve;
Come, with your guilt and fear opprest.
And make this last resolve.'

"I had never seen such a sight—I had never heard these words before—I was all attention. He dismounted, and fastened his horse to one of my lower limbs. He said that he had gone to the camp-meeting which broke up that morning at Broxton's Bridge, a very wicked youth—had behaved badly after he got there—that he more than once made sport of the services—that on Sunday he heard the presiding-elder, the Rev. H. A. C. Walker, preach a very impressive sermon, from the words, 'How long halt ye between two opinions?'—that he was deeply convicted of his sins—that he felt awful—that at night he went with the mourners to the altar for prayer—that among them was the young Captain, A. B. Stephens, who was at last among others happily converted—that he went back to his seat more distressed than ever. He said, that he was then returning to his home on Jackson's Branch—that he was afraid his day of grace was gone, and his sins never would be pardoned. He now fell down on his knees, crying and saying,

> ' I can but perish if I go,
> I am resolved to try;
> For if I stay away, I know,
> I shall forever die.'

"I now heard voice of persons unseen speaking above me. One said, 'Let us stop here awhile in our rapid flight, for this mourning soul is near salvation;' and another voice replied, 'We will wait, for he will soon be converted; and then we will carry the glad news to heaven, and tell his mother and sister that the still much-loved one on earth is saved, and the prodigal has come back to his Heavenly Father.' I listened now more intently than ever, and was so glad that the birds were listening too, and the winds were silent also. He still prayed on, and struggled in his agone, and cried out aloud, and begged the Saviour to have mercy upon him, and he said, 'I will pray for pardon till I die.' The sun had gone down now, and the evening star was shining. Now he sprang to his feet, and said, 'O! I have found my Saviour! I have got the blessing! I am so happy!' And he clapped his hands and shouted, till the woods rang around. I now heard a voice overhead saying, 'Let us carry the glad news to heaven: the dead is alive, the lost is found.' He then looked up, and said, 'O! that my dear mother and sister were here to rejoice with me.' He then mounted, and rode off, saying,

> ' Nothing but sin had I to give,
> Nothing but love have I received;
> Now will I tell to sinners round,
> What a dear Saviour I have found.'

"This was the happiest day of all my life. But a sad change has come over me since. My much-loved old State is ruined now. Many of the noble youths are sleeping in their soldier graves in distant lands. The old house near me was burned down; the merry voice of childhood I no longer hear; my loved friends are all gone—I hope to a better world than this. I am sick at heart, and tired of life. Every time the thunders roll and the lightnings flash near me, I say to myself, 'O! that my death was come.'

"Farewell! Roving Preacher of the gospel. I hope, if you ever pass by here again, you will find me prostrate on my mother earth. I have heard that you Methodist ministers love to pray at the twilight hour. I beg you, when you bow your knees in private this evening, to ask the great Eternal to hasten my overthrow; for I long for my destruction."

Let me here say, my friends, that the writer of the "Stray Leaves" feels very sorry for the old homestead near Nimmons' Mill, on the Bamberg circuit, and also for the venerable and melancholy old oak that stands near Rivers Bridge, on the Great Saltketcher. My friends, excuse these mournful thoughts in which I have been so long indulging.

On Saturday, I arrived at the St. Peter's Church. I had not been there for many years. I expected to find a waiting congregation, but only two persons were present—my much-respected friend, Henry Solomons, and his little son. Even the Gaius of the old Black Swamp circuit was so situated that he could not come, though I spent some pleasant hours at his house that evening—Major W. G. Roberts. All the dear friends of the happy years gone by seemed glad to see me. I had the pleasure once more of meeting the Honorable Edward Martin, still, I hope, on his way to the happy land far away. I rejoiced and praised the Lord together with that whole-souled man—Brother R. Davis. While with him, "or ever I was aware, my soul made me like the chariots of Amminadab." I enjoyed myself very much with those Christian gentlemen—Dr. S. Smith and F. Maner. Sister Joseph Maner Lawton, I found living in what had been a servant's house, near where her noble mansion once stood. But, though her surroundings were so very different from what they had been, she was still the same gentle, heavenly-minded lady, worthy of her more than Roman husband at rest in the home of the pious departed. I enjoyed myself much here in the Lord, my strength, and my salvation.

The site of the old Black Swamp camp-ground was so changed, that I did not recognize it, until it was pointed out to me. Though almost forgotten by many on earth, heaven and hell still remember that famous battle-ground for the immortal powers. How sad the thought, that many who once heard the gospel preached there, are now lost forever. But let us praise the Lord for the hope, that many others, who were converted there, are now praising God in endless day, and singing the song of Moses and the Lamb forever.

Farewell! loved friends of the immortal Black Swamp circuit. May your future be much brighter in this life than your present is! and when life's pilgrimage is over, and the Jordan of death is crossed, may you rest forever in the green fields of Eden on the other side of the flood.

## LEAF THE FORTY-FIFTH.

#### THE CONCLUSION AND FAREWELL.

Preachers and people, saints and sinners, are often much troubled on account of the times. But, my friends, I suspect we have not confessed our sins to the Lord as we should have done—for, who of us have not sinned against Heaven, who of us have reformed and repented as we should have done—as much as we must do, before the Lord of Hosts will "cause his face to shine upon us, that we may be saved." Are not many of us, who profess to love the Lord, more cold and dead in religion than we used to be in the olden times? The writer of these "Stray Leaves" pleads guilty, and entreats his Christian friends to pray for him, that he may mend his ways, and do much better in the future.

The great trials through which we have had to pass, instead of humbling us more, and 'bringing us nearer to the Lord, have, alas! driven some of us farther from him. Many of us look too often at the dark side of the cloud; and some of us, I fear, almost doubt an overruling Providence. Some, who, years ago, loved the Lord, and were very valiant for the truth, have gone back entirely to the world; or, if they remain in the church, they are dead perhaps in trespasses and sins. Others have hung their harps on the willows, and refuse to sing the Lord's songs. Others have rent their robes, but not their hearts, before the Holy One of Israel; and they mourn over the sad times, still expecting them to be worse.

Now, I think we are doing very wrong. We should repent of our sins sincerely, and humble ourselves in the dust before God; and see if he will open the windows of heaven for us, and pour out a blessing "that there shall not be room enough to receive."

My friends, if you will only receive these "Stray Leaves" as kindly as you have ever done their author, he will feel that they have been treated much better than they deserve, and will be grateful, and will pray for the blessing of heaven, that maketh rich for both worlds, to rest upon you all.

Let us, friends, in these very troublous times, submit ourselves resignedly into the hands of our Heavenly Father—knowing full well that he ever knows what is right, and does what is best, for us all. Let us not, for a moment, think that we are utterly forgotten of the Lord, and that in anger he has forever shut out his tender mercies from us. Let us not, for a moment, think that the holy angels have ceased their ministrations to the heirs of salvation in the South; but, let us fondly hope that they pitch their tents around us as often now as ever. Let us not always look at the dark side of the cloud; but let us try by faith to see the bright side of every stormy cloud that may gather over us at any time. Let us never despair of finding forgiveness for our many sins, if we will only repent in dust and ashes before the Holy One of Israel, and seek him with all our hearts.

And now to you, my many personal friends in the different branches of the one true church of the ever blessed Saviour, who have so often welcomed me to your hearts and your homes, I respectfully bid farewell! We have often enjoyed ourselves much together in this vale of tears; may we, when done with the sorrows of earth, meet to part no more in the happy land far away.

> " And if our fellowship below,
> In Jesus be so sweet,
> What heights of rapture shall we know,
> When round his throne we meet!"

FINIS.

www.ingramcontent.com/pod-product-compliance
Lightning Source LLC
Chambersburg PA
CBHW020330250426

**43667CB00050B/1189**